LANGUAGE AND LITERA...

Dorothy S. Strickland, FOUNDI...
Celia Genishi and Donna E. Alvermann, SERIES EDITORS

P9-BYV-768

ADVISORY BOARD: Richard Allington, Kathryn Au, Bernice Cullinan, Colette Daiute, Anne Haas Dyson, Carole Edelsky, Shirley Brice Heath, Connie Juel, Susan Lytle, Timothy Shanahan

(Continued)

For volumes in the NCRLL Collection (edited by JoBeth Allen and Donna E. Alvermann) and the Practitioners Bookshelf Series (edited by Celia Genishi and Donna E. Alvermann), please visit www.tcpress.com.

Change Is Gonna Come

Transforming Literacy Education for African American Students

Patricia A. Edwards
Gwendolyn Thompson McMillon
Jennifer D. Turner

Foreword by Carol D. Lee

Teachers College,
Columbia University
New York and London

INTERNATIONAL
Reading Association
800 BARKSDALE ROAD, PO BOX 8139
NEWARK, DE 19714-8139, USA (302) 731-1600
www.reading.org

Published simultaneously by Teachers College Press, 1234 Amsterdam Avenue, New York, NY 10027, and the International Reading Association, 800 Barksdale Road, P.O. Box 8139, Newark, DE 19714-8139

Selections from Pat Edwards' NRC Presidential Address originally appeared in Rowe, D. W., Jimenez, R., Compton, D., Dickinson, D., Kim, Y., Leander, K., & Risko, V. (Eds.). (2008). *57th Yearbook of the National Reading Conference.* Oak Creek, WI: National Reading Conference. Reprinted with permission of the National Reading Conference and Pat Edwards.

An excerpt from "Booker T. & W.E.B." is from Randall, D. (1969/2009). In M. J. Boyd (Ed.), *Roses and Revolutions: The Selected Writings of Dudley Randall* (p. 103). Detroit, MI: Wayne State University Press; and appears by permission of Dudley Randall's Literary Estate.

A prayer by Marian Wright Edelman first appeared in *The Sea Is So Wide and My Boat Is So Small: Charting a Course for the Next Generation* (2008), p. xiii. New York: Hyperion Books. Copyright © 2008, and used by permission of Hyperion Books.

Library of Congress Cataloging-in-Publication Data

Edwards, Patricia A. (Patricia Ann)
    Change is gonna come : transforming literacy education for African
  American students / Patricia A. Edwards, Gwendolyn Thompson McMillon,
  Jennifer D. Turner ; foreword by Carol D. Lee.
        p. cm. – (Language and literacy series)
    Includes bibliographical references and index.
    ISBN 978-0-8077-5084-1 (pbk. : alk. paper)
    ISBN 978-0-8077-5085-8 (hardcover : alk. paper)
        1. African Americans–Education. 2. Academic achievement–United States.
    3. Language arts–United States. I. McMillon, Gwendolyn Thompson.
    II. Turner, Jennifer D. III. Title.
    LC2717.E394   2010
    379.1'53109788–dc22   2009053230

ISBN 978-0-8077-5084-1 (paper)
ISBN 978-0-8077-5085-8 (hardcover)

Printed on acid-free paper
Manufactured in the United States of America

17   16   15   14   13   12   11   10   8   7   6   5   4   3   2   1

This book is dedicated to our families, who instilled in us the desire to succeed and to encourage others to do the same. The book is also dedicated to parents, preservice and experienced teachers, administrators, researchers, school board members, community leaders, teacher educators, and policymakers, who must work together for the success of all children, especially African American children.

Contents

Foreword:
Looking Back to Go Forward

Patricia Edwards, in opening this book, seamlessly integrates her own personal narrative of growing up in the segregated Jim Crow South with the intellectual history of our nation's efforts to address the achievement gap in literacy. Her story is powerful because it embodies a core set of principles about human learning, which is based on a strong body of empirical evidence. That empirical evidence about human learning and development points to the plasticity of the human brain, the ways in which humans are genetically endowed by their evolution with the capacity to adapt to changing circumstances, and the dynamic relationships between risk and protective factors in influencing outcomes of development. We have additional evidence that displays of competence are context dependent. We also have evidence that as a species we are wired to have access to multiple pathways for development.

Despite these robust findings, the political metanarrative of policy and practice has at its center assumptions about cultural deficits—in language practices, in family functioning, in community cultural orientations—all of which characterize anything other than a presumed monolithic set of middle-class values and practices as deviant. The outgrowth of this metanarrative has been restrictive conceptions of literacy, scripted approaches to the teaching and assessment of literacy, and normative pedagogical practices that more often than not label students who do not fit the mythical norm as "incompetent." As Patricia Edwards accomplished in her personal story, we can feel the impact of this deficit positioning in the voices of the young people reflected in the opening chapter of this book.

The Sankofa image invoked in Edwards's Preface captures the axiom "looking back to go forward." The history of African Americans is replete with evidence of resilience in the face of the gravest of challenges. Enslaved Africans risked life and limb, literally, to learn to read and write. The first institutions African Americans developed—independent of government support—at the end of the Civil War were schools, some 1500 (plus 500 of what were called Sabbath or church-based schools). In the midst of the civil rights movement, freedom schools were created by the Student Non-Violent Coordinating Committee across the South, led by such inspirational teachers as Septima Clark and Ella Baker. Vanessa Siddle Walker documents how segregated schools in the Jim Crow South served as centers of community development and as sites of high expectations, preparing African American students to excel in spite of racism and poverty. From the African Free School in the 1700s to the independent African-centered school movement from the 1970s onward, African Americans have developed educational institutions that focused on centering young people in a cultural milieu that provides protective factors for resilience.

The challenge we face is in marrying the evidence of this history—mirrored across diverse communities facing racism and class bias—with the science of human resiliency. This challenge is both an agenda for empirical research and equally an agenda for practices with regard to teacher preparation, the professional circumstances of teaching, literacy standards, and assessments. It is an agenda that involves understanding what is entailed in complex reading and writing, the social and emotional demands of learning, and the sources of generativity and resilience in families and communities. It is among the most complex tasks of teaching because it requires highly specialized and integrated knowledge across multiple domains, and the ability to interrogate one's own beliefs and assumptions. It is among the most challenging tasks of policy development, where the question addresses the kinds of resources that are needed to create environments that support this kind of practice-based knowledge, which must be dynamic and culturally rooted.

This volume, *Change Is Gonna Come: Transforming Literacy Education for African American Students*, informs and inspires the quality and focus of the conversations needed if we are to gain traction.

—Carol D. Lee, Northwestern University
President, American Educational Research Association, 2009–2010

Preface

In Spring 2004, Pat was elected by her colleagues to serve as the first African American President of the National Reading Conference (NRC). As the world's premier reading research organization, NRC is a professional organization of literacy scholars who share an interest in research and dissemination of information on literacy. For more than 50 years, NRC has played an active leadership role in improving reading and literacy instruction around the world through the important research conducted by its members.

After all of the excitement of being elected, Pat began to think about her presidential address, which she knew had to be given 3 years later. Pat selected Austin, Texas, for her conference because 23 years earlier she had attended her first NRC conference there. Having the conference in Austin meant a lot to her, because it felt like she was coming full circle.

Pat knew that she had to do an outstanding job on her presidential address. Being elected president of NRC brought back to memories of her high school days when she was one of 24 Black students to attend an all-White school in Albany, Georgia, during the turbulent 1960s. She was taught that it was her responsibility to do well in school and give back to the community. Because of this teaching, Pat welcomed the invitation to Albany High School.

Many members of the Albany community doubted whether Pat could survive the academic pressures, and she had to prove them wrong. Even now, as a recent study by Dorinda Carter (2005) shows, Black students perceive that they have to "prove wrong" negative stereotypes about their intellectual ability and racial-group cultural patterns as a way to resist the racism of their school context. The "prove them wrong" phenomenon has been found to be common among some Black students in predominantly White colleges and universities. It was certainly a message Pat received from her parents, neighbors, and friends. Throughout her life journey, she constantly has heard, "Pat, make us proud."

And Pat wanted to do just that at NRC. She knew she wanted to share with her NRC colleagues something about the education of African American children. On the advice of past NRC president Donna Alvermann, Pat spent 2 years preparing her speech. And with Gwendolyn McMillon's and Jennifer Turner's assistance, she selected the topic *The Education of African American Students: Voicing the Debates, Controversies, and Solutions* (Edwards, 2008). Pat wanted to give the audience the experience of being in an African American church. When she was a child, she attended a Southern Baptist church that did not have air conditioning. Instead, worshipers used fans to keep cool. Pat told the audience, "It might get hot in here!" To enhance the authenticity of the church experience, colleagues passed out fans bearing a picture of the Sankofa bird and several quotes related to the education of African American children.

Pat's presidential address began with a video clip that opened with several pictures of the Sankofa bird (see Figure P.1).

Sankofa is one of many adinkra symbols used by the Akan people of Ghana, West Africa (see Brandon, 2004; W. Willis, 1998, for additional information). The adinkra is a cotton cloth produced in Ghana and used for special occasions such as weddings and initiation rites. The adinkra symbols also represent popular proverbs and maxims, record historical events, and express particular attitudes or behavior related to depicted figures, or concepts uniquely related to abstract shapes. The Sankofa bird has caught the imagination of a number of African American groups interested in our African heritage. The meaning of Sankofa is "looking back to go forward," suggesting that our ancestors can show the way to the future. The symbol is relevant to both Africans and African Americans today, in that it is useful for us to look back to our history as a basis for creating the kind of unity we need to go forward with knowledge and strength. Pat explained that African Americans, who were defined in the United States as slaves and property, often were characterized as having no history and no culture; it was as if our history began with our existence as slaves in the Americas. To transform us from African people into

Figure P.1.
The Sankofa Bird
Drawn by Todd Norman

American slaves, all efforts were made to deprive us of our history and culture so as to make us believe we had neither. Without question, African Americans have always been significant contributors to the history of this country. Pat argued that African Americans must look back at the totality of our history, accept the responsibility of defining ourselves in relationship to that totality, and acknowledge our rightful role in the Global Village.

In the video, music from Lou Rawls and the a cappella ensemble Sweet Honey in the Rock accompanied pictures of the Sankofa bird and, later, quotes from several prominent Black leaders–Frederick Douglass, George Washington Carver, W. E. B. Du Bois, Booker T. Washington, Carter G. Woodson, Marcus Garvey, and Langston Hughes. Songs like "Ain't Gonna Let Nobody Turn Me Around" and "This Little Light of Mine" moved the audience to sing along, clap their hands, and remember the violent, stressful 1950s and 1960s. The next segment in the video profiled the schools that African American children attended in the segregated South, reminding the audience of Rev. Dr. Martin Luther King, Jr.'s "I Have a Dream" speech and the church bombing in Birmingham, Alabama, where four Black girls were killed. Pat concluded the video with a statement that she often heard: "Education has always been an 'equalizer' for the African American community." Above this quote was a picture of her mother, Annie Kate Edwards, a teacher who instilled in her children the value of education, with Pat and her older sister Callie (see Figure P.2). The closing song in the video was "We Shall Overcome," a song that had and continues to have an indelible impact on Pat.

Figure P.2.
Edwards Family Photo
© *Pat Edwards*

That presidential speech inspired this book, which was born when Gwen and Jen worked closely with Pat on developing the four major debates/controversies surrounding the education of African American students: (1) the fight for access to literacy, (2) supports and roadblocks to "success," (3) best practices, theories, and perspectives on teaching African American students, and (4) the role of African American families in the literacy lives of their children.

In the process of putting together Pat's address, Gwen, Jen, and Pat often talked about the concept of "social location." Social location, according to Rev. Dr. Renita Weems (1995), Vanderbilt theologian, is a person's frame of reference, a perspective on life, identity kit, or fund of knowledge, that impacts his or her ways of thinking. Pat had two social locations in her life— Jim Crow and the promise of change. When she was young, Jim Crow laws touched every aspect of Pat's life. Jim Crow was more than a series of rigid anti-Black laws. It was a way of life and a legitimization of anti-Black racism. Under Jim Crow, African Americans were relegated to the status of second-class citizens. And Jim Crow etiquette, which excluded Blacks from public transport and facilities, juries, jobs, and neighborhoods, operated in conjunction with Jim Crow laws (Black codes), and both were undergirded by violence, both real and threatened. Blacks who violated Jim Crow norms risked their homes, their jobs, even their lives. Whites could physically beat Blacks with impunity. Blacks had little legal recourse against these assaults because the Jim Crow criminal justice system comprised all-White police, prosecutors, judges, juries, and prison officials. Violence was a method of social control, and Jim Crow was an autocratic giant in a nation that professed to be democratic. Pat didn't understand why Blacks were treated so badly. She often asked her mother, "Mama, are us Blacks being punished because of our skin color?" Pat's mother replied, "One day things will change."

So, Pat held on tightly to the second social location of her life, the promise of change that her mother often spoke of. Pat asked, "How will this change happen, Mama?" Her mother proudly responded:

> Education is the key to success. No one can take your education away from you. If you get a good education, you can make a difference, you can positively change your life and the life of others. I didn't have an opportunity to go to college, but I'm going to make sure that the three of you [Pat and her two sisters] go to college. I'm going to take off one day a month from my job to serve as a "room mother" and I'm going to work with the Parent–Teacher Association. I want to be an integral part of making change for you and your sisters become a reality.

Over time, Pat saw her mother's promise of change come true.

Gwen's social location is firmly grounded in her religion and finds a model of sacrifice in Jesus. She believes that she has a calling to make sacrifices, to go back to her old neighborhood (and similar communities), to lovingly bring hope through resources that will improve young people's quality of life. Gwen's social location was built upon a foundation of relationships—an intimate relationship with God, an unconditional love for family, and an agape (self-sacrificing) love for others (especially the unfortunate, the disenfranchised, the impoverished). The concept of denying oneself and taking up one's cross was taught to Gwen by the examples of her parents, who denied themselves over and over again to provide for their family, the children in the neighborhood, and the members of the church where Gwen's father was pastor and her mother taught Sunday school. Many considered the neighborhood where Gwen's family lived "the ghetto." During the day drug dealers and numbers men crept though the neighborhood earning their living, and the sound of gunshots and sirens was the twisted lullaby that put the children to sleep at night. However, this same neighborhood was the place where lifetime friendships were developed and where Gwen and other children learned to give and receive love and encouragement from many caring adults—especially her parents. Throughout her childhood in Saginaw, Michigan, she heard her parents repeatedly say, "Get a good education—it's the only way out of the ghetto," and "Once you have made it, reach back and help someone else."

Jen characterizes her social location through three images that she calls the "urban trinity": the ice cream truck, the crack house, and the library. Jen grew up in Mt. Airy, a Philadelphia community known in the 1960s and 1970s as a "good" part of the city. The image of the ice cream truck, with Jack and Jill or Mister Softee painted on the side, was symbolic of the good times and happy memories within this all-Black community. Jen fondly recalls getting popsicles from the ice cream truck and eating them on the front steps until the streetlight came on. But when the second image, the crack house, emerged in the 1980s, things began to change. Jen remembers when crack first appeared on her block. She had picked up one of the little vials that littered her driveway. Her mother saw her and screamed, "Give that to me right now!" Jen recalls the rainbow of blue, purple, red, and orange "caps" that littered the driveway, sidewalks, and, at times, the front steps. Jen never thought crack houses would be on her block, but after several years of seeing people that she and her friends called "zombies" walking up and down the street, with filthy clothes, rotting teeth, and dead eyes, and numerous police raids, she knew that the violence and crime had changed her neighborhood forever. But the local library offered some hope for Jen and her siblings. Jen's parents were avid readers and allowed their children to walk to the library to check out books and signed them up for summer reading programs and other special events. The library is still very important to Jen's family, and when the mayor recently announced that the library would close due to budget cuts, Jen's mom and dad joined hundreds of people in the community to protest. Jen is proud to say that the protestors saved the Wadsworth Library, and now her 9-year-old niece is able to continue checking out books.

We have written a book at this critical time because while literacy is the new civil right (Henry, 2001), the solution for improving the literacy achievement of African American students remains an enigma. Over the years, scholars from varying disciplinary backgrounds, including sociology, anthropology, history, and psychology, have provided other explanations and orientations to address the literacy challenges of African American students. We feel, and you might agree, that many books that represent passionate pleas about the schooling of African American children are quite theoretical and therefore seem disconnected from the lived experiences and work of classroom teachers and principals (e.g., Bell, 1993; Du Bois, 1903/1995; Perry, Steele, & Hilliard, 2003; West, 1993). Other popular books that were born from the Civil Rights and multicultural movements present compelling practices and pedagogies for African American learners that are very connected to teachers and schools (e.g., Hale-Benson, 1982, 2001; Ladson-Billings, 1994; Lee, 2007; Morrell, 2004; A. Tatum, 2005), but the practices have not yet been adopted by many mainstream teachers and schools because White teachers and even some Black teachers do not have the deep knowledge and understanding of African American culture to implement them.

Many other texts have been published to help African American students learn in school. Some texts have focused on pedagogies related to multicultural education and cultural responsiveness (Banks, 2001; Gay, 2000), but we believe these texts address general education issues that are difficult to translate into practices that literacy teachers can take up readily in their classrooms and schools. Consequently, we work hard in this book to address these issues and we take the critical step of providing some specifics to show readers how to begin to move these practices into the mainstream. Finally, some books have highlighted Afrocentric pedagogies and schools (Asante, 1987; Murrell, 2002); however, not only are these practices highly controversial, but they don't mirror the realities of schooling in diverse settings. Clearly, there are a variety of discussions and conversations about the challenges of African American education. However, these books typically offer a single perspective or message, with each book representing fragmented bits and pieces of the "puzzle" of African American education. In this book, we attempt to address all of these frustrations.

Our book serves three main goals. First, we discuss the enigma of educating African American literacy learners in a holistic way, from multiple perspectives (e.g., school, family, community). Second, this book provides more than just an emotional discussion to evoke feelings of compassion concerning African American students and their literacy challenges. It is written to empower teachers, parents, principals, and teacher educators in their work with African American children by unlocking the paths toward successful literacy teaching and learning. Thus, a primary objective of our book is to connect theory, research, practice, and history in ways that help literacy practitioners transform their classrooms and schools. Third, this book fills a need for high-quality, research-based pedagogies for African American literacy learners. Such emphasis on literacy is crucial because the recurring debates and controversies throughout American history have been focused on access to literacy and equal opportunity to learn to read and write in schools.

The book is divided into six chapters. In the Introduction, we provide an overview of the state of African American education today. In Chapters 1 through 4, we address the four major debates we introduced earlier: (1) the fight for access to literacy, (2) supports and roadblocks to "success," (3) best practices, theories, and perspectives on teaching African American students, and (4) the role of African American families in the literacy lives of their children. In discussing each debate, we highlight the educational struggles of African American students in the United States and consider how valuable lessons learned from the past can inform a more successful future for our children. In the final chapter, we propose solutions, drawing on our broad analysis of current research, as well as our practical and professional knowledge of approaches that support literacy development of African American students. We address how responsibility for these solutions must be shared across the policy, research, community, family, and classroom levels. We believe that these five levels of solutions are needed, because the debates and controversies are complex and multilayered, and defy a "one-size-fits-all" approach.

Our overarching metaphor throughout the book, as in Pat's speech, is the Sankofa. We "look back" to examine the historical contexts of the debates and controversies related to educating African American literacy learners, while "going forward" to analyze the contemporary contexts of literacy education and the issues, debates, and controversies related to working in today's classrooms and schools. We "look back" to pull from the strength and wisdom of the African elders who taught their apprentices the importance of community-building and instilled values that motivated parents to take ownership in the education of their children. We "go forward" to share practical ideas that will challenge educators, parents, policymakers, community leaders, and other members of "our American village" to respond to the call to action voiced in this book. By moving back and forth between the historical and contemporary debates and controversies in literacy education, we aim to (1) inform readers of the rich historical legacy that African

American people created as they struggled to become literate in schools, (2) advance new visions, conceptions, and understandings of African American literacy education rooted in the knowledge of African American culture and history, and (3) provide information about high-quality, research-based literacy instructional pedagogical approaches and strategies that will empower teachers, principals, teacher educators, parents, and community leaders to transform classroom practices and school learning environments for African American literacy learners.

We invite you to adopt and adapt the practices described in this book, making them your own, molding them to fit the specific strengths, experiences, and needs of the African American children in your school community. And we challenge you to begin talking with colleagues, and to share this book with parents, preservice and experienced teachers, administrators, researchers, school board members, community leaders, teacher educators, and policymakers, who together must establish the policies that empower all literacy learners, especially African American learners.

Patricia A. Edwards
Gwendolyn T. McMillon
Jennifer D. Turner

Acknowledgments

No one walks alone, and when one is walking on the journey of life, just where do you start to thank those who joined you, walked beside you, and helped you along the way? Pat wants to begin by thanking her two brilliant co-authors, Gwendolyn McMillon and Jennifer Turner, for their support of her 2007 NRC Presidential Address, which inspired this book. Gwen and Jen looked at what Pat was doing, read, wrote, offered comments, and helped her shape the content. They were the inspiration that drove Pat onwards. They kept Pat focused. They let her be quiet when she wanted to be quiet, and when Pat wanted to be noisy—well, that is another story.

Gwen and Jen especially want to thank Pat for being a true friend and mentor in every sense of the word. She has provided numerous opportunities and expected us to "step up to the plate." We have certainly learned from the best.

Pat thanks Donna Alvermann, Kathryn Au, and Taffy Raphael, all past NRC presidents, for their great advice and constant encouragement. They shared their knowledge, their ideas, and numerous tips, all of which culminated in the completion of this book.

The three of us—Pat, Gwen, and Jen—want to thank Carol D. Lee for her awesome Foreword. Her words appropriately capture our illustrious history and future. As African American female scholars we are proud to be able to share this moment with a "real sista" who has inspired us once again to continue to strive to make a difference in the lives of children who look like us.

We would also like to thank the colleagues in our departments at Michigan State University, Oakland University, and University of Maryland College Park. Special mention is made of Julie Schrauben, doctoral student at Oakland University, who gave us valuable help.

We thank our Acquisition Editor, Meg Lemke, whom we fondly refer to as "our editor of the year," who has an abundance of talent, patience, and skills. She read our drafts, understood our message, and helped us to say what we wanted to say. More importantly, we thank Meg for keeping us on track and giving lots of virtual and face-to-face pats on the back when we experienced short completion deadlines.

We thank Karl Nyberg, our Production Editor, who was heroic in not only clearing up our words, but also in keeping us honest when we drifted off course. He was patient, tireless, and meticulous as we polished everything up to get it ready for final production.

Our deepest gratitude goes to our families for their unflagging love and support: John and Annie Kate Edwards (now deceased), who prepared Pat to face a very uncertain world and gave her the confidence to serve as a good friend, mentor, leader, and teacher; Rev. M.T. (deceased) and Pecola Thompson, Gwen's first and most important literacy role models, who taught her to have hope and follow God's will for her life; and Larry and Shirley Danridge, who prepared Jen to be a "border crosser" as well as a good scholar, teacher, and mother. We also thank our family members, teachers, and all of the children who allowed us to include their voices for sharing their rich stories, experiences, and perspectives in our book.

And last, but not least, Pat thanks her two nieces Andrea and Demetrice, her nephew Sam, her grandnephew T. J., her three grandnieces TaMyia, Amira, Tamara, and her two sisters Callie and Sandra; Gwen thanks her sons Morgan, David, and Joshua, her husband Vincent, her brothers and sisters, nieces and nephews, and the students, teachers, principals, schools, and others from her community; and Jen thanks her sons Isaiah and Elijah, her husband Michael, her niece Amani, her sisters Jocelyn and Jessica, and her brother Joshua, for all their love, support, and encouragement.

Change Is Gonna Come

Transforming Literacy Education
for African American Students

Hope, Literacy, and the State of African American Education Today

If you accept the expectations of others, especially negative ones, then you never will change the outcome.

—Michael Jordan

This book was written in the spirit of change. Change for African American children who walk the hallways of our schools, searching for wisdom and truth. Change for African American families and communities that nurture African American youth. Change for schools and teachers that serve African American students. Change for teacher education programs and governmental policies designed to promote equal opportunity to learn and to develop caring and competent educators.

We believe that fundamental changes must be made if African American students are to not only learn, but thrive in our schools. Our educational system certainly has had its share of reform, but the process of transformation must continue because so many African American students are being left behind by our schools. Consider the voices of several African American young people, and the persistent challenges that they have experienced in K–12 schools.

Timothy, first grade (suspended 12 times):

> Mama usta ground me when I got kicked out. But now she just say, "Oh well," and tell me to go play. She said that she tired of Mrs. Rudolph puttin' me out. She say they don't know what they doin' up in this school. Sometimes I get kicked out 'cuz Mrs. Rudolph wait too long to call on me. I raise my hand, but she must not see me 'cuz I'm always sittin' in time out with my back to everybody and my face to the wall. I don't care if she give me time out. Mama said I can still answer questions. I know all the answers 'cuz I'm smart. The reading lady told me

1

I read better than the fifth graders. I don't know why my teacher won't call on me. It makes me mad.

Fredriana, fifth grade (suspended nine times):

My mom tells me that I talk too much. Maybe I do, but I got a lot to say. I've had a kinda rough time in school these last few years. I loved my third-grade teacher, but she got sick with cancer and had to stay home to get better. We had so many substitutes that I can't even remember all their names. . . . That year was a bad year for me, but I was looking forward to having Mrs. Reimer for the fourth grade. I heard that she was good, but she was out having a baby and when the teachers got laid off something happened and she couldn't come back to our school. We didn't get a real teacher until the middle of the fourth grade. She was alright at first, but she just didn't understand me. Like I said I have a lot to say and sometimes she just didn't wanna listen. One day after she had been there for a while, I decided to be nice to her. I reached out to give her a hug and she told me, "Get back, I don't give hugs." I couldn't believe she fronted me off like that. I got tears in my eyes and went to sit down, but I thought I would try one more time 'cuz Mama told me to be nice to her. I said, "I just was giving you a hug." She told me again, "I said I don't give hugs." I've never heard that before. How could a teacher not give hugs? After that, I couldn't stand her anymore. She kicked me out of class just about every day 'cuz she didn't like me and I didn't like her either. I'm not a teacher, but I know it's important for teachers to love their students.

Tony, sixth grade (suspended three times):

I was a new kid at school. They closed my old school because the school district was running out of money. I didn't have any friends but my teachers leading up to my fifth-grade year were great! My fifth-grade year was the worst year of my life. The first teacher was my favorite; she was smart, funny, and cool. She read to us every day and challenged us to become better writers. We had writing workshop and Success for All reading sessions every single day. I have always been smart for my age, and she would reward me. If I got finished early, I would have to help students who were struggling. She told me that helping others would help me understand the material even better. A lot of days she would give me extra work that kept me interested because sometimes I get bored with the regular work. But she got laid off because the school district didn't have enough money to pay all the teachers.

I think it happens mostly in the African American community because I feel Blacks have a reputation of being seen as "less" than Whites by the government; therefore, most money goes to the White schools. I haven't heard about any of the White schools in the suburbs around here closing, and they still have their teachers. It just doesn't seem fair to me. When I got a new teacher was when everything went downhill. My self-esteem dropped, I didn't do my work, I got in fights, got suspended and most of all got bad grades. I was frustrated, angry, and sad because of the replacement. I felt as if everyone was against me. So I decided to just quit doing anything. My principal stepped in and convinced the teacher to let me turn in my work rather than get an "E" [failing grade] because she wanted me to go to the gifted middle school. Though I made bad choices, I still graduated from elementary and I will attend the gifted school this fall.

Tray, eighth grade:

I thought middle school would be great, but some stuff I didn't like in the first 2 years. Like in the sixth grade people thought they were all of that and they like to bully people. In Mr. Summerfield's class I did not get a good grade in math, and he didn't help me that much. And when it was time for homework assignments he talked very low and he knew that I sat all the way in the back of the class. Or when he would pass out homework sheets, I never got one. In seventh grade, I had some problems with people like the time when a kid shot a staple in my eye, and the substitute told us to go down to the Behavior Center. And when I went to school the next day I got suspended for 3 days, and I failed English Language Arts that marking period, because we had a test while I was suspended and they wouldn't let me make it up.

Calvin, twelfth grade:

I think it's a boy thing and a Black thing. Mr. Korf seems to hate boys and Black girls. He's a horrible geometry teacher and everyone knows it, but the principal and school board members won't get rid of him. I'm normally a good student with As and Bs, but Mr. Korf seemed to take pride in failing as many students as possible. Whenever I asked a question in class, he would try to embarrass me by saying, "I already went over that and I'm not wasting my time repeating anything." This was the canned response whenever a boy or a Black girl tried to ask a question. I finally got my report card and wasn't surprised when I had a D. My mother visited the school to ask if he would tutor me to help improve my grade in his class. Mr. Korf told her that it wasn't his job to tutor students before and after school, and he didn't have time during his lunch hour.

The words of Timothy, Fredriana, Calvin, Tray, and Tony illuminate the pain, frustration, anger, sadness, and longing for literacy that often is hidden behind the research and the statistics on African American education. We know that many African American students are doing poorly in school. Recent statistics suggest that 86% of African American students read below grade level, and results from the 2007 National Assessment of Educational Progress (NAEP) show that in fourth grade, only 14% of African American students read at or above the proficient level (with literal and inferential understanding of the text), compared with 43% of Whites, 46% of Asians, 17% of Latinos, and 18% of Native Americans. By eighth grade, 13% of African Americans read at or above the proficient level, compared with Whites (40%), Asians (41%), Latinos (15%), and Native American (18%). These statistics are sobering, but those which reveal the social difficulties that some African American students experience are even more heartbreaking. According to Skiba and Leone (2001), African American students are suspended at a rate two to three times that of other students, and African American students are more likely than their White peers to be suspended or expelled for the same kind of conduct at school. And these rates of expulsion are affecting even the youngest African American students. As Gilliam (2005) reported, African American children in state-funded *prekindergarten* are expelled at about twice the rate of Latinos and Whites. All of these statistics are staggering, yet after reading them, we may disassociate ourselves from the terrible plight of African American students because the numbers simply don't seem real. However, by sharing real stories about real African American students, we hope that we all will remember that "it's not just about literacy, it's about their lives" (A. Tatum cited in Edwards, 2008).

"I HATE SCHOOL": LOW LITERACY AND LOW LIFE CHANCES

Joshua, preschool: "I hate school. I'm gonna drop out!"

Mykene, third grade (suspended five times): "I'm ugly and I'm stupid and I hate school."

Malik, fourth grade: "Finally I made it to the fourth grade. I hated the third grade. My teacher and I just couldn't get along. We always argued. When one person would make her mad, she would take it out on everyone, and that's not cool."

All three of these African American children claim that they hate school. They are just babies; one is in preschool, while the others are in elementary, and they already perceive their schools, and their teachers, to be the enemy. When African American children hate school, they are likely to disengage from the enterprise of learning, which can have dire consequences for their educational and social lives. First, African American girls are more likely to have children as teenagers. Black American teenagers have higher pregnancy and out-of-wedlock birth rates than their White and Hispanic peers (Kaplan, 1997). Interestingly, some research has suggested that there is a moderate relationship between a young woman's reading score and her later risk of giving birth as a teen. In a study of teenage women from Philadelphia enrolled in Grade 8 in 1995–1996, Wildsmith, Bennett, and Johnson (2007) found that those with lower levels of literacy had a much higher likelihood of teenage birth relative to those with high levels of reading skill. They concluded, "Because poor early reading skill reduces the ability to learn material provided in school, girls who struggle with reading early on in school are unlikely to achieve in the academic setting and have strong attachment to school. In turn, these women are at a higher risk of having a teenage birth" (p. 2).

Second, African American students are more likely to drop out of high school. In an article in the *San Francisco Chronicle*, Nanette Asimov (2008) reported that 42% of African American students dropped out of California high schools, a higher percentage than Native Americans (31%), Latinos (30%), Pacific Islanders (28%), Whites (15%), or Asian Americans (10%). For those African American students who do stay in school, the struggles can be enormous, and after graduation these students often find that they still have not acquired the skills and knowledge that would prepare them for a prosperous professional life. For example, only 55% of all Black students in 2005 graduated from high school on time with a regular diploma, compared with 78% of Whites (Editorial Projects in Education, 2008). In 2002, 23% of all Black students who started public high school left prepared for the workplace, compared with 40% of Whites (J. Greene & Winters, 2005).

These statistics are alarming, but we want to remind you that there are African American students who graduate from high school and attend college. Yet while these students often are considered to be "exceptional," even they have difficulties graduating from college. In fact, in 2000, of the roughly 120,000 Black students attending 4-year institutions as full-time freshmen, half were enrolled in institutions that graduated under 40% of their Black students, and one in 10 attended institutions with Black graduation rates below 20%, while the average graduation rate for all students was 57%.

We believe that African American students want to like school rather than hate it, want to be successful literacy learners, and want to have more opportunities in life. And we hold firm to the belief that every African American parent wants his or her child to have a better quality of life than they themselves had. It is the American dream to be able to improve one's quality of life, but for many African Americans this dream has not been realized as a result of failure in school. Why has the American dream been deferred for so many African American students and their parents? In a brief review of the literature, we have noted three key answers to this question.

NARROW DEFINITIONS OF
LITERACY AND LITERATE PRACTICES

In schools, literacy typically is defined as reading, writing, speaking, and listening skills. According to Spears-Bunton and Powell (2009), these literacy skills represent the mainstream "style of speaking, writing, and behaving" (p. 7) endorsed by schools. They argue that while this view of literacy is highly valued in schools, it is also quite narrow, and it defines those who have differing forms of cultural practices, experiences, and literacies as "nonliterate." For example, the literate practices of White middle-class families, such as reading bedtime stories and going to the library, may not be practiced within African American families. Some African Americans, for example, may not take their children to the library because they did not go there as children (Diller, 1999). Consequently, in many schools, African American children and families are perceived as "disadvantaged" or "at-risk" because they do not have the traditional literate practices that are valued in school (Edwards & Danridge, 2001). Based on these deficit views, teachers may lower their expectations for African American students, emphasize basic skills, and limit their opportunities to engage in critical thinking (Hammond, Hoover, & McPhail, 2005).

However, we strongly believe that African American youth and families *are* literate. In their classic research, Anderson and Stokes (1984) identified nine domains of literacy: religion; daily living; entertainment; school-related activity (e.g., homework); general information (e.g., catalogs, advertisements/flyers); work; literacy techniques and skills (child and adult initiated); interpersonal communication; and storytime. These domains incorporate home literacy practices, such as reading recipes and cooking, reading religious texts, reading the newspaper, paying bills, and working on the computer, that are part of American life. We believe that Anderson and Stokes's research can be used as a framework to illuminate the literacy practices of African American students and families. As Maisha Fisher (2008) has argued, there are numerous

> "unexpected sources" of Black literate traditions in the twenty-first century in out-of-school and school settings [including] spoken word poetry, open mic venues often held in restaurants and cafes, Black-owned and operated bookstore chains as well as classrooms that use an open mic format to give students opportunities to share their original compositions. (p. 3)

While these sources of literate traditions are important to African American students, families, and communities, they often are ignored or overlooked in school literacy curricula. Powell (2009) notes that "textbooks and pre-packaged literacy programs often promote ritualized, mechanical responses that have little to do with students' lived experiences" (p. 9).

Yet the kinds of literacy practices enacted in African American families and communities can be used to build bridges to school literacy. In his classic book, *Shooting for Excellence: African American and Youth Culture in New Century Schools*, Mahiri (1998) offers strong practical examples of curricular interventions that (a) acknowledge the literate practices that African American youth engage in outside of school and (b) draw upon their out-of-school literacies and popular cultural practices for English instruction in diverse secondary schools. For example, Mahiri used a variety of literature (e.g., *The Color Purple, Joy Luck Club*), newspaper articles, and popular media texts (e.g., interviews in hip-hop magazines like *Vibe*) to teach reading and writing to African American (and other) adolescents in school. While this book, and many others that have been published more recently (e.g., Morrell, 2004; A. Tatum, 2005; Young, 2007), offer rich insights into this kind of teaching, we wondered how White teachers, and even some Black teachers, who may not be as familiar with or confident in using African American youth literacies, would be able to implement this kind of pedagogy. Importantly, Mahiri worked with some of the teachers on his research project to help them enact these kinds of pedagogies; however, most teachers do not have access to this kind of professional support. We have found that many classroom teachers want to teach African American students in responsive ways, but they do not have the deep cultural knowledge of African American youth, and they often do not know how to actually learn this cultural information because it typically is not provided in teacher education programs or professional development workshops (Ladson-Billings, 2005).

Many researchers believe that in order to improve the literacy attainment and schooling of African American students, teacher education programs must excel in preparing teachers and administrators who have an elevated level of authentic knowledge of African American culture; a deeper understanding of the impact African American culture has on behavior, learning styles, and preferred teaching styles; and a genuine appreciation for the valuable repertoire of experiences African American students bring to school (Banks, 2001; Gay, 2000; Irvine, 2003).

President Obama's proposed education policy is designed to better prepare teachers for their jobs. The Obama–Biden education plan will offer more pay for expert teachers who can serve as mentors and coaches to new teachers (Office of the Press Secretary, 2009). There will be more incentives and opportunities for teachers to improve their knowledge and skills. Additionally, the plan gives more pay for highly qualified teachers who teach in underprivileged schools. However, nowhere in the plan is it mentioned how the issue of preparing teachers *culturally* will be addressed. It is clear that the concept of developing teachers with deeper, authentic cultural understanding of minority groups is still an issue that needs to be brought to the attention of schools, administrations, and policymakers.

FACTORS THAT CONFOUND LITERACY ACHIEVEMENT

Schools have been viewed as the Great Equalizer in American society. However, there are many other factors besides race that mitigate African American students' equal opportunity to learn in school. Poverty, for example, greatly affects African American families and communities. For example, about 64% of African American students are being raised in single-parent households (*African Americans by the Numbers*, n.d.). In addition, there are a large number of single-race Black grandparents living with their own grandchildren younger than 18. In these households, about half of the grandparents are also serving as primary caregivers and guardians, oftentimes because their biological parents are unable to care for these children due to drug addiction, incarceration, mental illness, and so on. Health care issues are also very challenging, because almost twice as many African American children (19.6%) are uninsured as White, non-Hispanic children (11.3%).

The poverty rates in schools that African American students attend are also high. For example, more than 60% of Black students attend schools where more than 50% of the school population is identified as living in poverty, compared with 18% of White students (Orfield & Lee, 2005). Kozol's (1991) look at school poverty in the early 1990s opened our eyes to the appalling conditions of schools serving many African American and other students of color. Today, Black students are still more likely than White students to attend schools where trash is present on the floor (29% vs. 18%), graffiti is present (10% vs. 3%), and ceilings are in disrepair (12% vs. 7%) (Planty & Devoe, 2005). Limited financial resources for schools not only mean dilapidated buildings and scarce materials, but a less-prepared teaching staff as well (Darling-Hammond, 1997). In high schools where at least 75% of the students are low-income, there are three times as many uncertified or out-of-field teachers teaching English or science than in schools with wealthier populations (Department of Education, National Center for Education Statistics, 2004).

We know that teachers and schools are often frustrated by these factors because they do not have the power to change the economic conditions and family structures of their African American students, and yet they also are expected to teach these children effectively. But change in the family and community can lead to school success for African American youth. In *Whatever It Takes: Geoffrey Canada's Quest to Change Harlem and America*, Paul Tough (2008) describes the systematic efforts that Geoffrey Canada has undertaken to transform a Harlem community. In his work, Canada viewed the problem of African American students' underachievement from a different angle; rather than just working on the schools, he aimed to "transform every aspect of the environment that poor children were growing up in; to change the way their families raised them and the way schools taught them as well as the character of the neighborhood that surrounded them" (p. 19). Canada's work has been extremely successful, and the African American students in the Promise Academies he founded are thriving. President Obama even mentioned Canada's work in his speech to the African American Congress on the 100th anniversary of the NAACP. We certainly applaud Canada's work. But because so many teachers are working with African American students from fragile families, without the benefit of these community supports and resources, we need to know much more about how to make these successes a reality across the country. What kinds of policies need to be in place to support African American children and families? And are there lessons that we can learn from the Promise Academies that can help teachers work with African American students in families and communities that are not heavily supported?

LANGUAGE ISSUES

When discussing the African American Vernacular English (AAVE) versus Academic English debate, language arts instruction must take into account the specific historical and cultural features of language use in the African American community (Moore, 1996). In fact, these issues cannot be addressed completely without placing the discussion in the larger context of the African American struggle for access to equity in education. The language discussion becomes much more complex when concerns about power and dominance are addressed. Hilliard (1983) asserts that "no full understanding of the issues associated with language and the education of African American children can be gained unless the history of the role and dynamics of language in the context of oppression is developed" (p. 24). Author and literary critic bell hooks (1994) further supports the idea that a discussion about language must include issues of power when she states, "Standard English is not the speech of exile. It is the language of conquest and domination" (p. 168). She suggests that African American culture includes among its characteristics resistance to and distinction from the dominating culture. In other words, as bell hooks suggests, some African American students are simply resistant learners, rather than incapable of learning and using Academic English. They may consider changing the way they speak as surrendering or succumbing to a racist society that perpetuates inequities.

Fordham and Ogbu (1986) affirmed this idea when they learned that some students consider speaking in Standard English as "acting White." They found that some students resist using Standard English as an act of resistance to society and allegiance to their own culture. Elaine Richardson (2003) discusses this issue in *African American Literacies*, explaining what she believes to be some confusion in the literature on African American students and their rejection of some of their high-achieving peers. She refers to Carter Woodson's belief that most African Americans received a culturally biased education that taught them to sever ties with the Black community and cultural activities. Woodson and Richardson have a problem with Blacks who have no interest in making a commitment to help less fortunate Blacks, expecting them to pull themselves up by their bootstraps. Richardson believes that people in the Black community see this as "thinkin' that you betta than somebody," and ostracize the educated Black person from the Black community. She explains that this is the phenomenon of "sellin' out" or "acting White." Richardson explains that "acting White" is not simply about trying to achieve academically; it also means refusing to help others achieve. However, when successful Blacks are committed to assisting others in their community, they often are welcomed by community gatekeepers.

In her book, Richardson also discusses her experience of being ill prepared for college, although she thought she was smart. She states, "My goal was to go to school, try the American way, and get a 'good job'. Maybe teach school or something—I didn't know for sure. I just felt that I was smart, and never really found out I was illiterate until I went to college and got placed into dummy English" (p. 3).

Although Richardson was successful in high school, she learned that mastery of AAVE was not enough for her to get through college successfully. (A more detailed discussion of this issue appears in Chapter 3, Teaching African American Students: Approaches and Best Practices.) Richardson's experience is not unique. Numerous African American students are successful in high school, but suffer in their college classes because they have not been appropriately taught how to negotiate the cultural borders between African American Vernacular English and Academic English. Their schooling experience is laden with issues of power and dominance and involves determining how to be successful within Delpit's (1995) "culture of power" and effectively function from Du Bois's "double-consciousness" perspective. Richardson raises important issues that must not be addressed superficially, for these issues are "hot lava" topics in the discussion of successfully educating African American children. How do we get beyond the discussion and actually develop specific ways to help our children become border crossers? We need models that can be implemented in the classroom on a daily basis to ensure that our budding scholars do not fail when they enter institutions of higher learning. Part of the answer may be in our early approach to out-of-school learning. We cannot afford to compartmentalize our teaching. Instead, we must learn to embrace out-of-school literacy experiences and develop ways to utilize them to make our classroom literacy teaching and learning more effective.

In his book, *What They Don't Learn in School: Literacy in the Lives of Urban Youth,* Jabari Mahiri (2003) features a self-authored essay entitled "Street Scripts: African American Youth Writing About Crime and Violence" that discusses the use of out-of-school literacies to resist and replace the dominant (and often oppressive) scripts forced on students in school. Understanding this process of resistance and replacement can help us learn how to develop a "stance of intervention" that can motivate students, according to Mahiri, who believes that economic empowerment, not increased literacy, is often the goal that youth are striving toward. Mahiri's ideas are fascinating because he tries to help readers think about how literacies may change access to resources. The principal theme in the text is that school is not the only place where rich literacy experiences occur. Three other authors in Mahiri's book represent levels of challenge for literacy teachers of African American students. First, Samuelson's "I Used to Go to School Now I Learn: Unschoolers Critiquing the Discourse of School" asserts that many young people who are engaged in the unschooling community do not hold traditional ideas about discourse and challenge literacy teaching and learning in unique ways. Unfortunately, some educators may quickly conclude that the "unschoolers" are the students who are unreachable and simply turn a deaf ear to them. Second, Sutton's chapter, entitled "Spoken Word: Performance Poetry in the Black Community," challenges teachers to consider the "miseducation" of several spoken word poets who are literary leaders in their community. The poets candidly share experiences of being disconnected with literacy, and especially writing in their high school classes, through an imposition of form (students were forced to utilize specific poetic forms rather than being given a choice), uninteresting materials used in class, and very limited opportunities to have their passion nurtured. Finally, Morrell and Duncan-Andrade provide a contemporary example illustrating how to use hip-hop as a bridge to canonical texts.

In *African American Literacies Unleashed: Vernacular English and the Composition Classroom,* Ball and Lardner (2005) provide a comprehensive study of AAVE, skillfully laying the groundwork for reversing the cycle of underachievement for African American students who speak it. They assert that teachers must make a three-part change in order for the transformation to be successful: (1) knowledge; (2) self-reflection; and (3) personal and professional classroom change. Teachers and teacher educators are required to learn AAVE and unlearn racism in order to transform their attitudes about the subject. Ball and Lardner use personal narratives, student texts, interactive discourse, and examples from community-based organizations, and provide 12 changes that teachers can make if they want to change their classroom practice. They also provide an exceptional framework for teachers to follow if they want to move beyond rhetoric and transform their practice. However, their work focuses on secondary education, and we are concerned that elementary teachers may not attempt to transfer the knowledge. We believe that it is imperative for elementary teachers to begin working with students as early as possible to help them become fluent in both AAVE and Academic English. What would Ball and Lardner's model look like in an elementary classroom? The issue of language use is one that causes many hardships for African American students, including some who are considered academically successful. We need more elementary and secondary education models that can be implemented in classrooms.

MOVING FORWARD WITH HOPE

Even though scholars have spent more than 30 years trying to explain why African Americans continue to perform poorly in school, Dummett (1984) laments that "the enigma remains" (p. 31). We believe that narrow definitions of literacy and literate practices, factors that confound literacy achievement, and language use are complex issues, and they contribute to the low literacy achievement that African American students have experienced. They are part of the reason why African American children, for so many years, have not had an equal opportunity to learn and have had many of their dreams deferred. Despite these difficulties and challenges, however, there are also what we call "pockets of hope" that emerge, which remind us that something *can* be done to transform the educational experience of African American students. Unfortunately, because these pockets of hope seem to remain small, isolated islands of success, they do not reach the thousands of African American students who are lost within our public education system.

In this book, we aim to make these pockets of hope deeper and wider by providing historic and current "snapshots" of issues within literacy education for African American students in K–16 schools (looking back) and offering solutions that will help teachers, schools, parents, teacher educators, and policymakers move forward in transforming schooling for these students. Our personal narratives and the voices of students and teachers keep us grounded in reality, as we activate our belief that "change is gonna come."

CHAPTER ONE

The Fight for Access to Literacy

For what do I go to this far land that no one has ever reached? Oh, I am alone! I am utterly alone! And Reason, that old man, said to her, "Silence! what do you hear?" And she listened intently, and she said, "I hear a sound of feet, a thousand times ten thousand and thousands of thousands, and they beat this way!" He said, "They are the feet of those that shall follow you. Lead on! Make a track to water's edge. Where you stand now the ground will be beaten flat by ten thousand times ten thousand feet." And he said, "Have you seen the locust how they cross a stream? First one comes down to the water-edge and it is swept away, and then another comes and then another, and then another, and at last with their bodies piled up a bridge is built and the rest pass over." She said, "And, of those who come first, some are swept away, and are heard of no more; their bodies do not even build the bridge?" "And are swept away, and are heard of no more— and what of that?" he said. "And what of that—" she said. "They make a track to the water's edge." "They make a track to the water's edge—" And she said, "Over that bridge which shall be built with our bodies, who will pass?" He said, "The entire human race." And the woman grasped her staff. And I saw her turn down that dark path to the river.

—Olive Schreiner, *Dreams*

From the Middle Passage on, African Americans have been forced to fight for civil rights: freedom; equal employment opportunities; the right to vote, to live in their neighborhood of choice, to equal access to public transportation and public facilities (e.g., hotels, restaurants, restrooms, etc.); and other civil rights. Many of these battles have been won, at least at a superficial level. Some of our ancestors gave their lives, and others sacrificed their livelihood, to increase our chances of becoming a literate race. Like the woman in the opening poem, they made a track to the water's edge. Yet, in the 21st century we continue to fight in America's classrooms for access to literacy.

The stories of Rev. Thompson, Elena, and others are examples of the persistence that Blacks continue to exhibit in their fight for access to literacy. Despite sacrifices made for their families, they refused to abandon their dream to become educated. They are heroes in their own right and their stories should be told for generations.

NARRATIVE BEGINNINGS—
REV. M.T. THOMPSON: "LIFTED FROM RED CLAY BY RED WORDS"

Born in Alabama during the Great Migration, M.T. (15 months) and his older sister, Letha (2 years, 6 months), lost their mother during childbirth. The midwife's limited medical knowledge was not enough to save her. Their father, whom they lovingly called "Papa," was devastated. Several years later Papa met and married Laura, who loved M.T. and Letha as her own. M.T. and Letha could not start school right away because they had to work in the fields to help take care of their family. Finally, when M.T. was 8, he started going to school. He loved learning and worked hard to try to learn to read, but after a few months his father told him and his sister that they would have to quit school because there just wasn't enough money to feed and take care of the family. Letha wept bitterly–she dreamed of becoming a nurse. The next day she got dressed to go to the fields, but M.T. told Papa, "Please let Sista keep going to school; I'll pick enough cotton for me and her." Papa agreed because he knew that M.T. could do it. M.T. was allowed to attend school sporadically over the next several years. He tried to catch up with the other students, but it was difficult. He was embarrassed when called upon to read aloud–many of the much younger children could read better than he.

At the age of 17, M.T. left his sharecropping job and, like many other Blacks during the Great Migration, moved north seeking a better way of life. His older cousin, John Henry, told M.T. that he could live with him in Michigan, get a job at the foundry, and make a good living. M.T. landed a job with General Motors and met a beautiful young lady, Pecola, whom he married. Although his foundry job improved his quality of life, M.T. was never at peace with his semiliterate state. He loved books and taught himself to read. M.T. became a preacher in 1960, and was called to pastor at New Mount Calvary Baptist Church in 1962. His desire to learn increased more than ever. He felt compelled to become more knowledgeable–especially about the Bible. He desired to be able to read and understand the words of Jesus, which appeared in red in his Bible. As a full-time General Motors iron pourer, full-time pastor, and father of eight children, M.T. started attending adult education courses. He would study at the dining room table with his children, reading and writing, always emphasizing the importance of getting a good education. Sacrificing everything, Rev. M.T. Thompson quit GM in 1969 to focus totally on his ministry as pastor. When M.T. Jr. graduated from Oakland University in 1973, M.T. Sr. graduated from adult education. At that time, adult education did not have commencement exercises, but Rev. Thompson wanted to celebrate his great victory. He got permission to march with Buena Vista High School's class of 1973. M.T. Sr. and M.T. Jr. took their cap-and-gown picture together–proud of each other's accomplishment. Four years later Pecola graduated from high school, a year before her youngest child. Did M.T. and Pecola win the fight for access to literacy? Definitely! Collectively, their children have 11 college degrees, including a doctor of ministry, doctor of philosophy, and law degree; their grandchildren have five degrees already, and seven of them are currently in college (Thompson et al., 2009).

Reverend Thompson grew up at a time when many African Americans had to work to help their parents take care of their siblings. Although we still find some older siblings with similar responsibilities in today's society, it is much less common. What is found more frequently in the contemporary classroom are cases where African Americans are given limited access to literacy as a result of being diagnosed with learning disabilities and/or behavior problems. In the next section, a student named Elena tells her story of being forced into special education—one that is shared by too many African Americans.

THE FIGHT FOR ACCESS IN A CONTEMPORARY CLASSROOM— ELENA: "I DON'T BELONG IN SPECIAL EDUCATION, AND I'M NOT STAYING THERE"

I never understood why they decided to put me in special ed, but I knew that something wasn't right. A few of us in Mrs. Simbulski's math class were strugglin'. To me, she wasn't a good teacher. She didn't explain stuff like my teachers back in elementary. Most of the time she was hollering at somebody . . . they was always actin' up in class. I told Mama that I didn't like the class 'cuz the teacher couldn't control her students at all. They just took over the class every day. I kept tryin' to get the stuff, but the teacher finally stopped tryin' to teach. She would just come up in class and give us a page number and expect us to understand. I told her she was the teacher and she oughta be able to do something about her students actin' a fool.

When it was time for us to take some test—I don't even remember the name of it, I didn't understand the questions, so I answered the best I could. Next thing I knew they had called my mother and told her to come to a meetin' at the school. They had something called IEP or IAP [Individual Education Plan written for students with disabilities] or something like that, and told her that I was too slow for the regular class. Me and my mother didn't understand becuz' my grades in my other classes were not that bad. My mother refused to sign the papers and decided that we would move.

At my new school in a city across the state, I did much better because the teachers and students were much more serious. I ended up having all A's and B's for the rest of my sixth-grade year and my seventh-grade year. At the end of the seventh grade, Mama decided that it was okay for us to go back home becuz we missed the rest of our family, and she was sure that I would be okay in school after having such a good year.

When I got back to my old school, I wasn't ready for what was about to happen to me. After a few days, my mother got a telephone call to come out to the school. They had received my records from downtown and she was goin' to have to sign the papers for me to go into special ed. She showed them my grades for the past year, but they told her that she had to sign. Mama ain't no joke and she refused to sign, so I had to go home. She kept calling different people tryin' to get help. She cried and I cried and finally I told her maybe I am slow and I just wanna go back to school and be with my friends, but she told me, "No Baby, sometimes you just have to fight. We ain't givin' up." Mama finally talked to some lady who was the head of the Special Ed Department for the city or somethin' like that, and she told Mama that she had to go through some process for me to get out of special ed. I couldn't just get out. Mama was fed up with those people and she told her what to do with the process. I had been out of school for over a month, and I was mad cuz' I was missing volleyball season.

Mama moved us again. But this time we just moved to the little city outside of where we lived. It was mainly a White area, but Mama had talked to them about everything and they told her that they would accept my sixth- and seventh-grade report cards. They didn't put me in special ed and they even let me play on the middle school volleyball team right away. Of course, I made a lot of friends right away cuz' I helped the team win the rest of their games. I went on to their high school and pretty soon I got used to my new friends. I did pretty good in classes, except math. I think that old teacher messed me up, but when I got to algebra class, my new teacher really liked me. He worked with me and tutored me, and told me to stop thinking about what happened to me before. I worked hard, and I passed the class.

I turned 18 during my senior year and decided to move out on my own. I was just tired of everything and my boyfriend wanted me to spend more time with him. Mama was real upset but I told her that I'm goin' back to finish school. She worked so hard to help me, but I just got tired of the whole thing. I don't know, I think all that stuff back in middle school always stayed on my mind. I still wonder if maybe somethin' is wrong with me. I mean, why did they do that if it ain't nothing wrong with me? My high school teacher and counselor are upset. They told me that I'm good enough to play college sports. They told me that I'm smart enough to go to college. They keep calling, telling me to finish. I don't know. I'm confused. I think I'll go back soon.

Students like Elena find themselves at the mercy of educators who are frustrated with student behavior and suffer from a loss of confidence in their own ability to reach and teach the students in their classrooms. We realize that some students have problems that require them to receive assistance through a special education curriculum, but we believe that the disproportionate number of African American students in special education classes reveals a deeper issue—the fact that students are not receiving appropriate instruction and assistance in their regular education classes. When students like Elena are forced into special education, it often damages their self-esteem and diminishes their self-worth to the point that they begin to question their ability.

LOOKING BACK TO GO FORWARD: A HISTORICAL PERSPECTIVE

To address the current issue of access to literacy in schools and communities, we "look backward to go forward." In his award-winning text, *The Education of Blacks in the South, 1860–1935,* James Anderson (1988) helps us develop a better understanding of the issues that Rev. Thompson, Elena, and other African Americans had to address in their fight for early access to literacy. He asserts that history books include a standard story that has some truths, but the real stories of African Americans' literacy development influenced the nation's "complex and contradictory attitudes" much more than many realize. We share the belief with Anderson that the story of the African American quest for access to literacy is a story that is not necessarily found in history books, and the story changes depending on the storyteller's experiences. Slaves, sharecroppers, abolitionists, journalists, educators, Rev. Thompson, and Elena have different stories to share concerning their fight for access to literacy, but common threads of suffering, sacrifice, persistence, and victory can be found in each story. Each case illuminates the complex and contradictory attitudes of a nation that claims to be founded upon principles of individual freedom and equality, yet allows individuals to experience physical and mental bondage and continuous discrimination.

Coming to America—Involuntary Immigration

Coming to America as involuntary immigrants, most Blacks were enslaved and considered property. The first 20 slaves were brought to the United States in 1619 as indentured servants (Harley, 1995) who served a limited amount of time and eventually were freed. However, a slave market was created as Europeans brought more African slaves to the United States. Farmers and plantation owners were unable to cultivate large pieces of land alone, and they made requests to slave traders for increasingly large numbers of slaves. As the slave trade grew, certain plantation owners made requests for slaves from specific geographical locations because they seemed to be better "fit" for certain types of work (Sobel, 1988).

The Physically Enslaved Seek Mental Emancipation

The African American struggle to acquire literacy began during the 17th century. Alliances included advocates of slavery who favored the education of Blacks, but believed being enslaved helped to enlighten them concerning the Gospel message of Christianity. Missionaries were the first educators of Blacks because their responsibility was twofold: to teach Blacks to read and, more important, to proselytize them, often using Bibles as textbooks (Woodson, 1933). The early education of Blacks in America by missionaries was based on three main principles: (1) educating slaves for Bible reading, to make them Christian, (2) the idea that all people should be free and should support Christian efforts to abolish slavery and provide equal access to education (supported mainly by Quakers), and (3) the belief that slavery should be abolished to enable Africans to take their rightful place among the other citizens because the country emerged from a concept of individual freedom. "Rightful place" did not necessarily mean "equal status." Many well-known abolitionists, such as John Jay, Harriet Beecher Stowe, Benjamin Franklin, and others, supported education for Blacks to gain their rightful place, based on their words and actions (Morgan, 1995), while President Thomas Jefferson vacillated on his beliefs concerning whether Blacks should be given all individual freedoms offered to White citizens.

State records reflect the efforts of various individuals and organizations that attempted to assist African Americans in their quest for literacy acquisition and development. As early as the 1630s, French Catholics were providing education for all laborers, regardless of race, in Louisiana. The Society for the Propagation of the Gospel in Foreign Parts financially supported missionaries and schoolmasters who taught slaves and free persons of color how to read and write (Gordon, 1971). However, what was considered "progress" to Blacks and advocates for their education was threatening the economic futures of some slaveholders, and they set out to cease the rapid growth of literacy development among Blacks. Many slaveholders were afraid that educated slaves would be more difficult to manage because they would be able to read documents and might begin to believe that they could have a better life. Literate slaves could navigate their way from slavery to freedom more easily and perhaps might encourage others to seek freedom, as well. In the early 1700s, a series of laws prohibiting the teaching of slaves was enacted in many states (Woodson, 1933).

With the forming of a new nation, questions arose concerning whether the U.S. Constitution would address the "legal" citizenship status of African Americans. Access to public schooling was based on citizenship status, and free African Americans were especially concerned with this issue. But the United States was founded on a belief in White supremacy and was considered a White man's country. Illuminating this belief, during a meeting in the First Congress of the United States in 1790 (Takaki, 1979) the "founding fathers" limited naturalization to White aliens. Although this limited the citizenship of "newcomers," it did not address the issue of people who were already in the country during its inception, such as African Americans.

Individual states were left to make their own decisions; southern states continued with institutionalized slavery, and northern, midwestern, and western states' belief in White supremacy became evident by the laws that they passed, including orders for Blacks to leave the state or receive lashes (Ohio and Oregon). Blacks actually were beaten if they remained in the state, and their lashes often were increased for second offenses. The federal government supported the degrading actions of these nascent states by allowing them admission to the union. African Americans were not allowed access to education, and their education was left up to the benevolence of Whites in their state and often depended on their citizenship status as Blacks. This connection of citizenship and rights to education provided the rationale that many Whites needed to feel comfortable limiting Blacks' access to literacy.

Quakers opened a number of schools in response to slavery proponents, including schools for "Colored" children in Rhode Island and Boston (Morgan, 1995). In 1780, Black and White children were allowed to attend school together in Pennsylvania and New Jersey. The Quakers were especially responsible for opening integrated schools for poor children (Morgan, 1995). Members of the Quaker community provided funding for the education of Blacks on a local basis, and they encouraged fellow Quaker members to share in their efforts throughout the country, but they were more successful in the North than in the South (Morgan, 1995).

The Quakers formed the Manumission Society in Philadelphia and New York to protect slaves from bounty hunters, with a trustee list of very important people. Alexander Hamilton, one of the authors of the *Federalist Papers,* and John Jay, the first Chief Justice of the United States, were Manumission Society trustees. Jay believed that slavery diminished the national character, and therefore he supported antislavery movements and schools for African Americans. Cornelius Davis left his job at a White school to teach 40 children at the African Free School (Morgan, 1995). Most of his students had slave parents. After a female teacher was hired in 1791, girls were admitted to the school, and by 1796 the school had its own building, which later was destroyed by a fire—a target of racist arson. The City of New York had donated land for the construction of African Free School Number 1, and African Free School Number 2 was built in 1820 to accommodate 500 pupils (Morgan, 1995). School administrators worked hard to increase the interest of the powerful trustees, who were not involved. Although they sat on the board, the trustees did not utilize their influence to gain support from others in the community. In an attempt to increase support from trustees for their school, administrators invited international scholars and educators to observe the school's program, and received exceptionally favorable responses. Describing some of the school's accomplishments, Morgan (1995) states:

> This pragmatic mission of empowerment for free Blacks gave rise to a concentration on direct instruction in reading, writing, natural history, astronomy, arithmetic, navigation, and moral education. Joseph Lancaster had developed a unique approach to instruction, materials, and supplies in the teaching of poor children in England, and the Lancasterian system was adopted by the African Free School. The African Free School gave to education some of our earliest examples of special classes for the gifted, called "merit" classes, and the use of pupils to tutor younger pupils in lower grades. In later years the school expanded its curriculum to include globe use, composition, map making, and linear drawing. (p. 42)

Several African Free School graduates became successful leaders, especially in other parts of the world. In Europe, Ira Aldridge became known as one of the greatest interpreters of Shakespearean characters; James McCune Smith, the first Black pharmacist in New York City, graduated from the University of Scotland and became the medical director of the Colored Orphan Asylum in New York; and Edward A. Jones became the first African American college graduate, earning his degree from Amherst College in Massachusetts in 1826. John B. Russman, editor of the first African American newspaper, *Freedman's Journal,* became the superintendent of schools in Liberia, and eventually the governor of the Colony of Cape Palmas in Liberia. Martin DeLaney, an 1852 Harvard Medical School graduate, participated in halting a cholera epidemic, but could not get enough support to keep his private practice in business. After serving in the Union army during the Civil War, he worked as editor for his own newspaper, *The Mystery,* and worked for Frederick Douglass's *North Star.*

Many African Free School graduates struggled to find positions in their areas of training, although their schooling experiences were exceptional. The United States limited Blacks' access to employment, and Blacks who were not fortunate enough to attend special schools were the most vulnerable to the discriminatory practices of a prejudiced society.

Blacks Strive to Educate Themselves

While most attempts to educate Blacks were for the purpose of proselytizing them, free Blacks also took a leadership role in establishing the means to educate themselves and their people. As early as 1790, the Brown Fellowship Society in Charleston sponsored many Sunday schools for the purpose of educating free Negro children. At the end of the Civil War, there were about

600 Negroes attending Baltimore Sunday schools. Sunday schools were one of the most important educational institutions for Negroes, and churches and ministers encouraged parents to send their children to whatever schools were available. In 1825, courses in Latin and French were offered day and night, and 4 years later an African Free School was opened by the Oblate Sisters of Providence (the first successful Roman Catholic sisterhood in the world established by women of African descent). St. Frances Academy is the oldest continuously operating school for Black Catholic children in the United States and is still educating children in Baltimore.

Although African Americans also were actively seeking ways to ensure that their children received a secular education, Christian education was especially emphasized during this time. The first Black Sunday schools were established to teach values—and literacy skills. These schools had four basic characteristics: (1) they were modeled after public schools; (2) their students were members of the congregation; (3) they existed for training in morality; and (4) they were sponsored by a local church (Ward, 1998). Before public schooling was offered to Blacks, many children attended Sunday school on Sunday and returned to the same building—the African American Church building—to attend school Monday through Friday, because it was often the only building in the community owned by Blacks. Students did not pay to attend school and they were offered a curriculum modeled after public schools. Sunday school and school during the week often were funded by church offerings and philanthropists who believed in literacy development for Blacks.

Many Blacks made extreme commitments to gain access to literacy and to assist others in their quest to become literate. The teaching experiences of abolitionist and former slave Frederick Douglass are an example of the risks that were taken to help Blacks gain access to literacy. Douglass spent a portion of his childhood in Baltimore (from 1826 to 1833), where he was given the responsibility of looking after Tommy, the son of Hugh and Sophia Auld. Sophia taught Frederick to read until her husband forbade it. Frederick continued to teach himself to read in secret and began reading newspapers about the debate over slavery. At the age of 12 he bought his own copy of *The Columbian Orator* and taught himself public speaking. In 1833, he was moved from Baltimore to St. Michaels by his master and began operating secret schools. After hearing that Douglass taught two slaves with whom he worked to read, other slaves in the community wanted to learn also. Douglass decided to meet regularly with all who were interested at the house of a freedman. In the summer, Douglass held class under the shade of an old oak tree. He had as many as 40 men and women in regular attendance on Sundays for "Sunday school," most of whom managed to bring old spelling books to the meetings with them (Douglass, 1969). He also met with some of his fellow slaves three evenings a week during the winter. In his opinion, the people met with him regularly for one main reason.

> These dear souls came not to Sabbath school because it was popular to do so, nor did I teach them because it was reputable to be thus engaged. Every moment they spent in that school, they were liable to be taken up, and given thirty-nine lashes. They came because they wished to learn. . . . Their minds had been starved by their cruel masters. . . . They had been shut up in mental darkness. . . . I taught them, because it was the delight of my soul to be doing something that looked like bettering the condition of my race . . . (and) I have the happiness to know, that several of those who came to Sabbath school learned how to read. (Douglass, 1969, p. 84)

Learning to read was certainly a form of emancipation to many Blacks. A Black soldier being tutored by a missionary stated that he believed that being a reader was in itself a form of freedom. Father Joshia Henson, who was once a slave, provided his perception of his own literacy learning as an intellectual awakening. About learning to read, he wrote:

> It was, and has been ever since, a great comfort to me to have made this acquisition; though it has made me comprehend better the terrible abyss of ignorance in which I had plunged all my previous life. It made me also feel more deeply and bitterly the oppression under which I had toiled and groaned; but the crushing and cruel nature of which I had not appreciated, till I found out, in some slight degree, from what I had been debarred. At the same time it made me more anxious than before to do something for the rescue and the elevation of those who were suffering the same evils I had endured and who did not know how degraded and ignorant they really were. (see Genevese, 1976, pp. 562–563)

Many educated Blacks were committed to helping other Blacks learn to read. However, most plantation schools were conducted by literate slaves who had only rudimentary reading skills (Genevese, 1976). They generously and heroically shared their limited knowledge with their fellow slaves. In the early 1800s, a newspaper article published in Richmond, Virginia, charged that Black children were learning to read and write during Sunday school (Berry & Blassingame, 1982). Supposedly, someone had witnessed students carrying schoolbooks to church on Sunday. In response to the accusations, a group of Richmond city policemen stormed the African American church and found that students were being taught reading, writing, and mathematics. The school at the church was discontinued.

African American public and private schools invariably were met with some form of confrontation (Wood, 1968). Blacks and Whites involved in helping Blacks gain access to literacy were harassed by those who did not believe Blacks should be educated. They were ostracized and dismissed from church registers and organizations, and suffered verbal harassment, mob violence, and lynching. Black schools–and the books that were used for teaching in them–were burned and teachers were beaten. There was especially a fear that educated Blacks were a danger to the existing social order after the slave insurrection of Nat Turner, and rebellions of Denmark Vesey and Gabriel Posser (Wood, 1968).

The path to literacy for Blacks had many twists and turns, and those who learned to read and write persevered through many trials and tribulations. A major roadblock in the path to literacy was the linkage between citizenship and the right to public schooling.

The Struggle to Become Citizens

The legal status of African Americans was not defined by the federal government until the Dred Scott decision (1857), which ruled that people of African descent, whether or not they were slaves, could never be citizens of the United States. Unwilling to allow Blacks to participate equally in the American society, Whites utilized the legislative system to perpetuate racism. Toward the end of the 19th century and the dawn of the 20th century, a series of decisions had a great impact on the lives of Blacks in their pursuit of freedom. In 1896, in the *Plessy v. Ferguson* case, the Supreme Court ruled that "separate but equal" facilities were constitutional. In 1898, Louisiana originated the "grandfather clause," which qualified males to vote if their fathers or grandfathers were eligible to vote on or before January 1, 1867 (Harley, 1995). This clause excluded most Blacks, and by 1910, Georgia, North Carolina, Virginia, Alabama, and Oklahoma had adopted the clause. In 1907, the Supreme Court ruled that railroads could racially segregate passengers traveling between states, even when segregation was illegal in the states in which the train was traveling. These court rulings are representative of the political climate during this time and indicative of the legislative and judicial support for overt racism in the United States.

Septima Poinsette Clark's work for equal access to education and civil rights for African Americans several decades before the rise of the national awareness of racial inequality (McFadden, 1993) led her to be known as the "Queen Mother" or "Grandmother of the Civil Rights Movement" in the United States. She also helped to establish "Citizen Schools," which taught reading to adults throughout the Deep South.

The fight for access continued with the case of *Brown v. Board of Education* (1954). The Supreme Court combined five cases (those from Delaware, Kansas, South Carolina, Virginia, and the District of Columbia) into a single case. At issue in the case was Reverend Oliver Brown's objection to his daughter, Linda Brown, having to pass an all-White school in her neighborhood to attend a distant, all-Black school.

Well over 50 years have passed since *Brown* v. *Board of Education*, but the words of W. E. B. Du Bois (1903/1995), from more than 100 years ago, still ring true: "The problem of the 20th century is the problem of the color line" (McMillon, 2009, p. 120). Institutional racism continues to erode the foundation of America's promise to its children. Statistics illuminate pronounced differences in education (assessment scores, graduation rates, college admission rates, retention rates, special education referrals, gifted program referrals, etc.), employment (hiring, salaries, promotions, etc.), and other areas between Whites and minorities. The issue of "the color line" is addressed also by Cornell West (1993) and Derrick Bell (1983, 1993) when they argue that "race matters."

Black Literacy Leaders Emerge

After slaves were emancipated, several Black "literacy leaders" emerged. Booker T. Washington wanted Blacks to get a vocational education and stop fighting against Whites. He stated that they should become better trained in vocational areas, which would ensure them gainful employment (as blacksmiths, housekeepers, etc.). Many White philanthropists supported his efforts wholeheartedly. However, many Blacks considered him a "sellout" to Whites because he encouraged Blacks to attain a vocational education in areas that could be of service to Whites rather than a liberal arts education. They felt that he was doing his own people a great injustice in exchange for the fame and fortune that he received from the White population. Two of his greatest opponents were W. E. B. Du Bois and William Trotter. In 1903, Trotter, a publisher, was arrested for heckling Booker T. Washington at the Columbus Avenue African Zion Church in Boston (Harley, 1995). Trotter explained that he confronted Washington publicly because Washington held a monopoly on the American media, and opposing views on race relations were not heard. Du Bois also spoke out about his belief that Blacks should get a liberal education to prepare them for social mobility. In 1905, W. E. B. Du Bois held a conference for Black leaders and organized the Niagara Movement, which was dedicated to aggressive action on behalf of Black freedom and growth. Also, in 1909, W. E. B. Du Bois and others, including some Whites, met and advocated a civil rights organization to combat the growing violence against Black Americans. This meeting led to the founding of the National Association for the Advancement of Colored People (NAACP). National religious organizations were very involved in politics and social justice; however, it became apparent that an organization was needed that strictly focused on issues in these areas.

The following is an excerpt from "Booker T. & W.E.B.," a poem written by the famous Black poet Dudley Randall (1969/2009) that describes the contrasting educational philosophies of W. E. B. Du Bois and Booker T. Washington:

> "It seems to me," said Booker T.,
> "It shows a mighty lot of cheek
> To study chemistry and Greek
> When Mr. Charlie needs a hand
> To hoe the cotton on his land,
> And when Miss Ann looks for a cook,
> Why stick your nose inside a book?"
> "I don't agree," said W.E.B.,
> "If I should have the drive to seek
> Knowledge of chemistry or Greek,
> I'll do it. Charles and Miss can look
> Another place for hand or cook.
> Some men rejoice in skill of hand,
> And some in cultivating land,
> But there are others who maintain
> The right to cultivate the brain."

Another Black leader, Marcus Garvey (see Grant, 2008), argued that since Blacks were being prevented from gaining civil rights in this country, they should return to Africa. Garvey was born in Jamaica, the son of a mason and domestic worker/farmer. At the age of 14 he left home and found employment in a printing house, where he became a master printer and foreman. However, he was blacklisted after joining the union and participating in a strike. He left Jamaica and traveled throughout Central America, working in Costa Rica and Panama, and moved to London for several years. During Garvey's travels he became convinced that uniting Blacks around the world was the only way to improve their conditions. He founded the Universal Negro Improvement Association in 1914 as a way of uniting all of Africa and its diaspora into one organization with the goal of founding a country and absolute government of their own. After corresponding with Booker T. Washington, he arrived in the United States in 1916 to lecture and raise money to start a school in Jamaica modeled after the Tuskegee Institute, which focused on teacher training, equipping students for jobs in the trades and agriculture, and providing a practice-oriented education that encouraged high morals and cleanliness. Garvey moved to the United States and began a series of successful attempts to garner support for his "Back to Africa" movement. He returned to Jamaica to become a politician after being challenged by W. E. B. Du Bois, being disconnected from the NAACP, and meeting with the imperial giant of the Ku Klux Klan. Du Bois believed that Blacks should fight for access to literacy and a better quality of life in the United States by becoming educated and dedicating themselves to helping others. Du Bois valued the diverse experiences of an integrated society and vehemently opposed the idea of the all-Black society that Garvey proposed. A number of Black leaders requested that the U.S. Attorney General incarcerate Garvey after he became connected with the KKK. They felt that he had gone too far to garner support for his request that all Blacks leave the United States and become citizens in his proposed all-Black society. Although his ideas and methods were exceptionally unconventional, it is important to note that Garvey is credited for traveling to Geneva and presenting the Petition of the Negro Race, which outlined the worldwide abuse of Africans to the League of Nations. But, at the same time, Garvey was an opponent of integration—he wanted a segregated all-Black country, run by an all-Black government.

Integrated, But Not Equal

> Learners do not develop knowledge and literacy exclusive of their social histories, cultures, and immediate contexts for using knowledge; . . . the presence of schools, classrooms, and teachers does not ensure necessarily that learners have access to literacy.
>
> —Virginia Gadsden,
> "Literacy, Education, and Identity Among African-Americans," p. 358

The fight for access continued after integration (Hacker, 1992; Kozol, 1991). In fact, the policy called *integration* eroded much cultural strength among African American communities. While the stated goal of integration was equity in education, segregation of the highest order and inequities have been maintained through integration policies. At the same time, these integration policies resulted in African Americans losing community control and cultural maintenance. This has occurred because the policy of integration never took on the true cause of inequity as measured in our institutions and our history as a nation: racism. In their books, Hacker and Kozol discuss in detail the racism that still divides Blacks and Whites, even today. Hacker contends that African Americans remain a subordinate class because "being black in America bears the mark of slavery. Even after emancipation . . . blacks continued to be seen as an inferior species, not only unsuited for equality but not even meriting a chance to show their worth" (p. 14). Hacker believes that these convictions persist today and are the basis for the existence of two nations within the United States—nations that are separate, hostile, and unequal. Kozol describes the effects of poverty and inadequate funding on education. He eloquently argues that the American education system is still separate and unequal over 50 years after the historic desegregation decision, *Brown* v. *Board of Education.*

What are some of the ways that the public education system remains separate but unequal for African American students? We highlight three key institutional policies and programs that limit African American students' access to school literacy in significant ways: (1) ability grouping and tracking in classrooms; (2) disciplinary policies; (3) special education programs and gifted education programs.

Ability grouping and tracking in classrooms. In many classrooms, teachers use ability grouping "to accommodate instruction to the diversity of their students' needs, interests, and abilities. The assumption is that students will learn best when the instructional content is matched well to their current knowledge and abilities" (Braddock, 1995, p. 155). Robinson (2008) supports Braddock's notion of ability grouping when he states that "ability grouping is a term that denotes two distinct forms of organizing students for instruction; (a) between-classroom tracks and (b) within-classroom ability groups" (p. 143). Typically, elementary and middle school students are placed into three groups of readers: above average, average, and struggling readers. In theory, ability groups should help teachers differentiate reading instruction and adjust to students' needs and interests. Yet previous research has shown that often these reading groups create de facto tracks, with students remaining in the same reading groups throughout their careers in elementary school (Hiebert, 1983; Rist, 1970). The differentiated instruction that occurs in ability groups is not always better for students. Allington (1980, 1983) found that teachers teach good and poor readers in very different ways; they provide good readers with more time to practice during their reading groups, interrupt them less frequently, and help them to direct their attention toward making meaning and understanding texts. Currently, many schools encourage teachers to "flexibly" group their students; however, some research suggests that ability-grouping practices (which may result in limited movement across groups) remain prominent in elementary reading instruction (Chorzempa & Graham, 2006; LeTendre, Hofer, & Shimizu, 2003).

Darling-Hammond (1997) and Robinson (2008) contend that the patterns established by ability grouping in elementary literacy classrooms are more formalized through tracking in secondary schools. Tracking is defined as "the separation of students into separate instructional strands with differentiated curricula based on presumed or tested ability levels" (Darling-Hammond, 1997, p. 127). Significant research has shown that tracking has detrimental effects on students, especially those in the low academic tracks, because lower-level courses offer a much less challenging curriculum, and their pedagogy emphasizes basic skills rather than higher-order thinking and critical reasoning (Lleras & Rangel, 2009; Oakes, 1985, 1992, 2005). Dekker, Krou, Wright, and Smith (2002) believe that the overrepresentation of minorities in special education is a result of discriminatory testing procedures. They provide evidence that 45 out of 50 states have a statistically significant overrepresentation of Black children in special education programs, and that African American and Hispanic students frequently are placed in lower-level classes even with equal or higher test scores than White students. Dekker and colleagues (2002) further claim that many minority students are placed in special education programs with the intent to help them catch up with their peers and reenter general education classrooms, but they actually receive inferior instruction and fall further behind. Additionally, Robinson (2008) asserts that lower-tracked students often are placed with lower-quality teachers, which also affects achievement. Students placed in lower-level academic tracks have fewer opportunities to learn, which ultimately limits their access to knowledge and impedes their school success and literacy achievement (Darling-Hammond, 1997; Oakes, 2005; Robinson, 2008; Rubin & Noguera, 2004).

Equally problematic, tracking reproduces a form of de facto segregation by placing White and Asian students in the highest academic tracks, and African American and Latino students in lower tracks. According to Darling-Hammond (1997), tracking has "created a form of educational apartheid" (p. 267), because research studies have shown that in integrated schools, African American and Latino students are more likely to be assigned to vocational courses, remedial classes, and other low-track classes (Braddock, 1995). Yet the deleterious effects of tracking, and the racial separation it produces, are seen vividly in the halls of American secondary schools. For example, while teaching in a culturally diverse high school in the San Francisco Bay Area, Mahiri (1998) noted that the highest academic tracks in the school, the Advanced Placement classes, were about 85% White and Asian, while the lower-level courses had about 85% Black students. He also noted that the students, both Black and White, perceived the tracking in their classes as limiting cross-cultural interaction. One student explained, "I think that the reason we are segregated at lunch and after school and all that is because we don't have classes together. How can we interact if we don't have classes together?" (Mahiri, 1998, p. 95). When students are socially segregated via tracking, there is little opportunity for democratic communities to grow within secondary schools.

An example of the negative effects of ability grouping and tracking can be found in a personal story shared by Vincent (Gwen's husband).

I wasn't recognized as one of the smart kids because most of those kids were put in a different room and section of the school. In the sixth grade, I wanted to be put in that room with my other friends, but I was put in Mr. Bowman's room where there was always some clowning going on. Mr. Bowman's room was located on the second floor. Often, I was selected to hand deliver something to the office located on the first floor. The class that I wanted to be in was directly across from the office. Whenever, making a delivery to the office, I would peek into the other room, I'd see my other friends reading and studying. That classroom was always quiet and seemed to be orderly. I remember somebody saying that the people in that class were smart. Nevertheless, Mr. Bowman was my first Black teacher and I remember connecting with him. He was a good teacher but we lost him halfway through the school year. It was great having a Black man to connect with in the classroom. Later in life I learned that he had made a decision to change career paths for better pay. Before him I had lazy teachers who didn't challenge me and quite frankly I became bored with school. Given this opportunity to unpack my thoughts, I can say that my elementary school years were staid. I don't feel as though my teachers took a real interest in me.

By the time I got to junior high [middle school] I was exposed to drugs and a culture of violence. For me this was a shock; at least I didn't feel threatened in elementary school. It was just about survival—being knowledgeable about drugs, gambling, and protecting myself. With a father and mother who were committed to providing for and raising their family of three in the turbulent 1960s and 1970s, I was taught to avoid the traps of the violent drug culture. I knew that the consequences of bad choices were not just about getting hooked on drugs or getting into trouble. I would have to face parents and other family members who taught me the importance of having a good reputation, and a sense of community. I wasn't a part of the so-called "smart, or popular, group." I had (among other basic junior high school classes) wood shop, metal shop, and printing or typesetting—using old antiquated machines. Students who were enrolled in these classes were generally considered average or below average, and probably not on their way to college.

In high school I don't feel as though I was steered in the right direction. Again, in addition to other vocational classes I had wood and metal shop. I graduated but I never remember sitting down with a counselor and having input in my academic track. I played football and hung out with my friends, but I wasn't aware of anything at school being offered that was of interest to me. I knew some of the kids who were taking classes that I couldn't take because early on I had not been prepared to do the work. I had not been challenged. Some of the football players and others were the ones in the shop classes with me. Today, I don't feel as though anyone took an interest in me. It would have made a world of difference if someone at the schools I attended had taken an interest and pushed me in a more academic direction. There's no doubt in my mind that I could have been a student who could have shined, but it didn't happen that way for me.

not Prepared

As an adult I was angered when I realized that I was not prepared academically. My formal education had not prepared me for the academic challenges of a collegiate environment. The further I went along in my professional life and learned how policy was made, I became even more incensed. At the state level I could see how money was being taken out of education and put into building prisons.

I fault myself for my own shortcomings. There is an old adage my parents taught me, that "when you learn better, you do better." Life struggles and circumstances sent me back to a vocational training school for adults where I learned some of the things that I should have gotten in high school. I realized that I had to reinvent myself. I started taking classes at Delta College—unsure about what I wanted to do, but knowing that I needed to work toward a better quality of life. Although I had a career-oriented way of thinking by then, I still did not know what that career would become. However, I had been taught a good work ethic and was willing to do whatever it took to set a new course in life for myself. Finally, after working at Cox Cable (as a technician) for a few years, I knew that I needed to revisit my own insecurities and think more seriously about a career, not just a job. My family and church responsibilities provided more stability and motivated me to pursue a college degree. I attended Saginaw Valley State University and finally met teachers who took an interest in me and nurtured my learning process. After graduating with honors, I was accepted into an accelerated master's program at Michigan State University and received several scholarships and an internship to cover the costs.

Showing their confidence in my abilities, Saginaw Valley State University hired me as an administrator in the president's office, where I remained until I became a full-time pastor. I am currently a candidate for a doctor of ministry degree at Ecumenical Theological Seminary in Detroit, Michigan. Gaining access to certain levels of literacy was a difficult battle for me, because I didn't always have teachers who cheered me on. In fact, sometimes it seemed that some even tried to prevent me from achieving. My old friends who were in the elementary classroom with the "smart kids" look at me now with respect and admiration. I remember how things were "back then" and realize how far I have come with the help of my God, my family, and a few good educators who saw something special in me.

Disciplinary policies. In addition to tracking, disciplinary policies and procedures may mitigate the educational opportunities of African American students. According to the National Education Association (2007), minority students have higher rates of office referrals, suspensions, and expulsions from school, and students with disabilities who are from African American, Latino, and Native American backgrounds are 67% more likely than their White peers to be removed from school by a hearing officer. Black males are more likely to receive more severe punishment than White students for the same type of behavior, and low-income Black males in special education have the highest suspension rates of any subgroup (National Education Association, 2007; Townsend, 2000).

Cultural clashes between teachers and African American students may contribute to disciplinary problems in schools (McMillon, 2001). Teachers may misinterpret African American students' behaviors, speech (e.g., rapping), and dress (e.g., baggy jeans, backward baseball caps) in negative ways, and these cultural misunderstandings may lead to inappropriate or inequitable disciplinary actions (Cartledge, Tillman, & Johnson, 2001; Schwartz, 2001). Even more problematic, such disciplinary policies do not seem to help African American students access and acquire the conventions, interactional styles, and behaviors that are highly valued in schools. Rather, as West-Olatunji, Baker, and Brooks (2006) contend, "The higher rates of discipline referrals, suspensions, and expulsions do nothing to ameliorate the classroom behavior of African American students. A domino effect leads to other debilitating consequences such as grade retentions, school drop out, and academic failure" (p. 3).

Special education and gifted programs. Disproportionality in two critical school programs, special education and gifted and talented education, remains a persistent problem in American schools. According to Blanchett (2006), disproportionality "exists when students' representation in special education programs or specific education categories exceeds their proportional enrollment in a school's general population" (p. 24). African American students are overrepresented in special education classrooms. According to the Council for Exceptional Children (2002), while African American students accounted for about 15% of the general population of students ages 6 through 21, they made up 20% of the special education population across all disabilities. Even more disturbing, Artiles, Harry, Reschly, and Chinn (2002) reported that the actual proportion of all African American students placed in mental retardation classes was 2.54%, which is significantly higher than Native Americans (1.31%), Whites (1.13%), Latinos (0.74%), and Asian/Pacific Islanders (0.49%). More current statistics show an alarming increase—Skiba and colleagues (2008) report that African Americans currently make up 17% of the school-aged population, and 33% of students identified as mentally retarded (now called intellectually disabled).

While states use varying eligibility criteria for special education programs, the National Education Association (2007) contends that "teacher referral is a strong predictor of eligibility for special services" (p. 6). Artiles and colleagues (2002) further elaborate on the prominent role that teachers play in the referral process, noting that "although the existing empirical evidence on referral bias is equivocal, there is some evidence middle class elementary school teachers possess greater proclivity to racial biases with regard to achievement expectations and perceptions of student maturity" (p. 7). Others (e.g., Ladner & Hammons, 2001) found that districts with more White teachers had a greater rate of minority special education enrollment. Ruben (2009) further emphasizes this pattern when he lists the possible causes of disproportionate special education representation:

> psychometric test bias, sociodemographic factors, unequal opportunity in general education (the most consistent findings in education research is that students achieve in direct proportion to their opportunity to learn), teacher ethnicity (as the percentage of African American teachers increased, overrepresentation of African American students in the emotionally disturbed category decreased); and special education eligibility and decision-making processes (teachers referred minority children more often than nonminority children and tended to refer minority students for behavioral rather than academic issues). (pp. 6–7)

Like Blanchett (2006), we believe that "these realities suggest that 'race matters' within special education" (p. 24).

Some African American students may benefit from special education services. However, researchers have concluded that because African American students are likely to be overidentified for special education services, there is a high level of misidentification (Artiles et al., 2002). Schooling can have long-lasting harmful effects on students misidentified for special education services because (a) the curriculum offered in special education programs may be limited and less rigorous than in general education courses; (b) racial separation can occur, because African American and other culturally and linguistically diverse students are more likely than White or Asian/Pacific Islander students to be in separate classrooms or schools; (c) students may perceive themselves to be less intelligent and less capable than their peers; and (d) special education courses become permanent "tracks" for most students, who remain in their program throughout their entire school careers (Artiles et al., 2002; Blanchett, 2006; Harry & Klingner, 2006; National Education Association, 2007).

Additionally, African American students are underrepresented in academically accelerated programs like gifted and talented programs and/or honors classes (Ford, 1998; Ford & Harris, 1994). The National Education Association (2007) has identified a variety of factors that may negatively impact the identification process for culturally and linguistically diverse students, including:

- Cultural differences in communicative style (e.g., language)
- Stereotypic or deficit-oriented views of students and families
- Lack of culturally responsive assessments
- Lack of access to academic resources (e.g., extracurricular activities and programs, tutoring)
- Narrow definitions of academic "giftedness" that are not responsive to cultural and linguistic differences

In contrast to special education, teachers are less likely to refer African American students for gifted services, and research has shown that teachers are less reliable and less effective than parents in identifying culturally diverse children for gifted education (Ford, 1998). For example, in 2000, fewer 12th-grade Black students took Advanced Placement (AP) examinations than their White or Hispanic counterparts. In 2003, fewer eighth-grade African American students took algebra courses than their White and Latina/o peers. In addition, in 2003, fewer 11th- and 12th-grade African American students took AP courses than White or Latina/o students (National Center for Education Statistics, 2003). Bonner and Jennings (2007) also conclude that the lack of identification of African American males for gifted and talented programs has led to underrepresentation by as much as 50%.

GOVERNMENT INTERVENTION

Over the years, our government has attempted to level the playing field for children of color in this country. Most states have mandated a standards-based curriculum. However, one of the most politicized fights for access is the No Child Left Behind (NCLB) Act of 2001. Because of NCLB, closing the achievement gap became a national priority. Schools are now held specifically accountable for the annual progress of African American as well as all other students. However, the process of accountability often is questioned by educators—especially classroom teachers. *Testing, assessing, collecting information, developing baseline data,* and several other terms are used when referring to the unprecedented number of required assessments that are given to K–12 students. Schools should be held accountable for properly educating their students; however, institutional racism and discrimination against the impoverished are still alive and well. Inadequate classroom materials, limited access to technology, burned-out and inexperienced teachers, cuts due to limited funding, and many other problems occur more frequently in both urban and rural schools, and perpetuate the inequities between "the haves" and "the have-nots." Schools must be given adequate resources if they are expected to meet the high standards established by NCLB. The problem is, however, that schools most in need of the extra funding that

NCLB offers cannot receive it because their scores are not high enough. In this way, NCLB seems to perpetuate the problem by withholding additional help until after a series of "disciplinary actions" have been taken, which put the schools in a negative light. Rather than offering immediate assistance to schools with low scores, extra funding is withheld and threats of a future take-over by the State Department of Education force many administrators and teachers into a "teach to the test" mode. While data-driven instruction offers many benefits, it is important that teachers implement their curriculum from a proactive rather than reactive perspective. Reactionary teaching seems to cause teachers to emphasize the areas that they think students need to know for their assessments, whereas a proactive teacher will focus on an integrated curriculum that helps students become knowledgeable in various areas and prepares them for future educational opportunities. Many schools that serve predominantly minority students find themselves in the reactionary mode due to low scores on the assessments. As a result, minority students, who were already suffering from inequities in their education, are now falling further behind in areas that are not covered in a "teach to the test" curriculum.

THE STRUGGLE CONTINUES

The fight continues even in the new millennium. Woodson (1933) asserted more than 75 years ago that the process of *mis-education* had impeded the progress of African Americans. He argued that the majority of "educated" Blacks were all but worthless in the liberation of their people, in that their education was too basic and technical and had not prepared them to critique their own condition. In 2005, Craig Saddler argued that African American youth are not only mis-educated but actually "de-educated." The term *de-educated* is used to shed light on the fact that, as a whole, African American youth are being systematically excluded from the education system and/or being systematically destroyed within that system.

The de-education of African American students, especially boys, is referred to as "the cradle to prison pipeline" (Children's Defense Fund, 2007), indicating that school is no longer considered "the great equalizer," but perceived as an institution that "prepares" Black males for prison by methodically decreasing their self-worth and potential through a process of "educational malpractice." Proponents of the belief that Blacks are not receiving an adequate education can use recent graduation rates as evidence that Blacks (especially Black males) still lag behind their White counterparts. The high school graduation rate for Black male students in the United States was 47% in 2005–2006, compared with 75% for White male students (Schott Foundation for Public Education, 2008). When Black students graduate from high school and attend college, they face numerous obstacles that could prevent them from attaining their undergraduate degree, such as limited financial resources, lack of preparation from their K–12 education, absence of a family college tradition, low ambition, and underdeveloped study habits. The national average graduation rate for Black students is 43%. Unfortunately, 34 historically Black colleges and universities have much lower graduation rates than the national average, with Texas Southern (15%), LeMoyne-Owen College (14%), and the University of the District of Columbia (8%) ranked the lowest ("Black Student College Graduation Rates," 2007).

With limited options, Black students may begin to consider alternatives to a college education and career, such as a life of risk and crime. In the United States, as of June 30, 2007, the custody incarceration rate for Black males was 4,618 per 100,000, and for Hispanic males it was 1,747 out of every 100,000. At midyear 2007, the estimated incarceration rate of White males was 773 per 100,000 (Sabol & Couture, 2008). Based on the estimated numbers of Black, White, and Hispanic males in the U.S. resident population, Black males are six times more likely (and Hispanic males a little more than two times more likely) to be incarcerated than White males. Many believe that the U.S. penal system is a prime example of institutional racism. There are more Black men in prison than in college. Rather than investing in properly educating Black boys by providing intense tutoring when their reading scores are inadequate, money is spent on building prisons to house them as adults. Statistics show that 11% of the Black male population is in prison, at an average cost of $45,000 per year to take care of a prisoner, compared with only $18,326 (in-state) and $29,193 (out-of-state) per year to attend college ("College Board Releases 2008/2009 College Cost Figures," 2008). In the past, prison was considered an institution for rehabilitation, but the current penal system offers few education programs for the incarcerated. Since 1994 when Pell grants were withdrawn, college funding for U.S. prisons has been supported entirely by nonprofit organizations, foundations, and volunteer hours and skills (Obah, 2004).

In conclusion, history tells us that we have moved from no access, to limited access, to segregation, to desegregation/integration, to mis-education, to de-education. Recognition of continued inequality and denigration in education is the first step toward our ultimate goal. The struggle continues for African Americans, even though it takes different shapes and forms. We can't and won't give up our fight for true equality in American education, for our fight is crucial for the education of African American students.

CHAPTER TWO

The Multiple Meanings of Success: Tensions, Conflicts, and Crises for African American Students

I have learned that success is to be measured not so much by the position that one has reached in life as by the obstacles which he has had to overcome while trying to succeed.

—Booker T. Washington

Booker T. Washington's oft-quoted words remind us that everyone, regardless of race or ethnicity, must face some challenges in order to attain success. However, African American people face unique obstacles to success based upon their social positioning as a "minority" within the United States, and the racist and discriminatory forces that work to oppress, marginalize, and isolate them (Hacker, 1992). In this chapter, we explore some of the complex challenges that African American students, from kindergarten to college, have experienced on the road to school success. We first turn to an issue that is salient for many African American youth: the development of racial identity. In her story, Jennifer describes her own racial identity development by highlighting the "acting White/acting Black" dilemma.

NARRATIVE BEGINNINGS—JENNIFER D. TURNER: "SUCCESS IS TRYIN' TO MAKE IT IN TWO WORLDS"

What is success? All of my life, I have been straddling two worlds, a White cultural world and a Black cultural world. Now, you might think that this is because I am biracial, but I'm not. Both of my parents are African American, yet they have always deeply believed that my siblings and I should know about and be comfortable in the White world. I was born and raised in Philadelphia, but unlike many "city kids" who never left their neighborhood, I had many early experiences within the White community. From the time I was about 6 years old, we went to a Mennonite church in Lancaster,

Pennsylvania. My father worked for a telecommunications company in the suburbs of Philadelphia, and had become good friends with a man who lived in Lancaster and attended this church. He and his family lived in a very rural community, and we often visited their house after church. Needless to say, we were the only Black people in this congregation, and as I grew older, I remember that this began to trouble me. I thought my father's friend and his family were very accepting, but some of the members of the church would slide off the pew and move to another part of the church when we came in, or they would not touch the napkins after we had taken one during the midday meal that the church served in the fellowship room. I remember asking my parents about this in the car one Sunday afternoon during the hour-long trip back home, and they shrugged it off and told me, "Some people feel that way but it has nothing to do with you." But I felt that it had everything to do with me, and I wondered why they seemed to treat me differently.

We stopped attending that church soon after, but I attended a predominantly White, parochial school for Grades 4 through 8. Again, I thought that things were fine; my best friends were an Italian girl and another African American girl who was bused to this suburban school like me. But there were some White kids who let me know that I didn't belong. I remember all the kids on the bus singing, "Oh you can't get to heaven" when we went on field trips. The first part of the song talked about being redeemed by the blood of Jesus and the power that it had to wash away your sins. But the other part of the song talked about all of the things that wouldn't get you into heaven, like wearing dirty blue jeans (God didn't have a washing machine) or wearing roller skates (You'd roll right past those pearly gates). One of the verses also said: "Oh you can't get to heaven with nappy hair, 'cause God don't have no grease up there." On the day that this verse was sung, I remember feeling my cheeks burn with embarrassment, and a child peeped around from the seat behind me and said, "Well I guess *you* won't be going to heaven." I was stunned. I felt so ashamed and I remember quietly saying, "Yes I will go to heaven." I felt that I might not have the "good hair" or right color to get into heaven, but I would do everything in my power to "act White." I was always shy and quiet as a child, but after that incident, I became excessively polite and obsessed with behaving impeccably. At that point, success for me was about fitting in and making certain that I interacted in a way that would be pleasing to White people. I knew that being smart and getting good grades was part of "making it" in the White world, but I also knew that talking and behaving in certain ways were also critical components of the success that I craved.

At the same time, I also wanted to have success in the Black world. Although I traveled back and forth across the boundaries between the White and Black worlds, I always knew that I was Black. I grew up in Mt. Airy, a community that had the reputation of being "nice" and "uppity" compared with other neighborhoods in Philadelphia. When my parents first moved into their house in the mid-1970s, I was 5 years old, and nearly all the neighbors on our block were White. There were a few Black families, too, and I quickly became friends with those kids. We played at one another's houses, had slee-povers, and went to the movies together and to the library. Over time, our families became so close that we went on vacations together, and my family decided to attend the Black church that one of our close friends went to so that we could all go to church together. I felt so comfortable at this church, and I was really excited when my family officially became members.

At the church, and with my friends on the block, my Blackness was never called into question. But I learned early on that others could and did judge my Blackness. In my own family, we had members who thought that we were not "Black" enough. My cousins and aunts and other family members on my father's side always called my siblings and me "Whitebred" because of the way we talked and acted. "You talk funny, just like a White girl," they would laugh and point at me, and we all would fall silent to stop their teasing. Some relatives even made fun of my father, who had been told in high school that he was not "college material" and encouraged to enter the military, where he ended up fighting in the Vietnam War. However, this never quelled my father's love of learning, and he kept reading and taking classes until he completed his bachelor's degree in the late 1990s. Rather than encouraging my father's educational pursuits, my uncles scoffed at him, saying things like, "Them books ain't gonna do nothing for you. You still a N-word no matter how much you think you know." My uncles' state-ments remained with me for years, and I couldn't help thinking that *choos-ing* to become educated in the White world meant that you automatically failed in the Black world.

Questions about success, race, and identity continued to intensify for me in high school. I attended the Philadelphia High School for Girls, an institu-tion known for its academic rigor and high standards of educational excel-lence. The school was diverse, drawing girls from a variety of racial, ethnic, linguistic, and socioeconomic backgrounds. I enjoyed going to school in such an environment, and made friends of many social and cultural backgrounds. But there were two groups of African American girls who seemed "untouch-able" to me. One group comprised the "fly girls," the pretty girls who wore the latest designer clothing and sneakers, had the most expensive purses and jewelry, and wore trendy hairstyles. The other group was also very attrac-tive and wore nice clothes and jewelry. However, these girls were members of Jack and Jill, an exclusive social club for African American children, and they had an untouchable air of sophistication due to their social status and upbringing. I didn't fit neatly into either of these groups. I was a nerd; I wore thick glasses and terrible clothes, and as the oldest of four children, I could not afford the numerous trips to the beauty shop necessary for keeping my hair coiffed in the latest styles.

I was attracted to the strong African American cultural knowledge and identity that the Jack and Jill girls had, but I knew that I could never fit in with them because my family didn't have the wealth or the social connections necessary for an invitation to join. But I thought I could be successful in attaining the kind of Blackness represented by the fly girls. So I worked to earn money and bought contacts, new purses, and "fresh" new sneakers. During the late 1980s, big gold chains, earrings and rings with your name etched into them, and big belts were considered fashionable in urban neighborhoods, and I was wearing them by senior year. Because I wasn't allowed to listen to secular music, I listened to my father's Walkman at night to sneakily learn all the latest R&B and hip-hop songs. I became adept at code-switching, using slang when I talked to the guys around my neighborhood, and "Standard" English at home. Code-switching became even more important to me when I began dating, and because I wanted desperately to be cool, I went out with several guys who were into criminal activities. I did all of this because I wanted to be "Black" in the same way as my cousins and those girls at school. And I felt that I had indeed achieved this level of Blackness. I have a scar on the right side of my face resulting from the removal of my birthmark, and in my freshman year at the University of Pennsylvania, all of the gold jewelry and the athletic wear made me look so tough that several students asked if I gotten that scar in a street fight. I remember laughing while simultaneously feeling proud that I had finally captured such an authentic level of Blackness. I felt that I had finally proven that I wasn't an Oreo—someone who was Black on the outside but White on the inside.

Thankfully, my experience at the University of Pennsylvania helped me redefine my understanding of Blackness. As a sociology major, I took several courses to learn more about African American culture and people. I read books like *The Mis-Education of the Negro* by Carter G. Woodson (1933) and *The Souls of Black Folk* by W. E. B. Du Bois (1903/1995), who I was pleased to learn conducted seminal sociological research at Penn in the 1890s. I also was nurtured, guided, and challenged in my thinking about African American culture by two extraordinary African American professors. They cultivated my spirit of inquiry and helped me develop questions that represented my passions and interests in urban culture and African American life. This was an important breakthrough for me, because it was the first time that I truly believed that I could be both Black and an intellectual. Later, I took a class on African American and Afro Caribbean women's literature, which helped me to see what various images and meanings of Black womanhood there were, and as I devoured books by Toni Morrison, Paule Marshall, Alice

Walker, and Edwidge Danicat, I began to also realize that I had the power to name myself, to tell my story with my own voice, and it was OK if it was a mixture of Black and White and common and elitist and religious and secular. I learned that my identity as a Black woman should not be defined by others, even if they are Black people whom I admire, or members of my own family. I do believe that race matters, and that our racial identity is a critical part of who we are. But after leaving Penn, I also believed that I could define Blackness myself.

But I still haven't resolved all of my race-related identity issues. Several years ago, when I worked as a high school counselor in the Philadelphia neighborhood where I grew up, I was talking on the phone with my supervisor, and after I hung up, one of the students said to me, "Miss Jen, you were talkin' like a White girl on the phone." For a split second, the word "Oreo" flashed in my mind, and I got angry. Then I realized that I had already defined my own racial identity: I am Black, and academic excellence and educational success are part of my culture. But this young lady was obviously trying to figure out these differences between White and Black, educated and ignorant, nerd and cool, and she needed help breaking down those false dichotomies, just like I did. But as strange as it may sound, I did not have the words to help her, or to allow her to critique what she had said. I had thought that I had healed, but the wounds were still too raw, too personal, and too painful. And I still come back to that place, because now I have children, and I want my boys to understand that they, too, have the power to define their own racial identities. But I am still struggling with the right words that will help my children, as well as other African American children, define success in their worlds on their terms.

STORIES FROM AFRICAN AMERICAN ELEMENTARY STUDENTS: TRYING TO BE "COOL" IN CONTEMPORARY CLASSROOMS

Jennifer's story of schooling centered on identity issues that stemmed from the acting White vs. acting Black dilemma that many African American students experience. But this may not be the entry point of identity conflict and turmoil for some African American students. In today's classrooms, African American children, especially boys, are enmeshed in dilemmas stemming from a different identity-related phenomenon: being cool.

The stories told in this section were formed from conversations that Jennifer had with three African American, elementary-aged children. Isaiah (8 years old) and Elijah (6 years old) are Jennifer's sons, while Amani (10 years old) is Jennifer's niece. Isaiah and Elijah attend an elementary school in a large district along the eastern seaboard. The elementary school is small, serving about 400 students, and is somewhat diverse. Isaiah and Elijah are part of a handful of students of color in their classrooms, and often they are the only African American boys. In contrast, Amani lives in Philadelphia and attends an all-Black elementary school in her neighborhood. All three are excellent readers; Elijah was reading at a first-grade level in kindergarten, and both Isaiah and Amani tested into their respective schools' gifted and talented programs. However, all three have been confronted with issues of being cool in the past year and have begun to consider what it means to be cool, particularly in relation to literacy.

Eljiah's Story

Elijah completed kindergarten in the 2008–09 academic year. He likes reading fairytales and other fiction books, and listed *Cloudy with a Chance of Meatballs* and *The Three Little Pigs* as two of his favorite books. However, when asked if he liked to read, he shouted, "Nooo!" and told this story:

> I don't like reading because reading is not cool. Reading is for babies. I like to play video games like *Lord of the Rings* and *Madden* and *Wii Sports Resort.* And I play soccer and football at recess and I would play with my friends, and we like to play tag. And we would play spy on the girls.
>
> Being cool means to be popular. That means you have a lot of friends. Being a friend means helping people. I am a good friend, and I was cool and I had a lot of friends. And I had a great birthday party and everybody said it was awesome! Everybody in my class is my friend and everybody in my class is cool.

Isaiah's Story

Isaiah, who completed second grade in the 2008–09 academic year and enjoys reading science fiction, fantasy, and adventure books, says:

> Being cool means that you have a lot of money, and cool clothes that are shiny and good and people want them, but they can't have them because they are too expensive. And, if you're cool, then you have a lot of friends. I think that there are cool people on television, like Carly, Sam, Freddy, and Fred [from *i Carly*, a popular show on Nickelodeon].
>
> My friends and I like to write during recess. We write *Lord of the Rings* stories. The other boys, they all play sports like soccer at recess. And I don't want to play because I like sports but I like writing better.
>
> I don't think I'm cool but I don't want a lot of friends. I only want two friends because then I don't have to be nice to everyone. You have

to work too hard to be nice to everyone. You can't just be mean to them. But if you're friends, you're friends, but if you're not, you're not. If someone doesn't like you, then they won't be friends with you and they won't sit with you.

Sometimes I try to be funny, and when I do things like walk funny or I'm being weird, then people laugh and say I'm funny. So then some of the girls said it and then everybody was saying it. And then sometimes even when I wasn't trying to be funny, they would laugh. But that was OK, because it made me cool!

Amani's Story

Amani completed fourth grade in the 2008–09 academic year, and she loves reading and math and playing video games that offer varying levels of adventure and challenge, like Pokémon. She enjoys mysteries, like the *A to Z* books and the *Nancy Drew* series. When asked about being cool and popular at her school, Amani told this narrative:

At my school, cool kids know everybody in the class, and lots of people outside of the class. Cool kids say "hi" to everyone, and everyone says "hi" to them. Cool boys in fourth grade are boys who play basketball and football, and sometimes they curse because they think that makes them sound cool. Cool girls know lots of sixth-grade boys, and they sometimes chase them. They wear fancy clothes, and they wear these boots and sometimes the boys will say that their boots are cute. Their hair is done almost every weekend and they change their hairstyle every week–sometimes they wear braids, or pony tails.

I'm not a popular girl, but I do have friends. Smart kids at my school aren't really popular, and I was one of the smartest people in the class. Sometimes kids wanted to sit near me, but that's because they wanted to copy off my tests and get higher scores. That made me really angry. I think that reading is cool, because reading can make you smarter and you can learn a lot more by reading than watching television sometimes. But other kids in my class didn't think that reading was cool at all.

Sometimes, I would try to be cool in school. I did not want to be in too much trouble, so I tried to get in a little trouble. My friend would drag me into her messes sometimes, and then I would get into trouble. Sometimes kids would tease me, and I didn't like that. They would say things like, "you are so smart, you're just trying to go to another school" or "you're so smart, you are gonna skip so many grades that you won't need school." They were just saying that because they want to be as smart as me.

> I feel like being popular is a good thing, but it gets harder and harder to be popular when you're smart.

We know that kids, whether they are White or Black, poor or rich, want to be cool and accepted by their peers; no one wants to be called a "nerd" or to be unpopular. However, these stories also reveal two critical functions of cool that impact the educational lives of African American students in very unique ways. First, African American students may recognize the pressure to be cool, and pursue popularity in school, very early in their educational careers. Beverly Tatum (2003) suggests that African American children are aware of race at early ages, but that racial identity conflicts and dilemmas, like acting White/acting Black, tend not to become an issue until the adolescent years. However, these stories suggest that African American children like Elijah can identify cool behaviors and cool peers in kindergarten, and that the tensions that arise from the social dilemma to "be cool or be smart" may emerge within the primary grades. Second, African American students may make the decision to pursue a cool social identity rather than academic achievement very early in school. Amani's peers were in fourth grade and, based on her story, they knew that doing well in school, and especially reading, was uncool and were moving further away from the social identity of "smart student." In contrast to White middle-class kids, and others who are attracted to cool culture, African American students do not have the social safety nets and structures to mitigate the negative consequences of these cool behaviors and social identities, which ultimately can destroy their academic careers (Kirkland & Jackson, 2009). So why would African American youth want to be cool rather than be smart? We explore multiple answers to this question in the remainder of the chapter.

LOOKING BACK TO GO FORWARD: RECLAIMING THE MEANING(S) OF SUCCESS

We begin this discussion about academic success and school achievement with Theresa Perry's (2003) words, because we believe that they are at the heart of our discussion about African American students and their literacy learning in schools.

> The prevailing assumption among many educators is that the task of achievement for African Americans as a group is the same as it is for any other group. African American children have to be able to do what all other children have to be capable of doing in order to achieve in American schools. . . . But since learning is fundamentally contextual, . . . there are extra social, emotional, cognitive, and political competencies required of African American youth, precisely because they are African American, if they are to be able to commit themselves over time to perform at high levels in school. (p. 4)

Perry's words highlight the notion that for African American students, school achievement requires additional social and cultural competencies that generally are not considered in our current educational conversation. This does not mean that learning literacy is more difficult for African American students due to cognitive or intellectual abilities; we believe that African American students are very bright and capable of learning in school. However, in a society that often devalues African American culture, the unique social and cultural positions that Black students take up fundamentally shape their experience of school and set up unique obstacles to achievement.

MULTIPLE MEANINGS OF SUCCESS

Three primary meanings of success shape African American students' understandings of and perceptions about literacy achievement and educational attainment. *Life success* is known in our national consciousness as "the American Dream"—owning a house and a car, having money and a comfortable life, and a family. The American Dream is propagated through a variety of media, including magazines, television shows, and movies. Even hip-hop stars celebrate the American Dream; the latest street anthem is Drake's 2009 smash "I Just Wanna Be Successful," which glorifies a luxurious lifestyle, complete with an abundance of cars, wealth, women, and clothing. While we contend that life success has many other kinds of definitions and ideals, when we think of prominent messages that African American students are receiving from the media and society in general, this definition is both pervasive and compelling.

Community (with a capital "C" *and* a lowercase "c") *success* is a term that we use to signify the cultural values, discourses, and norms of the African American Community. Because the term *community* has varied meanings and definitions, we use the capitalized Community to denote the African American Community at large. Historically, the African American Community has been vitally important to African American people. According to Billingsley (1968), before desegregation, the African American Community was an institution to which parents and children specifically looked for strength, hope, and security:

> In every aspect of the child's life a trusted elder, neighbor, Sunday school teacher, school teacher, or other community member might instruct, discipline, assist, or otherwise guide the young of a given family. Second, as role models, community members show an example to and interest in the young people. Third, as advocates they actively intercede with major segments of society (a responsibility assumed by professional educators) to help young members of particular families find opportunities which might otherwise be closed to them. Fourth, as supportive

figures, they simply inquire about the progress of the young, take a special interest in them. Fifth, in the formal roles of teacher, leader, elder, they serve youth generally as part of the general role or occupation. (p. 99)

Before desegregation, the African American Community was a "security blanket" for African American children and families (Belt-Beyan, 2004). Through local organizations such as the church and the school, the African American Community represented, enacted, and inscribed uniquely stylized characteristics and values. Intellectualism, freedom, collective success, and hard work were part of those core values, and the Black Community aspired to "pass along the knowledge that success comes with long struggle and requires patience and wit. . . . Children, as well as adults were expected to be resourceful and ever watchful for opportunities to meet any of their life's goals" (Belt-Beyan, 2004, p. 162). According to Belt-Beyan, many African Americans in the 19th century

> acted on the beliefs that their success and their children's success was inevitable and that the good always win in the end. . . . Many parents expressed the beliefs that even if they did not learn to read and write themselves, they would have considered themselves successful if their children did. (p. 163)

Through the years, these community-oriented values, beliefs, and dispositions have been encoded in long-standing cultural sayings such as "each one, teach one" and "we lift as we climb." Moreover, the standards of community success were transmitted through the African American literary tradition, which was built upon narratives by slaves or former slaves such as Phyllis Wheatley and Frederick Douglass (Belt-Beyan, 2004).

In addition to the historic African American Community, it is also important to note that for Black adolescents, success in the eyes of their social community, or peers, is crucial. We use the lower-case "community" to represent the cultural forms of interaction and communication that often are respected and valued by other Black youth. While youth culture in the United States may be representative of diverse cultures, Mahiri (1998) contends that "African American culture . . . has generative links to popular youth culture . . . in areas such as music and sports, where black achievements and styles set world standards of excellence" (p. 5). Although the links between African American culture and youth culture are apparent in music, professional sports, and other arenas, it is important to note that standards of success within the historic African American Community and the peer community may be quite different. For example, some Black youth see hip-hop superstars like Lil' Wayne, Jay-Z, and Kanye West as successful, while members of the larger African American Community may not perceive these artists as exemplars of success based on their standards.

Finally, *school success* embodies good grades, completed homework assignments, strong motivation to learn, good reading and listening comprehension, and critical thinking and interpretations of texts—all of the elements that we typically think of when we talk about "becoming literate" in school. However, we want to be clear that, for us, becoming literate in schools means more than simply learning to read, write, speak, and listen. Rather, becoming literate means acquiring a cultural backpack (Blake, 2009), which includes the discourses, language patterns and codes, symbolic systems (e.g., clothing), behaviors, conventions, and interactional styles of particular groups or communities. All children, regardless of their race, linguistic background(s), culture, or socioeconomic status, have their own cultural backpacks, and the discourses that they have inside these "backpacks" are integral to their social identities. Yet school success requires all students, regardless of their own cultural backpacks, to acquire and appropriately use the discursive conventions, norms, language codes, and practices within a "mainstream, white, middle-class" cultural backpack (Gee, 1991). As societal institutions, schools sanction the "mainstream" cultural backpack because these dominant literacies provide a significant amount of cultural capital within society and are accoutrements of the "culture of power" (Delpit, 1995; Powell, 2009). Consequently, from our perspective, school success and becoming literate are social, cultural, and cognitive processes that are neither neutral nor color-blind.

In this chapter, we have begun to discuss the multiple meanings of success that African American students encounter and negotiate as they learn literacy in school. But rather than focusing on teachers' and schools' notions of success, we believe that it is critically important to look at literacy achievement and school success "from the inside out, *from the perspective of African American youth as thinking, feeling, and social and intentional beings*" (Perry, 2003, p. 3, emphasis added). By emphasizing the perspectives of African American students, we illustrate how some African American youth might come to *resist school success* in their quest to attain life and community success, while others may *reclaim school success*. In describing two options available to African American students—resistance to or reclamation of school success—we hope to help teachers, parents, administrators, and policymakers to understand the range of experiences, dilemmas, and conflicts that African American youth may experience as they navigate literacy learning in school.

RESISTING SCHOOL SUCCESS

Students' resistance to school is not a new phenomenon. Researchers have studied how youth have resisted education and learning in school for decades (MacLeod, 1995). However, resistance for African American students may have persisted for so many years because literacy learning and schooling can be an assault on their minds, their culture, their identities, and their social existence. As Powell (2009) explains, for some African American students,

> a failure to learn *may be intentional.* That is, it is a resistance to literacy that is based upon a racist ideology of White privilege. It is a resistance to a literacy that for them holds no meaning or promise, that historically has failed them in their quest to overcome the hegemonic focuses of power in our society. And it is a resistance to a literacy that they find essentially irrelevant, that denigrates their cultural knowledge, that denies their voice. (p. 5, emphasis in original)

Powell's words not only highlight a number of reasons why African American students may resist learning literacy in schools, but also suggest that this resistance may be seen as a conscious choice. African American students may choose to resist literacy achievement, and school success, based upon their perceptions of, and reactions to, four types of dilemmas: (1) the acting White/acting Black identity crisis; (2) gender identity conflicts arising from "coolness"; (3) ineffective teacher–student relationships and classroom environments; and (4) limited, but realistic, opportunity narratives.

Acting White/Acting Black Identity Crisis

The identity crisis that emanates from the acting White/acting Black phenomenon can be a real issue for many African American students. Teachers and parents may not be aware of the identity tensions that African American students struggle with on a daily basis in school, because many keep these emotions to themselves. Indeed, some scholars have even challenged the veracity of the acting/White acting Black phenomenon. For example, in their study of eight high schools in North Carolina, Tyson, Darity, and Castellino (2005) found that Black students' academic achievement was not hindered by the acting White phenomenon, and that both White and Black students who were high-achieving were teased and/or ostracized by their peers. More recently, Diamond, Lewis, and Gordon (2007) interviewed Black and White students in a desegregated high school, and concluded that while Black students perceived race-based limitations to their opportunities for getting ahead and were cognizant of racial patterns of track placement within the local school context, there was no evidence that Black students opposed school achievement.

Yet there is compelling evidence that suggests that the identity crises arising from the acting White/acting Black phenomenon are indeed part of the lived school experiences of a significant number of African Americans across the country. Fryer (2006) cites a study conducted more than a decade ago in which a group of African American students were asked to identify "acting-White" behaviors. The students included a range of specific actions, such as speaking Standard English, enrolling in academically advanced courses, and wearing clothes from certain mainstream stores like the Gap. While not all of these behaviors are academically oriented, they do suggest that social popularity, race, and achievement may be interrelated. Harvard economist Roland Fryer has been studying this relationship and has found that, in racially integrated schools, African American students' social popularity drops significantly as their GPAs increase (Fryer, 2006; Fryer & Torelli, 2005). Fryer's work also suggests that adolescent males pay a higher social cost for academic achievement; African American males begin to lose friends at a lower GPA (3.25) compared to African American females (3.5), and they lose friends at a greater rate than their female counterparts. While some may contend that perceptions of acting White/acting Black are found only among low-income Blacks, research suggests that the acting White/acting Black phenomenon also may be a contributing factor for the academic disengagement and low achievement levels of Blacks in affluent suburban schools (Ferguson, 2002; Ogbu, 2003). Even President Obama, then Senator from Illinois, referenced the phenomenon in his speech at the Democratic National Convention in 2004, declaring that we must "eradicate the slander that says a Black youth with a book is acting White."

Where did the acting White/acting Black identity crisis come from, and why is it such a dilemma for so many African American students? Historically, White culture and Black culture have been socially constructed in diametrically opposed terms. Fordham (1996), an educational anthropologist who has extensively studied the acting White/acting Black phenomenon, noted that from the end of slavery to the rise of the modern Civil Rights Movement, people of African descent were forbidden to "act White." Jim Crow laws ensured that African Americans did not enjoy the same privileges and rights as White people, and as a result Blackness was defined as "not White." As Young (2007) observed:

> Legal segregation produced an intense social schizophrenia in blacks which they had to vigorously control in order to escape both legal consequences and the system of sanctioned vigilantism (i.e. lynching). Even when blacks . . . understood themselves to be no different from whites, they were forced, by condition, to be only black. Hangings, Jim Crow train cars, and "white-only" establishments reflect some known consequences of this condition. (p. 128)

After desegregation ended, African American people began to have access to the same institutions (e.g., schools) and privileges that Whites had. However, integration had several unintended consequences. According to Fordham (1996), Black people had more opportunities, but they were obligated to "act White" in order to compete in society with White Americans. Some Blacks actively resisted this obligation to act White, and fought for the right to maintain their cultural practices, through social movements such as the Black Panther Party (Young, 2007) and through the development of an oppositional identity (Ogbu, 1995). According to Fordham and Ogbu (1986), an oppositional identity constitutes "a sense of peoplehood in opposition to the social identity of white Americans because of the way white Americans treated them" (p. 176). Although African Americans did lose some of their native African language, customs, and traditions through American enslavement, some cultural elements remained intact and combined with other cultural practices to form new behaviors, conventions, and discourses that became their cultural backpack, or their frame of reference (Ogbu, 1995). Some African American people view their cultural frame of reference as a "boundary-maintaining mechanism" (Ogbu, 1995, p. 88) between themselves and White Americans, and often perceive "learning or speaking standard English and practicing other aspects of white middle-class culture as threatening to their own minority culture, language, and identity" (p. 88). Within this oppositional framework, there is no middle ground: African Americans must choose to be Black and enact practices that are part of that perceived cultural backpack or risk being rejected by their cultural community, including peers, and even family members, like the uncles in Jennifer's narrative.

Consequently, in schools, many African American students feel the "burden of racial performance" (Young, 2007, p. 131), and a significant number believe that they must choose whether they will be successful in the academic realm or in the realm of their cultural community. For these African American students, success in the academic realm means "acting White" and acquiring and enacting specific behaviors, norms, and conventions that are perceived as consonant with "White or mainstream" culture, while success in the community realm emanates from a close alignment to what they perceive as "Black culture." As a result, in some African American peer groups, those students who strive to succeed academically, speak "conventional" English, and engage in reading and writing at school are viewed as "acting White," while those students who are popular, are disengaged from school literacy, and speak other dialects (e.g., African American English Vernacular) are perceived as "acting Black." Therefore, some African American students resist doing well in school, not because they are lazy or unintelligent, but because they want to avoid the "racial schizophrenia" (Young, 2007, p. 131) that emerges from trying to be both academically and socially successful. By choosing to act Black rather than doing well in school, these African American students view themselves as having a successful Black identity based on the standards set by their peer group. Unfortunately, however, this type of community success does not correlate with school success, and the African American students who represent "acting Black" in such ways often undermine their achievement within the classroom.

Gender Identity, Racial Identity, and "Coolness"

For some African American students, the racial identity crisis emanating from the acting White/acting Black phenomenon has been exacerbated and complicated by gender. In recent years, the literacy practices and worlds of African American male adolescents have attracted major attention from literacy scholars (Kirkland & Jackson, 2009; Mahiri, 1998; A. Tatum, 2005). Previous research (e.g., Maynard, 2002) suggests that boys may resist and reject reading because they "view it as a passive, 'female' activity" (A. Tatum, 2005, p. 11). However, the link between masculinity and coolness may be even stronger for African American males. Young (2007) contends that "the difference between black boys and white boys is that black boys not only feel coerced to give up their masculinity if they do well in school, but they also feel forced to abandon their race—the ultimate impossibility" (p. 90). Consequently, in response to this "feeling of racial and gender endangerment" (p. 90), some African American males resist school success to pursue coolness.

Coolness is a "ritualized expression of masculinity that involves speech, style, and physical and emotional posturing . . . that many black males use . . . to evoke distance from, contrast to, and superiority over outsiders" (Kirkland & Jackson, 2009, p. 280). As exemplified by the African American boys that Kirkland and Jackson studied, many African American boys associate coolness with Black culture and with a particular racialized "identity kit," such as sports jerseys, clothing brands worn by hip-hop artists, and language codes hybridized from American English and hip-hop slang. Being cool, however, does not mean that African American adolescents are illiterate. Researchers like Alfred Tatum (2005) have shown that adolescent males are indeed literate, and that through practices that they perceive as cool, Black, and masculine, they can express the cultural, social, and emotional literacies in their lives. We recognize that African American youths' personal literacies are important, yet we are concerned that many of these boys shun school success because they associate academic literacy with the conventions, discourses, and identity of the "uncool" (nerdy, White) students.

While cool culture is viewed as the purview of African American males (Majors & Billson, 1993), there is growing evidence that a number of African American girls are pursuing cool literacies and identities as well. Recent research conducted by Sutherland (2005), Skinner (2007), and Gibson (2009) suggests that African American adolescent girls are reading and engaging with popular media texts that they perceive as "cool," such as hip-hop music magazines like *Source* and *Vibe*, reality television shows (e.g., *American Idol*, *America's Next Top Model*), and family sitcoms (*That's So Raven*). Also popular is urban fiction, a genre that incorporates slang/nonstandard English to address realistic issues such as sex, drugs, crime, and violence, through graphic imagery, resulting in a cautionary tale designed to help readers learn from the experiences of the adolescent female protagonist. Although some of the girls in these studies were good students, several had not attained high levels of school achievement and were disengaged from the literature and the discussions that occurred with their teachers during class. African American girls, like their male counterparts, are literate, and often these girls rendered interpretive perspectives and critiques of the texts they chose to read that were both sophisticated and nuanced. However, because these texts are not often sanctioned within the literacy curriculum, these African American girls are often positioned as "nonreaders" within the classroom and are "marginalized because they [do] not draw upon the same recourses as mainstream students who more closely emulate the roles, take up texts, and exhibit the practices privileged in traditional [classrooms]" (Skinner, 2007, p. 346).

Over time, this sustained marginalization and isolation in the classroom can lead to African American girls' resistance to school success in exchange for being cool (e.g., passing around urban fiction books to other girls, talking about them during and after class) and attaining respect and success within their peer community. Clearly, the literacy curriculum cannot include every text that interests adolescent African American girls. However, teachers can reduce the isolation that adolescent African American girls might experience in the classroom, and increase the "cool" factor of school literacy, by acknowledging that they are readers, learning about the ways that reading and writing impact their out-of-school lives, and helping them to think critically about popular media texts as well as those mandated within the literacy curriculum.

Ineffective Teacher–Student Relationships and Classroom Environments

We believe that teachers have been contributing factors in African American students' resistance to literacy learning and school success. We say this not to blame teachers, but to call attention to the fact that African American students *do* know when their teachers dislike them, and they are frustrated, hurt, and confused by this realization. Consider the voices of several African American teens in West-Olatunji, Baker, and Brooks's (2006) study:

Interviewer: How do you think your teachers feel about you?
Jamal: When my teacher go home, she probably be talkin' about me to her kids. She don't like me and . . . you know what I be sayin'? I don't like her neither.
Adam: Two wrongs don't make a right.
Brandon: My teachers hate me.
Jay: It don't mean *jump* to me! (p. 6)

Irvine (1990) contends that a *lack of cultural synchronization* and a *lack of cultural responsiveness* between teachers and African American students can create barriers to school success. A lack of cultural synchronization means that teachers and African American students do not share a common understanding of verbal and nonverbal language, manner of personal presentation, or ways of processing information and knowledge. As a result of these cultural misunderstandings, teachers sometimes "rush to judgment and hold false assumptions about [African American] children" (Edwards, Pleasants, & Franklin., 1999, p. 11). For instance, in her work, Michelle Fine (1995) noted that urban high school students were not only routinely dissuaded from drawing on their own personal experiences, language, family traditions, and community practices in class, but were also warned by their teachers on numerous occasions: "You act like that, and you'll end up on welfare" (p. 211).

In other classrooms, a lack of cultural responsiveness results in negative expectations by teachers and by the students themselves, as well as in a pattern of differential teacher–student interactions and behaviors that cause tensions and conflicts. For example, two types of problematic interactions between teachers and African American students in classroom contexts are *racial spotlighting* and *racial ignoring.* Dorinda Carter (2005) argues that teachers sometimes *spotlight* Black students as *Black* students, positioning them as hypervisible by Whites in the learning context when they do not seek to be. Racial spotlighting can occur in three ways: (1) the role of native informant (e.g., publicly asking a Black student to talk in class about slavery or a controversial racial issue like racial profiling); (2) racialized stares (e.g., looking pointedly at Black students when certain racial and/or culturally diverse topics are discussed); and (3) guilt by association. The latter is closely connected to stereotype threat, a phenomenon studied by Claude Steele. In his work, Steele (2003) reports strong empirical psychological evidence that when Black students believe they are being judged as members of a stereotyped group rather than as individuals, they do significantly worse on achievement tests. Along similar lines, the African American students in Carter's (2005) study reported that they perceived that they had to constantly "prove wrong" negative stereotypes about their intellectual ability and racial-group cultural patterns, and this was both psychologically and intellectually draining for them. Not even higher education provides relief from this burden, because research has found the "prove them wrong" phenomenon to be common among some Black students in predominantly White colleges and universities (Fries-Britt, 1998, 2002).

On the other hand, classroom teachers also can racially ignore African American students, positioning them in ways that render them "racially invisible" by Whites when they desire to be visible. Carter (2005) identifies three strategies for racially ignoring Black students: (1) devaluing of thoughts, meaning that teachers and/or students do not "take up" comments made by Black students; (2) no eyes on me, meaning that teachers do not call on Black students as often as other students, even when their hands are raised; and (3) dehumanizing, representing instances when teachers use racially derogatory slurs in talking with students. In *Black in America 2*, aired by CNN (O'Brien, 2009a), Bertram Lee Jr., a Black freshman at Haverford College, an elite private institution in Pennsylvania, described an incident where he was called the N-word by a course instructor.

In light of these challenging teacher–student interactions, some African American students begin to view school as a "cultural battleground" (Blake, 2009, p. 129). Over time, these students may grow weary of the battle and resist school success in a number of ways, including misbehaving in class, refusing to complete assignments, losing focus in class, and even dropping out of school (Fine, 1995).

Limited, but Realistic, Folk Theories on Upward Mobility

We have adopted Kim's (2006) metaphors of stepping stones and spring-boards to explain why some African American students do not perceive that school success is the most viable pathway to life success. Different groups of minorities have different folk theories, or collective stories, of getting ahead in America and attaining life success (Ogbu, 1995). Voluntary minorities are people whose families have willingly immigrated to the United States, and these groups tend to adopt White mainstream folk theories about getting ahead (e.g., working hard, getting a good education). Involuntary minorities are people who were brought to America by oppressive forces (e.g., slavery), and these groups hold very different folk theories because "in the course of many generations of barriers to opportunity structures, they . . . realize that advancement in this society requires more than education and more than individual effort and hard work to overcome the barriers to upward mobility" (Ogbu, 1995, p. 89). For African American children today, this means that the "go to school and get a good education for a great life" mantra may not have significant impact because they have learned that, due to structural forces such as racism and discrimination, this may not be the case. As Mickelson (1990) put it, "due to messages blacks receive from parents, friends, and neighbors, young blacks are not bewitched by the rhetoric of equal opportunity through education; they hear another side of the story at the dinner table" (p. 59). Thus, while African American students value education, and believe it is an important "stepping stone" to life success, they realize that their progress toward life success may be severely impeded by social barriers.

Stepping stone
Springboard

In contrast, African American youth tend to believe that alternative arenas, such as entertainment and professional sports, serve as springboards toward life success. Michael Baisden, a popular African American radio show
host, noted, "If you take a young black man and put him on the basketball
court with a white kid, automatically that black kid knows that he is gonna
kill that white kid. . . . There's something that, through his experiences, or
the media, or whatever, that tells him he's better" (O'Brien, 2009c). We agree
with Baisden, and because some African American youth believe that they
can excel in these arenas, they see them as springboards to the American
Dream. In many ways, the springboard metaphor is particularly fitting; it
propels you upward very quickly, you gain significant momentum, and very
little will get in the way of your upward movement. Similarly, young African
American men and women have become overnight celebrities, and sometimes instant millionaires, after signing movie, music, or athletic contracts,
and on the surface, it seems that very few structural forces like racism can
stop their upward trajectory. Consequently, some African American youth
stop pursuing education because it seems like just a "stepping stone," and
they begin to perceive these other "springboards" as more viable options for
life success. While this type of thinking holds great allure for African American youth, it is dangerous because only a few African American people will
achieve that level of success through entertainment and sports.

RECLAIMING SCHOOL SUCCESS

In order to be successful in school, in the community, and in life, African
American children must negotiate these multiple, and very complex, dimensions of success in ways that are psychologically, socially, and intellectually
healthy. Many of these students find that the path is both uncertain and
unknown, but they constantly strive toward reclamation of their academic
careers and literacy lives. Swann-Wright (2002) notes that the saying "making a way out of no way" is prevalent in African American epistemology
and folklore, because African American people had to create a new life for
themselves—one that they had imagined but never fully lived—after emancipation. Years later, African American students who pursue school success are
often trailblazers, sometimes the first in their family to graduate from high
school, college, or graduate school. We know that these students can't make it
alone, and there are often supportive families, schools, principals, and communities along the way. Yet African American students often walk the hard

road toward reclamation and success, using four strategies: (1) building resilience through double consciousness; (2) developing a cool, smart, and Black
identity; (3) connecting to school through community organizations; and (4)
engaging with caring teachers.

Building Resilience from Double Consciousness

Du Bois (1903/1995) used the term *double consciousness* to explain how African American people are simultaneously "an American, a Negro; two souls, two thoughts, two unreconciled strivings; two warring ideals in one dark body, whose dogged strength alone keeps it from being torn asunder" (p. 45). As African American educators and parents, we have talked about double consciousness as being "the best of both worlds," meaning, as Pat constantly says, "You understand Whiteness, and you know how to make it in the White world, but you still know who you are as a Black person." This kind of bicultural awareness seems to be the key to significant school achievement. In a recent article in the *Boston Globe* (March 2009), Meghan Irons reported on a "rising counterculture" of African American youth who are unafraid to acknowledge their intelligence *and* take pride in their culture, as participants in the W. E. B. Du Bois Society, an intellectual group comprising African American high school students from public, parochial, and independent schools.

Several scholars who were interviewed for the article argued that this is a new phenomenon that is beginning to catch on within the millennial generation. Neil Howe, co-author of *Millennials Rising: The Next Great Generation* (2000), noted that there are "growing islands" of American teens who are beginning to actively resist the culture of low expectations that surrounds them. In the African American Community, young people are working to break down the stigma that being smart and Black is uncool. For example, the Du Bois Society, which meets on Saturdays at Harvard University to study the works of prominent scholars, was co-founded by the Rev. Eugene F. Rivers III and his wife, Jacqueline in 2001. Since its inception, more than 300 African American youth have participated in the program, and many have matriculated into some of the nation's most selective institutions, including Harvard, Yale, Columbia, Dartmouth, Duke, Northeastern, and Boston College. Strong racial and cultural pride can lead to continued success in college, particularly for African American women. In a recent study, Cokley and Moore (2007) found that African American college women who see race as being a core part of their identity have higher GPAs than women who do not identify with their race. The researchers suggest that this difference in achievement stems from the need to be seen as a strong Black woman, an identity that entails high achievement in academics.

However, for many successful African American students, carrying two cultural backpacks can become an unbearable psychological, social, emotional, and intellectual burden, for two important reasons. First, the perspectives of smart African American students are not always affirmed in schools. In her study of an eighth-grade language arts classroom comprising African American, White, Latina, and Native American students, DeBlase (2003) found that the African American girls were often vocal participants; they formed critical interpretations of texts, and offered these perspectives as contributions in class discussions. However, the girls' explicitly racial interpretations of texts were rarely taken up in the classroom, despite their best efforts to steer conversations in this direction. For example, during one classroom discussion, the teacher became frustrated that the students were bringing up points about race when she wanted them to talk about another theme in the text. The teacher makes several attempts to redirect the conversation by asking questions, and the African American girls in the class respond to them. However, the conversation becomes so stilted and exasperating that one of the girls says to the teacher, "But that's not the question we want! We already told you [the answer]. Now can we get back to race?" (p. 305). In this case, the African American girls were taking up the role of "good student" by responding to the teacher's initial question, actively engaging in the conversation by raising a new question, and expressing willingness to think critically about the assigned text. However, the teacher consistently resisted explicit discussions on race, and over time some African American girls were marginalized and silenced within the classroom. DeBlase (2003) concluded that

> the enacted curriculum of this class did not acknowledge the ways in which race was implicated in the gendered lives of the girls in this classroom. Consequently, the girls were often left with only their own individual efforts as a means to work through issues of raced identity and its implications as a construct for understanding self in relation to texts. (p. 308)

Schools also may have a difficult time recognizing the academic achievements of African American males. As a student in a predominantly White junior high, Malcolm X (Haley, 1987) was first in his class. He told his favorite teacher that he wanted to become a lawyer, and while the teacher supported the aspirations of the White students who were less intelligent than Malcolm, he told Malcolm to become a carpenter. Similarly, in Jennifer's narrative at the beginning of this chapter, she describes how a high school counselor told her father that he was not "college material" and encouraged him to enter the military. Jennifer's father had done well in high school, especially in math, and went on to have a 25-year career in the telecommunications field. Yet the counselor could not see his academic talent and believed that he was better suited for the military.

A second problem facing African American students who embrace double consciousness is that, while it may appear to solve their identity conflicts, the cost of this "twoness" is often psychic turmoil, as Du Bois argues. Indeed, the internal conflicts and tensions caused by the "two warring ideals" often are experienced by African American students who have been successful in school, but who perceive themselves to have attained less success within the peer community. In her story of schooling, Jennifer highlighted the pain of not being White enough to fit into the White Christian schools and churches she attended but not feeling Black enough to fit in with the popular Black girls in her high school. Similarly, Vershawn Young (2007), an African American professor, describes the "racial schizophrenia" (p. x) he experienced (and still experiences) with these poignant words:

> Because I ain't no homeboy–though I long to be and would do anything short of killing to gain that identity–I'm not ghetto enough for the ghetto. Because I'm not a white boy, I'm not white enough for white folks. And because I wasn't born in to the middle class, I'm not completely accepted by the mainstream . . . the psychoemotional pain that this luminal existence creates, the pain of negotiating multiple cultural and racial worlds, is too great for many. I've been doing it for a long time and have been able to cope only by transforming my personal problem into an intellectual one. . . . but far too many are not able to do this. (p. xvi)

Both Young's and Jennifer's stories illuminate the "peculiar sensation" that Du Bois explains as emanating from this kind of double consciousness. African American students can draw upon both cultural worlds to achieve school success, community success, and life success, yet an unintentional consequence of this "border crossing" is that they eventually may feel as if they do not belong to either world. Du Bois (1903/1995) offers one solution to this problem: "to merge his double self into a better and truer self" (p. 45). But the question of how looms large, for there is no instant solution, no magic formula that we can share with African American students. This is why we firmly believe that successful African American students learn to "make a way out of no way," breaking new ground, creating new identities and expressions of Blackness and American-ness that feel authentic to themselves, and seeking out new relationships with other like-minded African American youth.

Being Cool, Smart, and Black

Michael Turner, Jennifer's 38-year-old husband, is an African American man who has defied the stereotypes and been successful in attaining school, community, and life success. Having earned a bachelor's degree in finance from the Wharton School of the University of Pennsylvania and an MBA from the University of Maryland, Michael is now an independent IT contractor who has worked with some of America's leading companies. Born the second of five children, Michael grew up in Fort Worth, Texas, in a two-parent family under tremendous turmoil and stress. As a child, Michael longed to escape his home and his neighborhood and achieve something greater. Such dreams are very common among African American children, but what made Michael unique was his ability to do well in his classes at the magnet high school, play football and basketball, and ultimately win an athletic scholarship to the University of Pennsylvania. When Jennifer asked Michael how he was able to accomplish this, he told this story:

> I don't know how or who taught me, but I started reading early. And my mom would leave magazines out for me. We had subscriptions to *Newsweek, Time, Forbes, Money*. And the more I read, the more I learned, and I don't know when it hit me, but I realized that education is important. Growing up, education was a way to get out. I would read bios of people in magazines, and those people always had graduate degrees. And they were always from Harvard, Yale, Princeton. I didn't understand what that meant, but I knew they went to school for a long time. So it never occurred to me to play football in the NFL. Or play basketball in the NBA. I liked playing sports, but for me, I had read enough in those magazines to realize that those people who were profiled were shown to have a lot of money. And back then, rap was pretty new, and rappers weren't making a lot of money. So I thought I could be successful by going to school.
>
> I was in a school with a magnet program [an advanced academic program for gifted and talented students] that whole time, and everybody was doing well. I think for the longest time, I just did well because everyone around me was doing well. And then, I realized that I wanted to get out of my neighborhood–it was so violent. And in high school, I wanted to get out of my house and I didn't know how to do it. My family would tease me, and my sisters and brother would call me a nerd. But that never bothered me because once I decided I needed to get out, I didn't care. My goal was just to go to college. So I studied hard. Sometimes I would go the library and study during lunch and before basketball or football practice. So I tried to do well in both.
>
> There were two [African American] kids in the magnet program with me, and they played basketball. They were good players. And they both dropped out of the magnet program in high school, freshman year, because it was hard. In both of those cases, their parents didn't force them to stay in the magnet program. Because to those parents, it was better that they have time to play basketball than to focus on school. I don't think either of them went on to college, because in my school, if you weren't in the magnet program, you weren't ready for college.
>
> School and sports were both important for me. And at the time, I felt that both made me cool. And the guys around my way would say, "That Turner, he's smart, but he can ball! So don't mess with him." Now, I think cool is feeling confident and not always needing to look to your friends for your confidence builders. And I think success is having a

certain amount of money. I have always been thinking about becoming a millionaire and that thought is always there. But I have two sons [now] and they need time with their family. And if you are chasing money, you just leave them behind. There are things that they need to learn from me and if I don't teach them, it will be much harder for my boys to get it later. Reading is a big part of it. I also want them to have enough time with Dad. So it is my job to make sure that they get all the time they need from me and to figure out how to still make enough money so that we can become millionaires. That would be success for me: if my sons feel like, "Hey, my dad was there for me. He taught me all these things that other people take for granted," and I can earn that extra money.

Michael's story is important because in many ways, he has been able to achieve a cool, masculine, and smart African American identity. Like Jennifer's narrative, the story that Michael tells is one of self-determination, of breaking down the false dichotomies of sports/school, Black/White, nerd/athlete, to develop a sense of self that is personally meaningful and fulfilling. Clearly, Michael did have obstacles in his life, but he had begun to define success according to what mattered to him: being a dad, raising two sons, and providing for his family. While we admire Michael's story, we have been disheartened by the fact that more stories about Black men who are honor students *and* star athletes have not been publicized in the media, and therefore remain invisible to Black youth. For example, the story of Myron Rolle, a 22-year-old African American football player who graduated pre-med in 2½ years from Florida State University and postponed playing in the National Football League in order to accept a Rhodes Scholarship at Oxford University, was not nearly as well publicized as other stories about professional Black male athletes (Cherner & Weir, 2009). Rolle's success story is important because it shows African American men attaining school success, success within the African American community and respect from their peers, and life success. According to Michael Baisden, a popular African American radio talk show host, "What young black men see are rappers and athletes. They're not seeing enough intellectuals, and they are not seeing enough people who are actually impacting us on a scientific level through engineering, medicine, and we need to do more" (O'Brien, 2009c).

Perhaps President Obama, an African American man who was educated at one of America's most elite universities, plays basketball, has a strong family life, and is the most powerful man in the world, will change this. He has become the "new standard" of cool, gracing the covers of magazines like *Ebony, Time,* and *Rolling Stone.* However, one thing remains certain: Without these critical intellectual role models, African American boys may not be able to emulate this kind of "inclusive" identity.

Connecting to School Through Community Organizations

Nationally recognized community organizations, such as the YMCA/
YWCA, Big Brothers/Big Sisters of America, and the Boys and Girls Clubs
of America, have played a critical role within the African American community. According to Fashola (2002), these organizations are the cornerstones of
many African American communities because they "provide opportunities
for young children to be introduced to new skills and to develop new talents
. . . [and] enrich and expand the opportunities of all children by exposing
them to a variety of activities" (p. 32). Journey for Change is an example of
the kinds of powerful opportunities afforded by community organizations.
Founded by Malaak Compton-Rock, Journey for Change is a program that
sought to empower and inspire low-income African American youth at the
Bushwick Salvation Army, a center in Brooklyn, New York. In August 2008,
30 kids, ages 12 to 16, were chosen to go with Compton-Rock on a 2-week
trip to South Africa, and documented their experiences playing with babies
in orphanages, dancing in the streets, and talking to elders about their lives.
Since returning home, the youths have been busy doing community service
projects in Brooklyn, such as serving food in homeless shelters, working in
a center for abused children, and cleaning up the neighborhood. When the
group was featured on CNN's *Black in America* program (July 2009), several
of the students who participated in this program talked about how trans-
formative the experience was for them; some were motivated to study and
improved their grades and behavior in school, while others talked about
the self-confidence, compassion, and hopefulness that they gained from the
program. Along similar lines, prominent African American celebrities, such
as Denzel Washington and Chris Rock, also have spoken passionately about
their life-changing experiences in community-based programs. In addition
to these powerful testimonials, there is also some empirical evidence that
community-based programs help to improve the literacy skills of participating students (Fashola, 2002; Fashola & Cooper, 1999). However, the extent
of the impact of community-based organizations on the academic lives of
African American youth remains unclear because the research literature on
program effectiveness is quite limited.

Engaging with Caring Teachers

Like other students in our schools, African American students are willing to connect with and will eagerly learn from caring teachers. In research
conducted on African American elementary and secondary students' views
of effective teachers and schools, these youth consistently reported that (a)
relationships between teachers and students affected their academic achieve-

ment, (b) teachers' responsiveness to their personal lives generated positive feelings that led to increased effort in school, and (c) they preferred that teachers establish classroom environments that "felt" like their homes or communities (Hollins & Spencer, 1990; Howard, 2002). As Linda Darling-Hammond (1997) explains:

> Relationships matter for learning. Students' trust in their teachers helps them develop the commitment and motivation needed to tackle challenging learning tasks. Teachers' connection to and understanding of their students helps those students develop the commitment and capacity to surmount the hurdles that accompany ambitious learning . . . success depends as much on the strength of these relationships . . . as on knowledge of students' learning styles and technical skills. (p. 134)

Historically, African American teachers in segregated schools were able to build close teacher–student relationships. Research conducted by prominent scholars like Vanessa Siddle Walker (2001), Adam Fairclough (2007), Michelle Foster (1997), and Arlette Willis (2002) has consistently shown that "the African American teacher is a critical figure in a web of caring adults who placed the needs of African American children at the center of the school's mission" (Siddle Walker, 2001, p. 752). In her book *Black Teachers on Teaching*, Michelle Foster (1997) noted that Black teachers also enacted an ethic of care by demanding academic excellence of their students, disciplining their students when necessary, holding high expectations for academic achievement and social behavior, motivating students to excel, and providing resources to address perceived needs. Some argue that after desegregation, when African American students began attending integrated schools, the disappearance of caring African American teachers and administrators negatively affected the self-esteem and racial pride of African American children (Edwards, 1993). While we do not wish to romanticize segregated schools, we also recognize that these sustained, nurturing, caring teacher–student relationships did not seem to be as available to African American students after desegregation, because

> When black children entered integrated schools, they were met generally by white administrators and teachers who were unprepared to deal with their cognitive styles, social values, beliefs, customs and traditions. Because of the discontinuity that developed overnight between home and school cultures, these personnel began teaching black children with preconceived notions and stereotypical views about how they functioned. (Trent & Artiles, 1995, p. 244)

Consequently, in the approximately 55 years since the *Brown* v. *Board of Education* decision, African American students have been taught primarily by White teachers. However, we want to emphasize that White teachers who care about African American students also can support their school success and literacy achievement. For example, in her autobiography *Project Girl*, Janet McDonald (1999) describes the pivotal role that two White educators played in her journey from living in a crowded Brooklyn housing project with her family to becoming an international lawyer in Paris. McDonald was smart and loved to read, and although she graduated from high school at age 16, she was not adequately prepared for college. Frustrated and lost, Janet enrolled at Harlem Prep, an alternative school directed by the Carpenters, a husband-and-wife team of White educators. McDonald thrived intellectually and socially in the nurturing, familial atmosphere that the Carpenters created, and with their encouragement and support, she applied to Vassar and was accepted. There, McDonald did extremely well, and eventually graduated from Columbia Law School and became an international lawyer.

Perhaps the most moving story we have heard about a caring White teacher comes from D. L. Hughley, the famous African American comedian. During an interview with CNN's Soledad O'Brien (2009b), Hughley was brought to tears talking about the teacher who made a difference in his life: his fifth-grade teacher, Lang Boston. Hughley said that Boston saw his potential, and believed in him when no one else did. Ruddell (1995) calls teachers like Lang Boston "influential teachers" who make a profound and long-lasting impression on their students by inspiring them to learn, motivating them to excel, or insisting they never give up on their dreams.

These success stories offer compelling evidence that White teachers have been able to reach out to Black students in ways that profoundly changed their lives. Research has corroborated this critical theme. In her classic work, Ladson-Billings (1994) studied eight teachers who were successful with African American students, three of whom were White, and more recently, Turner (2003) investigated the language arts practices of three White teachers who were effective with African American elementary students. Looking across these studies, the White teachers were able to develop and sustain a positive, nurturing relationship with their African American students, providing them the academic and emotional support essential for successful learning (i.e., intellectual and social achievement) in classrooms.

One teacher can make the difference in the life of an African American student. However, Black students are finding it extremely difficult to find White or Black teachers who can develop those kinds of relationships with them. Many teachers feel harried by curricular demands, increasing class sizes, tight assessment schedules, and accountability pressures, and they don't feel they have the time to personally connect with each student. Other teachers may want to connect with their African American students, but don't know how to do that because they have very little experience talking and interacting across racial lines (see Chapter 3 for a more substantive discussion of these points). Unfortunately, African American students may have one caring teacher, but without a social network of such teachers in their school careers, they may experience significant challenges in attaining school success through positive relationships with teachers.

THE STRUGGLE CONTINUES

This chapter described the multiple meanings of success that African American students must negotiate as they learn literacy in school: life success, community success, and school success. In writing this chapter, we have been captivated by the powerful messages that African American youth glean from various aspects of the African American Community, and how their interpretations of these messages may lead them to resist school success, and try to attain life success and community success through alternative means, or reclaim school success in ways that enable them to attain success in school, community, and life. Neither road is easy for African American youth to tread, and the intellectual, psychological, and socioemotional toll that both low- and high-achieving African American students pay in K–16 classrooms is extremely heavy.

Although we have attempted to illuminate the perspectives of African American students in this chapter, we cannot help but wish to see more African American students taking the path of reclamation. As we can attest, this road is very uncertain, mainly because African American students, to some extent, must make their own way toward literacy achievement, respect from their cultural community, and success in life. But like Marva Collins (1992), we believe that there is a brilliant child locked inside every African American student. Therefore, we believe that African American youth need some support in making their road, and that is where teachers can help.

Marva Collins (1992) argues that "the good teacher makes the poor student good and the good student superior. When our students fail, we, as teachers have failed also" (p. 32). We know that teachers of all racial and ethnic backgrounds can make a difference in the literacy lives of African American students. Hale-Benson (2001) argues that the solution to creating educational excellence for African American children is found in the classroom, in the activities between teacher and child, and in the teaching and learning processes that are nurtured and sustained throughout the academic year.

But what might these instructional strategies look like? And which ones are "best" for African American students? We address these questions in Chapter 3.

CHAPTER THREE

Teaching
African American Students:
Approaches and Best Practices

Children are who they are. They know what they know. They bring what they bring. Our job is not to wish that students knew more or knew differently. Our job is to turn each student's knowledge and diversity of knowledge we encounter into a curricular strength rather than an instructional inconvenience. We can do that only if we hold high expectations for all students, and convey great respect for the knowledge and culture they bring to the classroom, and offer lots of support in helping them achieve those expectations.

—P. David Pearson, "Reclaiming the Center," p. 272

As asserted by P. D. Pearson above, we believe that best practices and approaches for teaching African American students, and all students, include: (1) turning students' knowledge into a curricular strength; (2) holding high expectations; (3) showing respect for students' knowledge and culture; and (4) offering support to help them achieve expectations. These practices and approaches can be implemented in segregated and integrated schools by teachers of any race. One of the most important factors is a teacher's willingness to establish classroom practices that exemplify the characteristics suggested by Pearson. Gwen and her son David were fortunate to have such teachers. The narrative below illuminates several best practices and approaches implemented by Gwen's teachers in predominantly Black neighborhood schools in the 1960s and 1970s. David also shares a contemporary story about his educational experiences in a diverse neighborhood elementary school in the late 1990s and a middle and high school for gifted and talented students from 2001 to 2008.

NARRATIVE BEGINNINGS—GWENDOLYN THOMPSON McMILLON: "CONFIDENCE + CULTURE SHOCK = DOUBLE CONSCIOUSNESS"

While attending school, I did not think that my K–12 education was unique. I attended predominantly Black, inner-city elementary, junior high, and high schools. I walked to and from school every day with my friends in the neighborhood. We were not startled to see several police cars at a house that was being busted for drugs; gunshots and sirens were common noises in the night. Survival skills were taught in every home—and the stakes of learning were life or death. It all seems like such a dismal picture. However, we did not see our community as a terrible place. Instead, many of us still believe that our childhood was "the good old days" when we could laugh and play kickball, basketball, and four-square all day long. When I arrived at school, Black teachers and a Black principal who knew me by name greeted me. They knew my brothers, sisters, parents, and other family members, and I never wondered if they cared about me. Back then, teachers were like my second parents. I was fortunate enough to have the same teacher—Ms. Eva Wyche—for Head Start, first, second, and third grade. As one of the best teachers in the school district, she was asked to participate in several pilot programs, including one of the first Head Start programs in the United States (summer of 1964) and Project Brite (a math program that brought in college math professors to teach algebra to second graders). Now I realize that these were "privileged" educational experiences.

I developed a love for books at home before beginning school. My mother was my first teacher. One of my fondest memories is listening to my Mom read from the big red Bible storybook during Sunday school every Sunday. She read with such fluency—making each character come to life using a variety of voices. As soon as I could read, I read those stories over and over to myself. My father was a Baptist pastor who spent a tremendous amount of time reading and writing every week. I realize now that I had an exceptional childhood because I was blessed to have reading models in my home. My parents had great dreams for their children; they felt that every generation should improve. An education in "the realities of society" is what we were given on almost a daily basis. "You have to get there earlier, work harder, and be smarter in order to have the same opportunities that White children have," was one of my father's frequent messages to his children. My mother often would take a feminist perspective: "Get a good education so that you can get a good job and be independent . . . never depend on anyone else to take care of you." Hearing these messages at home reinforced the importance of an education, and when I went to school, I was an eager learner.

Ms. Wyche was a phonics pro. We had rhythmic drills that helped us learn the phonics sounds. She had three reading groups, based on ability. Of course, she never told us, but the students knew who was in the top, middle, and low reading groups. In the top group, we usually would read the text together, and complete our related assignments (i.e., answer questions, write a similar story utilizing vocabulary words, complete a crossword puzzle, etc.) independently. Ms. Wyche implemented differentiated instruction very effectively. I remember wanting to read ahead in the reading books. She never held me back; in fact, she would encourage us to take our workbooks home. Back then, we didn't have much homework, but if students voluntarily wanted to complete extra schoolwork, she would happily provide materials. At the end of the school year, she would always let us take our reading workbooks home and remind us to read every day during the summer. In class, reading, writing, and arithmetic were emphasized daily. We also kept up-to-date concerning current events by reading our *Weekly Readers.* In the fourth grade, I was placed in the "top reading class" with advanced sixth graders. Mrs. Calhoun—a local pastor's wife and family friend—motivated me to read longer chapter books by conducting daily read-alouds that made me feel like I was in the woods with Laura Ingalls Wilder or assisting Sherlock Holmes and Watson as they cracked a case. We couldn't wait for her to read the next chapter each day, and I often checked the books out and read ahead. As I moved into junior high, Mrs. Johnson, a Black language arts teacher, introduced me to many of the great African American authors and poets. She used Langston Hughes, James Weldon Johnson, Ralph Ellison, and others as models to encourage students to read and write poetry and essays that reflected our experiences. I usually wrote poems about staying in school and believing in oneself, displaying the concern that I had for my family and friends who struggled. Several junior high teachers recognized my academic abilities and forced me to work harder by giving me a different grading scale. I was expected to complete additional work and assist my fellow students with their work as well. While in the ninth grade, during one of my class periods I assisted the reading resource teacher with students in a remedial reading class. I remember being so angry that many of the students (some were neighborhood friends) could not read basic words. I couldn't understand why their teachers had not taken the time to teach them how to read. At the same time, at the impressionable age of 13, I had my first experience feeling the indescribable sensation when a student learns something really important. I taught several students to read that year.

In high school, I continued to have wonderful educational experiences, learning more about great African American poets and authors from Mrs. Floyd, whose father, a local pastor, was best friends with my father. In my first year of high school I decided that W. E. B. Du Bois's ideas were better than Booker T. Washington's ideas concerning the education and improvement of the Black race in the United States. Now, more than 30 years later, Du Bois is still my favorite Black historical person. In high school, I also was introduced to Shakespeare by Mr. Pratt, a White middle-class teacher who was known for demanding the highest level of excellence from his students. Feeling "smart," I had the audacity to take him twice, for mythology and college writing. They were my most difficult high school courses. As a researcher I still use some of the skills that I learned in college writing. My first assignment taught me a lifelong lesson. After reading over a friend's paper who decided to turn her paper in early for extra credit, I wrote a paper in a couple of hours that was much better written than my friend's paper. To my surprise, my paper was returned and Mr. Pratt told me, "Do it over. It's not your best work, and I won't accept it." After several days, I turned in my "best work," and received an "A." As he handed me the revised paper, he smiled his smug smile and said, "That's what I expect and no less." I have never forgotten the importance of doing my "best work," and not using others' work as a standard.

After graduating from high school with honors, and receiving a vote of confidence from my classmates by being voted "Female Most Likely to Succeed," I couldn't wait to go away to college. I was ready to get on with my life. But when I arrived at the University of Michigan, I went into "culture shock." I had never gone to school with White students, and their interactional styles were quite different from those of my peers at my old high school. It took me more than a year to adjust to the way things were in "the real world." I realized that my "normal education" had been quite unique. In fact, most of the Black students at U of M had attended diverse high schools where they had interacted with students from various cultures. I had a difficult time adjusting to the cultural climate at U of M. The professors' habits were difficult to adjust to, and I was not accustomed to such a competitive environment. At my old high school, teachers, administrators, and students were willing to help one another, and tended to cheer for each other, and celebrate victories together. U of M was a different kind of place. I felt isolated and frustrated because it seemed that hard work did not pay off. Grading on a curve seemed to always work against me. Many students were much better prepared than I. Eventually, I learned how to study and developed an understanding of the culture of the place. I graduated with a degree in economics and went on to become a financial consultant at Merrill Lynch. I was told that I was hired because I had attended a top-notch university and I must be smart enough to do well on Wall Street if I could survive U of M.

After working for Merrill Lynch for almost 10 years, I quit my job to stay home with my children during their formative years. I wanted them to have the privileges that I experienced during my early childhood.

A CONTEMPORARY SUCCESS STORY— DAVID BENJAMIN McMILLON: "I'M A BROTHA' WHO CAN DANCE, PLAY THE DRUMS, AND WIN THE SCIENCE FAIR"

I was fortunate to have elementary school teachers who took a special interest in me. My first-grade teacher complimented me on my writing skills early during the year and required me to write in complete sentences. I noticed that some of my friends didn't answer math problems in complete sentences, but she would check my paper and have me "correct" my answers if I tried to give a short answer. She told my mother that I was capable of higher-level work and she was going to challenge me. The following year, I conducted my first science experiment. My second-grade teacher loved science and had all kinds of interesting books that she allowed me to take home every day. I memorized the names and weights of all the whales and the distances between all of the planets on my own. At the end of the year, she gave me a box of books about whales, planets, snakes, and other interesting topics. I read them over and over again.

By the time I reached the fourth grade, I had the reputation of being "smart," and some of my classmates didn't like me because the teachers tended to use me as an example. I was often considered the "teacher's pet." Because of my reputation, and my brother's success on the spelling team the previous year, my fourth-grade teacher couldn't wait for me to become one of her students. Our school was well known for being competitive in the citywide spelling competition, but we had not been able to beat the gifted elementary school. The spelling coaches believed that they could win with my brother and me on the team. It seemed that the whole school cheered us on. Our parents and teachers drilled us after school at least three times each week. Then, the week of competition came, and one of our teammates was suspended 2 days before the city bee. But despite the setback, and because of our hard work, we were the 2000 City Spelling Bee champions. My brother and I were also the fourth- and fifth-grade individual winners.

Mr. York, my fifth-grade teacher, knew how to make every student feel special. He took our pictures, put them in the hallway, and told all of us that we were going to read more than we had ever read before. He brought in stacks of books and read many of them during class. He had a way of teaching that motivated every student to pay attention. Some of my classmates who had never bothered reading were spending lunch time trying to finish a book. On my teacher's advice, I read *Watership Down* and my life changed. At that time, I became an avid reader and writer because I chose to. I loved the creative way that Richard Adams and other authors used words, and I began to read more and more to expand my vocabulary, and always incorporated my newfound words into my writing. My love for reading and writing has benefited me greatly throughout my educational experiences, and especially in my scientific research pursuits.

My elementary experiences gave me the strong foundation and confidence level that I needed to be successful in the gifted middle and high school programs. My teachers paid attention and took time to identify my interests and special talents. They didn't teach all students at one level, but they encouraged me to complete work and participate in activities that challenged me and kept me interested in learning. Most children begin an identity crisis at the onset of adolescence, which can impede success and distract from the learning process. However, because of the surplus of confidence I acquired from my teachers' and parents' praise, and my resulting continued success, my identity crisis was very short-lived.

I believe that the key to success of any kind is social acceptance. Much of my success can be attributed to a healthy, encouraging relationship with peers, family, and teachers. At an early age I was exposed to many different cultures and learned to get along with people with all types of personalities, from a variety of backgrounds. It was not long before I realized that it was okay to be different from others, not only in terms of ethnicity, but also in terms of "the norm." And I developed a unique set of diverse abilities.

Even on my college campus, my "academic friends" and I do not participate in the same types of extracurricular activities; and my "social friends" and I usually do not share academic or research interests. I enjoy having diverse circles of friends who represent my diverse interests. For example, just as one would seldom find an experienced jazz drummer who majors in math and physics, one would seldom find a state science fair winner who wins hip-hop dance battles weekly. One might ask, "Do my Black friends perceive me as an 'oreo'?" No way! Oreos can't play the drums and dance like me. I don't have a problem fitting into my culture. Like James Brown, I can say it loud, "I'm Black and I'm proud!" I have been taught to embrace my culture and use my gifts and talents to improve the status of my race. When I was growing up I was taught to help students who didn't understand their schoolwork or their Sunday school lesson or had trouble on the playground. While in high school, I was a tutor for the NAACP ACT-SO Enrichment Program and a member of the Gamma Kappa Kudos Club—activities that further instilled the importance of academic success, cultural enrichment, and concern for advancing the African American race. Now, I'm still helping others. This summer I worked as a teaching assistant for the Bridge Program at the University of Michigan. Most of the participants were African American, and I had an opportunity to help them make a smooth transition from high school to college life. I taught one of the algebra sections, and encouraged my students to develop good study habits and live a well-balanced life that includes attending class, studying, going to parties, participating in study groups, going to office hours, hanging out with friends, working out at the gym, and eating good food.

My parents' decisions are largely responsible for my unusual social and academic success. During my 5th-grade year, I tested at a 12th-grade reading comprehension level. When I entered middle school, I tested into the Saginaw Arts & Sciences Academy—a gifted school for middle and high school students. At SASA, students are basically taught at approximately one to three grade levels above students in other schools. The student population was extremely diverse–students from all over the world attended SASA. With aspirations in scientific research, I concentrated in math/science. Each year, I was required to compete in the county science fair, and I learned how to conduct an intensive research project in the sixth grade. As my interests became more focused, I began conducting research in the area of physics and the space sciences. I won first place in the Michigan State Science Fair my senior year, and many other honors. I currently have two provisional patents on a discovery and an invention.

I began college at the University of Michigan in Fall 2008 and have not experienced culture shock of any kind. I was accustomed to the competitive environment and understood how to interact with my professors and fellow students. After I shared my research interests with one of my math professors, Dr. Mark Conger, he helped me receive a research internship that allowed me to continue working on my personal research under his mentorship. I am now double majoring in physics and mathematics; in fact, after school started, I chose to enroll in the honors physics classes. In spite of all my academic stress, I am still able to maintain a healthy balance with a social life in college. In fact, I just came from a Kappa party.

What can others learn from David's and Gwen's stories? Their K–12 educational experiences were exceptionally successful because they had teachers who creatively connected with their knowledge and interests, held high expectations, built on their knowledge and culture, and offered support that helped them achieve. Teachers can make a difference in the lives of their students. In addition to having a classroom and school atmosphere that supports them academically, Black children need to be taught (not just told) the "rules of the game." They also need to have opportunities to practice "playing the game" while receiving scaffolding from their parents and/or other adult mentors. Gwen was taught well and learned how to be Black and proud, but she was sheltered from the racism that exists in the "real world." Being told about racism does not teach Black children how to deal with it. They must be given opportunities to "spread their wings" and fly into the bitter society that they must deal with when they become adults. David came home from school several times with questions such as, "Why can't I get an A in Ms. X's class? I complete all of the work on time and I notice that some of the other children's papers aren't nearly as good as mine." Although David was an easy-going student (in middle school) and did not challenge his teachers, he noticed when he was treated differently. He complained several times that Black students did not get graded the same as White students in some of the classes. Not wanting to make assumptions, his parents told him to keep doing his best and everything would work out. However, after they checked with several Black and White students and parents, it was obvious that a few teachers made distinct differences in their grading. Gwen and Vince used this as an opportunity to discuss racism and help David think about strategies to deal with it. Gwen told him that he needed to do his best on "every single assignment" and begin keeping better track of his work. They documented everything, made copies, kept a folder, and at the end of the marking period, if there was a discrepancy, they asked for an explanation for the difference in grade calculations. This experience taught David the importance of documentation. Whether intentional mistakes or human error, teachers, supervisors, and other authority figures can make evaluation errors, and proper documentation provides evidence for correct grading.

Black children need to have opportunities to have exceptional educational experiences with other Black children, as well as with children from diverse cultures; and they need to be taught how to deal with racism—how to survive in school and society—while their parents and/or another knowledgeable adult scaffolds them through the process. School is not a place where students should be sheltered from societal issues; it is a place where students and teachers should have opportunities to think critically about various problems and brainstorm possible solutions.

LOOKING BACK TO GO FORWARD: TEACHING OTHER PEOPLE'S CHILDREN

It is important for teachers of African American students to implement culturally responsive teaching. One's culture does influence learning style, that is, the way we think about learning, including literacy learning, in the classroom (Hale-Benson, 1982; McMillon, 2001). Teachers must work to develop an understanding of how race and culture affect learning. However, as indicated in the narratives of Gwen and David, an important part of effectively teaching Black children is to teach them about the reality of racism and help them be prepared for it. Of course, we do not advocate for White teachers to take it upon themselves to teach their Black students a "lesson in racism" by implementing racist practices in the classroom. But we demand that all adults—parents, teachers, administrators, pastors, coaches, and so forth—admit that racism still exists and be honest when racist behaviors are being exhibited. Students need adults who are willing to help them learn how to effectively address situations. It is a fact that every teacher or professor is not going to make learning easily accessible and exciting for all students. Black students must be taught how to fight for their right to learn by respectfully demanding to be taught and developing the tenacity to "go the extra mile" to do well in class. Attending office hours and tutoring sessions, and developing a rapport with teachers who may not show an interest in their students, are a few of the activities that Black students must learn to participate in. With the changing demographics in the United States, schools no longer have homogenous student populations, but teacher education courses have not transformed with the changing times. Many universities still teach diversity as a single, isolated course. Diversity should be incorporated into *all* subjects, courses, and activities, especially in teacher education classes. We cannot change our student population, and we cannot immediately change the teaching population, which consists predominantly of White middle-class female teachers. Teachers should implement culturally responsive teaching, but when they do not, students must develop the fortitude to learn in spite of their teachers' inadequacies.

Great Debates in Literacy

Trent and Artiles (1995) expressed some concerns about teaching African American students in integrated schools. In particular, they reported that

> When Black children entered integrated schools, they were met generally by White administrators and teachers who were unprepared to deal with their cognitive styles, social values, beliefs, customs, and traditions. Because of the discontinuity that developed overnight between home and school cultures, these personnel began teaching Black children with preconceived notions and stereotypical views about how they functioned. (p. 229)

Integration did not necessarily impact the education of Black students positively. As indicated by Trent and Artiles, teachers were not prepared to teach Black children when integration initially was implemented. The question is: Has anything changed? After being told that teachers are not prepared to teach Black children, have teacher education programs changed? Since integration has been in existence for several decades, can teacher education programs truthfully say that their teacher education graduates are well prepared to teach students and connect with families from diverse cultures? Have school curricula changed to reflect the changing demographics of the student population? Have teachers changed their instructional ideologies to adapt to the students in their classrooms? Or have teacher education programs, school curricula, and teacher ideologies remained the same? If these changes have not occurred, should we be surprised that the enigma remains for African American students?

Several debates and controversies have surfaced over the years regarding the education of African American students. The sections that follow describe some of the continuing debates and controversies.

Race, Social Class, and Teacher Expectations. Jean Anyon (1981), Kenneth Clark (1965), Ray Rist (1970), and Jere Brophy (1983) are major voices in discussions about race, social class, and teacher expectations. In Anyon's widely cited article, "Social Class and School Knowledge," she reveals that even in an elementary school context, where there is a fairly "standardized" curriculum, social stratification of knowledge is possible. The differences that were identified among schools suggest that rather than being simply conserving or "reproductive," school knowledge embodies contradictions that have profound implications for social change. In Rist's seminal article, "Student Social Class and Teacher Expectations: The Self-Fulfilling Prophecy in Ghetto Education," he shows how a kindergarten teacher placed children in reading groups that reflected the social class composition of the class, and how these groups persisted throughout the first several years of elementary school. However, it is interesting to note that although Clark identified low teacher expectations as one cause of the low achievement of students in ghetto schools, it was not until publication of Rosenthal and Jackson's *Pygmalion in the Classroom* (1968) that the topic of teacher expectations "arrived" on the educational scene. In Brophy's review of the literature on teacher expectations, he reported that it is difficult to predict the effects of teacher expectations. Even with knowledge of teachers' expectations and an understanding of their level of commitment to motivate their students to meet those expectations, it is difficult to determine the effects of teacher expectations alone. Expectations interact with beliefs about learning and instruction to determine teacher behavior so that similar expectations may lead to different behavior. Also, students will differ in their interpretation of and response to teacher behavior so that similar behavior may produce different student outcomes.

African American Vernacular English. Many Blacks believe that the discussion about race and teacher expectations closely relates to the emotional feelings aroused by the Black English and Ebonics movement. Black speech is a dialect that often is misconstrued in our society (Dillard, 1972; Rickford & Rickford, 2000; Sims, 1982; Smitherman, 1986). One can note its negative connotations by the many terms that are used as labels to define this speech, such as "Black English," "African American Vernacular," "broken, inner-city English," and "Ebonics," just to name a few. The "Ebonics debate" has created much more heat than light for most of the country. For teachers trying to determine what implications there might be for classroom practice, enlightenment has been elusive. Most teachers of those African American children who have been least well served by education systems believe that their students' life chances will be further hampered if they do not learn Standard English. In the stratified society in which we live, they are absolutely correct. While having access to the politically mandated language form will not by any means guarantee economic success, not having access almost certainly will guarantee failure. However, teachers must approach the teaching of Standard English in a way that does not alienate students who speak African American Vernacular (Brock et al., 2009). Renowned literary scholar bell hooks (1994) asserts that some African American students are simply resistant learners, rather than incapable of learning and using Standard English. They look upon Standard English as "the language of conquest and domination" (p. 168). As teachers of African American students, it is imperative that we listen to the voices of the students and understand this resistance, while we help them understand the importance of learning the language that is used and valued in educational settings (Brock et al., 2009).

The Literacy Wars: Whole Language, Phonics, and Process Writing Instruction. Similar to the debate concerning Standard English and African American Vernacular, many Blacks feel that whole-language learning fails to provide many positive outcomes for a large number of Black children. Many of us are very familiar with the educational and political battle between proponents of a phonics emphasis in reading versus a whole-language emphasis. P. David Pearson (2004) and Kenneth Goodman (1989, 1998) are major voices in the reading wars debate. Proponents of phonics point to the declining reading test scores that they see as a result of whole-language instruction and to scientific studies that indicate phonics instruction produces better reading scores than other methods (Report of the National Reading Panel, 1998). Whole-language advocates point to other reasons to explain those declining reading scores and turn to ethnographic studies of students in classrooms to support their position.

Two critical books in the reading wars debate are *Broken Promises: Reading Instruction in Twentieth-Century America* (1989) and *The Struggle to Continue: Progressive Reading Instruction in the United States* (1990), both by Patrick Shannon. In his work, Shannon discusses the ways that educational reform changed reading into a technological rather than historical and cultural practice. Rejecting the notion of reading as a cultural practice that depends greatly on the interaction of students and teachers, programs were developed that diminished the value of human understanding, social interaction, and human intentionality. Underestimating the influence of these variables, schools have produced a decreased number of students engaging in meaningful interaction. As a result, students are becoming autonomous, self-motivated critical readers. Lisa Delpit, a prominent African American scholar and author of a widely cited article, "The Silenced Dialogue: Power and Pedagogy in Educating Other People's Children" (1988), and book, *Other People's Children: Cultural Conflict in the Classroom* (1995), complains about the lack of a display of power and authority in process-oriented classrooms: "The teacher has denied them access to herself as the source of knowledge necessary to learn the forms they need to succeed" (1988, p. 288). Delpit believes that African Americans should not be taught from a totally process-oriented perspective; they also should be explicitly taught literacy skills and patterns. We agree with Delpit's belief that African American children often learn more effectively with some direct instruction. The implicit teaching and communication that occur in classrooms are often the source of inadequate student learning (McMillon, 2001; McMillon & Edwards, 2000). Delpit further asserts that in addition to academic knowledge, rules or codes of power should be explicitly taught to African American students. The beginning narrative that describes David's experiences with racism, and his parents' intentional decision to teach him coping strategies, supports Delpit's notion that teaching the rules of the "culture of power" can help students become more successful.

Theoretical Approaches to Teaching African American Students

In addition to the aforementioned debates and controversies, there are a number of theories and perspectives for teaching African American children as well as other children of color. These theoretical approaches teach students to value and embrace their culture and heritage, challenge teachers to create an atmosphere that is more conducive to learning by building on their students' cultural values and beliefs, engage students in learning from materials in which they see themselves reflected in the text, and focus on antiracist curricula that empower African American children and their families. P. D. Pearson's characteristics, discussed at the beginning of the chapter, are reflected in most of these approaches, which include: (a) Afrocentric schools (Shujaa, 1994); (b) multicultural education (Banks, 2001; Grant, 1992; Sleeter, 2007); (c) multicultural literature (Bishop, 2007; Harris, 1990); (d) critical multiculturalism (Apple, 1993; May, 1999); (e) critical race theory (Ladson-Billings & Tate, 1995); and (f) critical pedagogy (Duncan-Andrade & Morrell, 2008; Freire, 1970; Giroux, 1988).

Afrocentric Schools. Afrocentric schools were birthed out of the belief that public education has failed African American students. These schools provide a cultural community that nurtures its students by providing Black adult role models (all teachers and administrators are Black at most Afrocentric schools) and teaching students about their rich African cultural heritage. Students are taught to utilize an Afrocentric approach, which focuses on considering how to contribute to the improvement of people of African descent, and to look at situations from a critical stance that enhances one's ability to identify discrimination and racism. Some believe that students are better prepared for global success because the curriculum is rigorous and includes history that incorporates the contributions of people of African descent. Shujaa (1994) uses Asante's (1980) Afrocentric transformation model as a justification for Afrocentric schools. Asante's levels of Afrocentric transformation are outlined below.

> (1) Skin recognition—awareness of skin color and heritage as characteristics that distinguish one as a person of African descent; (2) Environment recognition—awareness of discrimination and abuse within the environment attributed to one's skin color and heritage; (3) Personality awareness—recognition of individual preferences related to one's heritage; (4) Interest-concern—demonstration of interest in and concern about the issues of people of African descent; and (5) Afrocentricity—awareness of a collective and conscious will, and constant struggle to interpret reality from an African-centered perspective. (pp. 55–56)

Afrocentricity, Asante (1987) argued, "is above all the total use of method to effect psychological, political, social, cultural and economic change" (p. 125). It is a quality achieved "when the person becomes totally changed to a conscious level of involvement in the struggle for his or her own mind liberation" (Asante, 1987, p. 56). Two key terms to consider in Asante's (1980) conception are *consciousness* and *struggle*. Afrocentric consciousness implies a state of awareness in which one understands the need to evaluate symbolic reality as a social product that is never neutral. That is, symbolic reality always reflects a cultural point of view. The question Afrocentricity demands one address is whether that point of view reflects a reality grounded in the experiences of African people. Afrocentric consciousness enables individuals to recognize incongruities in their perceptions of reality and to reinterpret situations and phenomena in a manner that is consistent with collective interests of African people.

The use of the term *struggle* implies that achievement through Afrocentricity is a continual process in which individuals constantly interpret new social situations. The individual involved in Afrocentric transformation struggles to define social reality with Africa at the center of his or her consciousness. For African Americans this becomes an internal conflict in which Afrocentric consciousness is in constant conflict with Eurocentric hegemony. However, many proponents of Afrocentric schools, such as Carol Lee, professor at Northwestern University and founder of the Betty Shabazz charter school in Chicago, have found that these schools have had a great impact on the lives of their students. Their success is quite apparent—as of May 2009, 77% of the 825 students at Betty Shabazz scored at or above normal on Illinois state tests.

Multicultural Education. James Banks (2001), Carl Grant (1992), and Christine Sleeter (2007) are major voices in the multicultural education movement. They contend that little attention in professional preparation programs is focused on preparing teachers for pluralistic classrooms.

According to Grant (2008), the birth of multicultural education cannot be reduced to one defining moment. Instead, it began at several important times: when African Americans became interested in their history in Africa and America and decided to become educated about their role and participation in this rich history (Banks, 1994; Ladson-Billings, 1994); when Native Americans became educated on how to resist and live successfully around White Americans; when Asian Americans communicated with their families back in Asia concerning how to survive in the United States by resisting and getting along with White Americans; and when Mexican Americans began to interact with people from other cultures, including Whites, Blacks, and Asians. In other words, Grant asserts that communication within and between cultures about their relationships with people from other cultures required everyone to consider how to co-exist effectively.

Three forces converged during the mid-1960s that stimulated interest in the multicultural educational approach. The Civil Rights Movement matured, school textbooks were being critically analyzed, and assumptions underlying the deficiency orientation as a way of thinking about diverse children were reassessed (Gay, 1983). Deficiency orientation focuses on what one group lacks in comparison to the values and capital of another group. This deficit model suggests that mainstream values, beliefs, and ways of living are the standard or norm. Schools were severely criticized by members of the Civil Rights Movement, mainly because they perpetuated the deficiency orientation through institutional processes and teacher classroom practices. It also became apparent that many teachers knew very little about students of color and treated cultural differences (e.g., speech patterns, language differences, and ways of interacting socially) as deficiencies needing remediation because they were different from the "norm" (White middle-class ways of communicating). As Gay describes, this "new thinking about cultural differences provided the stimulus for the multiethnic education programs" (p. 561).

The multicultural education approach became an educational concept that most teacher educators professed to understand a great deal (even if they knew little or nothing about it), because policy mandates required the inclusion of multicultural content in teacher education courses (Sleeter & Grant, 1994). Even though the incongruence between preservice teachers' cultural insularity and children's pluralism became more well known, relatively little attention in professional preparation programs focused on preparing teachers for pluralistic classrooms (Grant & Secada, 1990; Liston & Zeichner, 1991; Sleeter, 1985). The marginal treatment of such issues in teacher preparation programs continued to reinforce a significantly monocultural approach to the preparation of teachers (Goodlad, 1990; McDiarmid & Price, 1990).

Multicultural Literature. Rudine Sims Bishop (2007) and Violet Harris (1990) are strong proponents of African American's children literature. They believe that when students from culturally and linguistically diverse backgrounds see themselves reflected in texts, it fosters motivation and engagement in reading. However, Harris is quick to point out:

> African-American children's literature has had a tumultuous past. That past included limited awareness among readers, school, and bookstores; and uninformed criticism. Several factors contribute to this state of affairs but one important factor is the existence of literary canons. (p. 540)

Needless to say, in today's ethnically diverse classrooms, it is essential that books reflect students' cultural backgrounds. Positive images of a child's heritage can make a real difference.

After researching possibilities, we developed the following guidelines for materials selection by adopting recommendations from various language arts and multicultural educators: Beilke (1986), Harada (1995), Harris (1990), and Pang, Colvin, Tran, and Barba (1992). They recommend that multicultural literature contain: (a) positive portrayals of characters with authentic and realistic behaviors, to avoid stereotypes of a particular cultural group; (b) authentic illustrations to enhance the quality of the text, since illustrations can have a strong impact on children; (c) pluralistic themes to foster belief in cultural diversity as a national asset, as well as to reflect the changing nature of this country's population; (d) contemporary as well as historical fiction that captures changing trends in the roles played by minority groups in America; (e) high literary quality, including strong plots and well-developed characterization; (f) historical accuracy when appropriate; (g) reflections of the cultural values of the characters; and (h) settings in the United States that help readers build an accurate conception of the culturally diverse nature of this country and the legacy of various minority groups.

The guidelines above are by no means an exhaustive list. They are meant to provide a starting point from which teachers can explore the many aspects of multicultural children's literature. In addition, teachers may wish to consult with colleagues, parents, and the local ethnic community, drawing upon their specialized knowledge and unique perspectives.

Critical Multiculturalism. May (1999) and Apple (1993) reveal that initial critical multiculturalism brought together two movements—multiculturalism and antiracism. It also addresses the crisis of representation: How does one represent the other? Students of color are not defined through a deficit model of instruction, but rather bring to the classroom their own "funds of knowledge" (Gonzáles, Moll, & Amanti, 2005). May and Sleeter (2010) believe that by integrating and advancing several theoretical threads, such as antiracist education, critical race theory, and critical pedagogy, they have developed a form of critical multiculturalism that offers a fuller analysis of oppression and institutionalization of unequal power relations in education.

Critical Race Theory. The earliest writings on critical race theory can be traced back to Derrick Bell as a response to critical legal studies. In his best-known writing, *Faces at the Bottom of the Well: The Permanence of Racism* (1993), he asserts that racism will not be eradicated unless Whites understand its devastating effects on them. Bell feels that many Whites fall prey to stereotypes about Blacks and are fearful that Blacks may unfairly get ahead of them. When discrimination occurs, many Whites respond with sympathetic nods or victim-blaming rationalizations. Bell believes that Whites often think of complaints of discrimination as "excuses put forward by people who are unable or unwilling to compete on an equal basis in a competitive society" (p. 5). According to Ladson-Billings and Tate (1995), critical race theory is a way of looking at racial relations, particularly within the United States, in a broader context than the traditional civil rights approach. They specifically argue for a critical race theoretical perspective in education similar to that of legal scholarship, by developing three propositions: race is significant in the United States; the American capitalist society is based on property rights rather than human rights; and inequities can be analyzed by looking at the intersection of race and property. The impact of Bell, Ladson-Billings, and Tate in educating African American students is far-reaching. If the influence of "race" is as great as they claim, it is quite evident why the academic achievement levels of African American students have not been able to improve significantly. How can students succeed in an environment that is intentionally established to fail them?

Critical Pedagogy. Giroux (1994) states that critical pedagogy utilizes the classroom as a site for critical reflection of power and structures. It recognizes how the classroom is a microcosm of society and acts as a reproduction mechanism in replicating systems of dominance and oppression. Critical pedagogy has its roots in the critical theory of Paulo Freire (1970), who focuses on the development of critical consciousness that produces personal and societal liberation from oppressive institutions and activities. Freire believes that the oppressed must take responsibility for liberating themselves, and that the oppressor often is victimized by his or her own actions. Rather than trying to liberate the oppressed, the oppressors must work to liberate themselves and ensure that they do not become an obstacle in the liberation process of the oppressed. Rather than an old "pick yourself up by the bootstrap" ideology, Freire believes that individuals must develop a mindset of liberation for themselves and a sense of responsibility to help others in their own group. According to Duncan-Andrade and Morrell (2008), it is not enough to simply increase students' critical consciousness; this consciousness must be linked to academic skill development. Their research includes work with urban teens in a high school English class utilizing elements of popular culture to develop social critique.

In response to these critical theories, there are a number of approaches for teaching students of color. One challenge that practitioners often experience when learning about various theoretical perspectives is that it is often difficult to develop ways to turn theory into practice. Pat Edwards often emphasizes that teachers want to know what to do on Monday morning with the 20 to 30 students in their classes right now. Although we recognize that teachers must acquire theoretical knowledge because they are professionals, we also understand that researchers need to assist teachers by developing practical ways to implement their theoretical ideas in the classroom.

BEST PRACTICES FOR TEACHING AFRICAN AMERICAN STUDENTS

In this section, we share best practices for teaching African American students that have been researched and published. This is not an exhaustive list. We are aware that many best practices do not become public knowledge because they are not documented and published. However, we have included as many best practices as possible, and we attempt to provide culturally transparent examples of classroom assignments and/or activities that reveal how each practice can be implemented. Examples include (a) culturally relevant teaching (Ladson-Billings, 1994, 2001) and (2) culturally responsive teaching (Gay, 2000; King, Hollins, & Hayman, 1997).

Culturally Relevant Teaching and Culturally Responsive Teaching

Ladson-Billings (1994, 2001) states that culturally relevant teaching is a theory of teaching that purposefully incorporates the cultural knowledge, experience, and frames of reference of ethnically diverse students to make learning more relevant for students whose cultural, ethnic, linguistic, racial, and social class backgrounds differ from that of the majority. Gay (2000) defines culturally responsive teaching as "using the cultural knowledge, prior experiences, and performance styles of diverse students to make learning more appropriate and effective for them; it teaches to and through the strength of these students" (p. 29). Based on these definitions of culturally relevant and culturally responsive teaching, we believe that the terms can be used interchangeably. Within the category of culturally responsive teaching there are a number of "best practice" strategies. These include the use of: (a) strategies for teaching African American males (A. Tatum, 2005); (b) hip-hop

(Morrell, 2004); (c) informational texts (Duke, 2000a, 2000b); (d) narratives (Juzwik, 2004, 2006a, 2006b); (e) cultural modeling (Lee, 2007); and (f) cognitive flexibility (Spiro, 1991).

African American Males. A. Tatum (2009), a researcher on best practices for teaching African American males, recommends that teachers provide meaningful reading material and encourage honest debate in order to help African American adolescent males embrace the power of text. He believes that specific texts and text characteristics that inform curriculum selection are missing from the literature concerning how to educate African American adolescent males. By selecting appropriate texts, Tatum believes that teachers can engage students by addressing four literacy needs: academic, cultural, emotional, and social. Tatum references several texts that he considers "enabling" texts because they resonate with African American males to encourage cultural uplift, economic advancement, resistance to oppression, and intellectual development. An example of an enabling text is *The Wretched of the Earth* (Fanon, 1963). In their autobiographical writings, both Frederick Douglass and Dr. Ben Carson discuss the impact that certain books had on their literacy development. Unfortunately, many African American males encounter "disabling" texts in their classrooms in schools. These texts focus on skills and strategies, and ignore the importance of connecting with student interests and cultural contexts.

Hip-Hop. Ernest Morrell (2004) uses hip-hop as a way of teaching African American youth. He argues that as the ethnic backgrounds, languages, and socioeconomic status of students change, teachers must adapt their teaching techniques and approaches to meet each and every student's needs. The great James Baldwin once remarked, "It is only in his music, which Americans are able to admire because a protective sentimentality limits their understanding of it, that the Negro in America has been able to tell his story" (cited in Norwood, 2002, p. 2). Baldwin also reminds us that music has always narrated the experiences of people of African descent in the United States.

In historical Black musical genres such as spirituals, gospel, blues, jazz, funk, and hip-hop, themes such as coping with the strife of social inequality and the constant presence of racism, political organization, self-(re)definition, and subversion are commonplace.

In their practice, Duncan-Andrade and Morrell (2008) use hip-hop related to students' daily lives to make parallels with classic novels. Students are taught to contextualize, critique, and respond to texts from popular culture, and they are taught how to utilize the same skills to understand canonical literature and to answer questions on standardized exams.

Informational Texts. In Duke's (2000a, 2000b) widely read articles, "For the Rich It's Richer: Print Experiences and Environments Offered to Children in Very Low- and Very High-Socioeconomic Status First-Grade Classrooms," and "3.6 Minutes per Day: The Scarcity of Informational Texts in First Grade," she looked for explanations for socioeconomic status (SES) differences in literacy achievement not in low-SES children's homes or communities, but in the schools and other organizations that serve them. She examined the print environments and experiences offered to children in 20 first-grade classrooms—10 in very-low-SES school districts and 10 in very-high-SES school districts. She found that the socioeconomic differences in print environments and experiences run wide and deep. Duke's research illuminates the fact that the low achievement scores of many African American students cannot be blamed on their home literacy environments. Inadequate funding and materials for classrooms also can affect student achievement.

The advantages of being exposed to informational texts at a young age can be found in David's contemporary story at the beginning of the chapter. His second-grade teacher helped identify his exceptional interest in science through her extensive library filled with informational texts. She nurtured his interests by allowing him to take books home during the school year, and encouraged him to continue pursuing his interests by giving him his favorite informational texts at the end of the year. During second grade, one of David's favorite books helped him memorize the distances between all of the planets. Is it a coincidence that 10 years later he won first place in the state science fair for space-related research? We believe helping students identify their interests, and providing early exposure to informational texts related to those interests, can improve students' literacy development by motivating them to read and learn.

Some students, such as David, tend to have a preference for informational texts, while others prefer narratives. Critical thinking skills can be taught using both types of texts.

Narratives. In her recent text, *The Rhetoric of Teaching: Understanding the Dynamics of Holocaust Narratives in an English Classroom,* Juzwik (2008) recommends using a rhetorical framework as a helpful model for understanding classroom talk about sensitive and difficult issues, such as the Holocaust, slavery, and race. Although they are sensitive and difficult topics, they should not be ignored or banned from the classroom. Many students are motivated to read and learn when they are exposed to sensitive and difficult topics. Juzwik suggests that because of the potential power and the potential dangers of oral narrative discourse in classrooms, it can be productive for teachers to investigate their own classroom rhetorics through narrative discourse analysis.

A rhetorical framework encourages multiple voices and perspectives. Teachers must be cognizant of their own values, beliefs, and attitudes, and how those ideas are voiced during conversations in the classroom. The assumption cannot be made that students will agree with teachers' perspectives. Instead, teachers need to know how to touch upon multiple perspectives from the students, understanding the sensitivity of the topic. Encouragement from teachers to voice their opinions about a text will help students develop critical thinking skills.

Cultural Modeling. Carol Lee (2007) defines cultural modeling as a way of designing instruction to make explicit connections between content and literacy goals, and the knowledge and experiences students share with family, community, and peers. While the focus is on literacy and African American students, Lee examines the functions of culture in facilitating learning and provides strategies for leveraging cultural knowledge in support of subject matter specific to academic learning. Similar to Delpit's (1988) beliefs concerning the need to explicitly teach African American students the rules of power, Lee asserts that students must be explicitly taught the patterns of various texts and comprehension strategies that scaffold the learning process. She believes that students have mastered many useful strategies in their everyday activities, especially the ways in which they tackle texts of interest such as hip-hop songs, and language play such as "playin' the dozen" (Lee, 1991). According to Lee, if teachers explicitly point out the strategies that students expertly implement daily, the students can begin to understand the process of approaching various texts.

Lee provides evidence for her theory by working with a group of at-risk high school students who scored in the lowest quartile on standardized tests. After participating in Lee's cultural modeling process, students were able to read classic texts and discuss them in terms of imagery, metaphors, figurative language, symbolism, and other literary devices, as well as pose questions that stimulated heated debates. Although the examples are chosen from an English class, eventually cultural modeling was adopted by the entire school and used across the curriculum in every content area.

Cognitive Flexibility. Rand Spiro (1991) developed the cognitive flexibility theory, which posits that no single perspective is adequate to the task of representing ill-structured problems. He believes a successful learner is one who can readily cast and recast knowledge in response to varying situational demands. To attain this flexibility, learners must understand problems in their full complexity and must "criss-cross" the landscape (problem space) in multiple passes in order to observe how shifts in variables and goals alter the space.

Spiro teaches cognitive flexibility through the use of technology. He uses multiple tapes of the same situation to show teachers scenes from their classroom. Using video clips taped from different vantage points in their classroom, teachers can evaluate their teaching practices. They can see what they did and what they said, observe student responses, and identify practices that facilitate and/or debilitate learning. If a teacher is able to look at snapshots from different perspectives, she or he can become aware of the students' perspectives.

Through the multiple perspectives, approaches, and voices represented in the culturally relevant and responsive approaches discussed so far, students are encouraged to engage with academics and their cultural heritage through a variety of practices.

Black Popular Culture

Culturally responsive teaching for African American students also may include texts that are embedded within Black popular culture. As Stuart Hall (1993) contends:

> In its expressivity, its musicality, its orality, in its rich, deep, and varied attention to speech, in its inflections toward the vernacular and the local, in its rich production of counter-narratives, and above all, in its metaphorical use of the musical vocabulary, black popular culture has enabled the surfacing, inside the mixed and contradictory modes even of some mainstream popular culture, of elements of a discourse that is different. (p. 109)

In our work, we define Black popular culture texts as those connected to the lives of African American youth. Hip-hop music, for example, can serve as one form of Black popular culture "text" that can be read by African American students. Hip-hop music is defined as "a cultural form that attempts to negotiate the experience of marginalization, brutally truncated opportunity, and oppression within the cultural imperatives of African-American and Caribbean history, identity, and community" (Rose, 1994, p. 21). Originating in New York City during the late 1970s, hip-hop music represents the fusion of four essential elements: MC-ing, DJ-ing, graffiti writing, and break dancing (Stovall, 2006). Although these four elements remain at the center of the hip-hop movement, the music itself has evolved over the years. Currently, there are three basic genres of hip-hop music: Gangsta Rap, Backpack Rap, and Popular Rap. *Gangsta Rap*, the most controversial genre, reflects the violent lifestyle of many inner-city youth. Rappers often defend themselves by saying that they are depicting inner-city struggles, not promoting them. *Backpack Rap* is socially conscious music that emphasizes a beat and lyrics inspired by the world around the producer/rapper. Finally, *Popular Rap* is described as a faddish style of music marketed as rap music due to its strong appeal within mainstream audiences (Quinn, 2005). While hip-hop has its roots within the African American urban community, the consistent demand for all three genres suggests that its influence has expanded to reach "not only Black urban youth, but many diverse youth groups nationally and globally" (Mahiri & Conner, quoted in Forrell, 2006, p. 29). In other words, hip-hop music is not just music on the radio; rather, it is at the core of a broader cultural movement for young people, especially Black youth, and is represented by and enacted through a number of related sociocultural practices such as music videos, television programming, movies/film, and advertising.

Elementary Classrooms. There are very few studies that demonstrate how hip-hop can be used in elementary classrooms. O'Gilvie and Turner (2008) reported on a case study of Mr. Jones, a fifth-grade teacher in an urban elementary school who used hip-hop to teach school literacy. By infusing a number of Black popular texts, including hip-hop lyrics (e.g., lines from "Hey Mama" by Kanye West) and movies (e.g., *Hustle and Flow*), into the literacy curriculum, Mr. Jones made connections to the lived experiences of urban students and enabled them to critically consider their world. Importantly, Mr. Jones still utilized the required basal series for literacy instruction, but he supplemented it with popular texts in ways that motivated his students to read and write, reinforced comprehension and critical thinking skills, and helped to build a strong literacy community in the classroom. Analyses of the case study revealed three specific strategies that Mr. Jones employed to infuse hip-hop into his literacy instruction: (1) building literacy community through hip-hop; (2) initiating "freestyle" instructional conversations; and (3) using hip-hop culture as text.

Middle/Secondary Classrooms. Much of the research on teaching African American students using popular culture has been situated in middle and secondary school settings (Lee, 2007; Mahiri, 1998; Morrell, 2002, 2004; Morrell & Duncan-Andrade, 2002; Paul, 2000; A. Tatum, 2000, 2005). The use of hip-hop or popular culture in a classroom setting is often extremely inviting to African American (and other) students who find it difficult to relate to traditional texts in the classroom. Morrell (2002, 2004), who has conducted extensive work on teaching hip-hop in urban classrooms, has designed lessons that incorporate hip-hop music and culture into the traditional high school English curriculum. In a poetry unit, for example, Morrell and Duncan-Andrade (2002) encouraged their African American students to see connections between hip-hop artists and poets from the post-Industrial Revolution. This integration of hip-hop and poetry proved to be an effective strategy, and the seniors became highly engaged in the project; throughout the unit, students became critical readers of hip-hop cultural texts and poetry, as well as cultural producers who developed their own poetry and raps that provided critical social commentary and promoted action for social justice. Similarly, Paul (2000) reported that her urban students enthusiastically engaged in a poetry unit that explored relationships between texts composed by classic poets (e.g., Emily Dickinson, William Shakespeare) and those composed by "street poets" (e.g., Arrested Development, KRS-One, Public Enemy).

Researchers also have reported that using hip-hop has led to gains in literacy achievement for some African American students. In his eighth-grade classroom, A. Tatum (2000, 2005) also used Black youth culture to teach vocabulary, utilizing music, television (e.g., "Movin' on Up," the theme song from *The Jeffersons*, which illuminated the meaning of *ambitious*), and urban films (e.g., Spike Lee's movie *Do the Right Thing*), to make connections to traditional texts, which enhanced his African American students' engagement with literacy and improved their vocabulary and comprehension skills. Similarly, Lee (2007) reported that her African American seniors demonstrated high levels of literary reasoning when they critically read and analyzed Black youth culture texts such as *Sax Cantor Riff*, a short film directed by Julie Dash, and "The Mask," a rap song by The Fugees. Interestingly, the African American students exhibited the highest levels of textual analyses when Lee did not dominate the conversation. Because of the extensive cultural modeling that was provided for the students, they were able to draw upon these skills to read canonical texts. In other words, their culturally relevant engagement with texts that they enjoyed helped them develop necessary skills that were transferable to the analysis of more "school-valued" texts.

Collectively, these studies show that using hip-hop music as an instructional tool transforms literacy learning because it gives voice and space to students who often are marginalized and powerless within their learning communities (Mahiri, 1998; Morrell, 2002). Equally important, teachers who use hip-hop as a pedagogical tool create more equitable opportunities for learning by incorporating students' lived experiences and culture into the official literacy curriculum, thereby building on learners' strengths rather than their perceived academic shortcomings (Paul, 2000; A. Tatum 2000).

Using hip-hop as a teaching tool for African American literacy learners is highly controversial. Most of the research highlights the positive aspects of hip-hop music and culture, and therefore lacks "significant analysis of hip-hop culture and its sometimes mass consumerism, heterosexism, misogyny, violence, and glorification of drug culture" (Stovall, 2006, p. 599). In fact, some teachers may believe that hip-hop music is inappropriate for African American students, or any other children, to listen to precisely because these messages are such a part of the culture. Lee (2007) makes the point that while some particular lines of certain rap songs may be violent, for example, this violence is no more disturbing than what occurs in *Macbeth, Crime and Punishment*, and some other canonical texts. We want to be clear that not all hip-hop artists or music falls into this category; in fact, there are some rappers whose messages of unity, love, and family are inspiring. It is important that teachers begin to acquaint themselves with music that their students enjoy, such as hip-hop music, and determine which songs can be used in class to increase student interest and motivation.

BEST PRACTICES FOR PREPARING TEACHERS TO TEACH AFRICAN AMERICAN STUDENTS

Over the years, teacher educators have developed several strategies for preparing teachers to teach in diverse classrooms. Despite much rhetoric and research, a fundamental question in preservice teacher education continues to elicit much debate: What do teacher candidates need in order to become effective teachers? Zeichner and colleagues (1998), Cochran-Smith (2003b), Duffy (2002), Turner (2006), and Kennedy (2005) responded to this question.

Zeichner and colleagues (1998) discussed three types of design principles for developing best practices in multicultural teacher education programs: (1) institutional and programmatic principles; (2) personnel principles; and (3) principles of curriculum and instruction in teacher education. They believe that under institutional and programmatic principles, the institution's mission, policies, and procedures should reflect the values of diversity and multicultural education, and the institution must show commitment to diversity through its funding, hiring practices, and other ways. Personnel principles should include admissions requirements that include multicultural as well as academic criteria. Also, faculty, staff, and supervisors must be committed to and competent in multicultural teacher education. Finally, curriculum and instruction principles have several tenets, among them that diversity perspectives should permeate the entire teacher education curriculum, including general and subject matter courses; the program should foster the understanding that power and privilege impact teaching and learning; the program should be based on the assumption that all students bring valuable knowledge, skills, and experiences that can be used as resources in teaching and learning; teachers must learn about students, families, and communities, and learn how to use cultural knowledge in teaching, learning, assessment, and so on; and field experiences must be offered that provide opportunities for students to explore learning in diverse settings.

Marilyn Cochran-Smith's (2003a) article, "The Multiple Meanings of Multicultural Teacher Education: A Conceptual Framework," provides a conceptual structure for interrogating the multiple meanings of multicultural teacher education. Cochran-Smith offers several examples of institutions that meet the standards established by her conceptual structure. She states that a few collegiate teacher preparation programs are committed to preparing teachers for urban schools or for social justice, for example, by building into their programs a process of ongoing faculty development intended to enhance the capacity of their institutions to carry out their goals. For example, faculty at the Center for Urban Educators of the School of Education at Long Island University, Brooklyn Campus, use a process of descriptive inquiry to interrogate their own work as urban teacher educators (Traugh, 2002). Similarly, faculty at Boston College engaged in a 2-year self-study referred to as "seeking social justice" to examine their mission of their teacher education program (Cochran-Smith & Lytle, 1999). On the other hand, at many institutions, there is enormous inconsistency in faculty members' knowledge, information, and depth of understanding about issues related to culture and teaching underserved populations (Kitano, Lewis, Lynch, & Graves, 1996), and no built-in structures for addressing faculty development along these lines. Also, in teacher education programs there are many variations in actual policies and practices. Some teacher preparation programs, such as the University of Wisconsin's Teach for Diversity Program (Ladson-Billings, 2001) and teacher education programs at Emory University (Irvine & Armento, 2001), for example, are designed explicitly to prepare teachers to construct culturally responsive curriculum and pedagogy.

In addition to the programmatic structures and policies that support teachers' development of effective teaching practices, the current work on vision (Duffy, 2002; Mercado, 2007; Rohr, Qualls, & Turner, 2007; Turner, 2006; Turner & Duffy, 2007; Turner & Mercado, 2009) reminds us that it is important to help teachers develop their own images and conceptions of "instructional effectiveness" in literacy classrooms. Duffy and Hoffman (1999) argue that teachers' own images of practice are important because there is no one-size-fits-all approach to effective teaching. Effective teaching is not scripted; rather, good teachers orchestrate productive literacy classrooms and pedagogy by using their own visions of practice to guide their instructional decisions (Duffy, 2002). However, many practitioners, particularly new teachers, need significant support in articulating and expanding their visions of practice in culturally and linguistically diverse classrooms (Turner, 2006, 2007). Given the realities of scripted curriculum, state/district mandates, and high-stakes testing, new teachers also need support to sustain their visions of practice in today's literacy classrooms (Mercado, 2007; Rohr et al., 2007).

Several researchers have worked tirelessly to prepare teachers to teach in diverse settings. Some examples of their efforts include: (a) the model of generative change (Ball, 2009; (b) early field experiences (Lazar, 2004);

(c) cultural self-analysis (Schmidt & Finkbeiner, 2006); (d) cultural imagination (Enciso, 1994; Florio-Ruane, 2001); (e) the autonomous model, ideological model (Au, 2006); (f) multicultural literacy (Diamond & Moore, 1995); (g) poetry writing (Rosaen, 2003); and (h) poetry pedagogy and performance (Apol, 2002; Apol & Harris, 1999; Certo, 2004).

Model of Generative Change

In her model, Arnetha Ball (2009) defines *generative change* as a process of self-perpetuating change that begins when teachers become inspired by the information acquired while taking courses or participating in professional development sessions. The knowledge becomes generative when the teachers take the information acquired and expand the knowledge by adding what they learn about their students, and develop instructional ideas that meet their students' needs. Ball found that as teachers were developing their voices on issues of diversity and becoming generative thinkers, their students were becoming more aware of diversity and becoming generative thinkers as well. Also, Ball asserts when teachers take a learning stance, they can use what they learn to enrich teacher–student interactions and improve literacy teaching and learning in their classrooms.

Internships and Cultural Self-Analysis

Althier Lazar (2004) allowed her preservice teachers the opportunity to participate in early field experiences and internships that gave them the confidence to teach in urban settings. In her research study, Lazar examined how her restructured internship helped interns to confront their preconceptions of children and their caregivers; understand the complex factors that shape literacy development within the community; and develop knowledge about culturally relevant teaching. Similarly, Patricia Schmidt (1998) created a model to help present and future teachers become culturally sensitive so they might begin to think about ways to communicate and connect with students and families from minority populations. Schmidt's model (the ABC model) requires teacher education students to compose an autobiography (A), write a biography (B) from information collected from interviews with a person as "different" from themselves as possible (e.g., skin color/race, ethnicity, language, religion, socioeconomic status, power/dominance), and complete a cross-cultural (C) analysis of similarities and differences between their autobiography and the biography. Students also are required to develop teaching strategies that incorporate the cultural knowledge learned from the ABC model.

Autonomous Model, Ideological Model

Au (2006) examined the literacy achievement gap experienced by students of varying racial and ethnic backgrounds from different perspectives: community, classroom, and school. Au believes that social communities often attempt to evaluate the academic success and failure of such students based on stigmatizing beliefs and overgeneralizations. Many people believe that schools should uphold only one form of literacy in mainstream society. As a result, the mainstream language becomes dominant, while the primary languages, family values, and cultural backgrounds of students often are devalued. In this paradigm, which Au calls the autonomous model, students of diverse backgrounds often are tested on their cognitive skills and literacy proficiency based on mainstream ideas that are as yet unfamiliar to them. Therefore, these students have difficulty developing a sense of ownership in the process of learning. The autonomous model does not teach students how to celebrate and respect differences in the processes of their literacy development. However, Au argues that not being proficient in one form of literacy does not mean that students are incapable of learning, because literacy development is the result of a process of social construction. Teaching students to value differences should be a fundamental emphasis in classrooms. She calls the concept of acknowledging multiple types of literacy the ideological model, indicating the comprehensive way that teachers can incorporate the multiple perspectives of their students.

Multicultural Literacy

Diamond and Moore (1995) helped inservice teachers organize their classroom instruction to mirror the new multicultural reality found in their classrooms. Specifically, for 3 years they worked with teachers and students from three culturally diverse school districts: a predominantly African American, economically deprived district; a racially balanced, economically varied population; and a predominantly White, economically sufficient population. Through numerous, regularly scheduled visitations to classrooms, they discovered ways to help teachers acquire a sensitivity to multicultural literature and ways to integrate multicultural perspectives across the curricula. The Multicultural Literacy Program includes three components: multicultural literature, a whole-language perspective, and the creation of a socioculturally sensitive learning environment. The literature highlighted the contributions of minorities and illuminated the injustices they experienced in society. Teachers and students found this type of literature much more meaningful than the previously used monocultural literature. Some of the multicultural literature-based activities included interactive reading and writing, Reader's

Theater, choral reading, journal writing, interactive discussion, mapping and knowledge-generated activities, and responding to literature through art, music, drama, and folk dancing.

Cultural Imagination

Through the use of and sustained conversations about autobiographical texts, Florio-Ruane (2001) introduced teacher education students and experienced teachers to the complex nature of culture. She understands culture not as a product reduced to a set of artifacts, foods, costumes, and ritual, but rather as a meaning-making process, noting that "culture is both meaning and the process of making meaning" (p. 27), where the cultural participant is both the weaver of this "web of meaning" and the strands woven. Using ethnic autobiographical texts as "representations" of an ethnicity is risky business. Such tactics create new stereotypes as well as reinforce held stereotypes. But Florio-Ruane shows that through sustained conversations, "the idea of an autobiography being reducible merely to an 'ethnic' one, the story of a 'them' different from an 'us' merely on the basis of nationality, mother tongue, or hue of skin, grew less and less appropriate" for the participants (p. 134).

Poetry Writing and Poetry Pedagogy and Performance

Rosaen (2003) used poetry as an opportunity for teacher candidates to explore aspects of their own culture and share their knowledge with one another. In particular, first she had teacher candidates read the first three chapters of *Roll of Thunder, Hear My Cry* (Taylor, 1991) and have a discussion about the Logan family's culture. Ideas from the discussion were listed on the board, followed by a student read aloud of "where I'm from" poems by Christensen (1999, 2000). Students then were asked to respond to questions and use the ideas to create a poem. Students were asked to make a Venn diagram to compare and contrast the content of their own poem with the information about the Logan family. Later in the semester teacher candidates were asked to share their poems with a partner before turning them in. Collected poems were organized, copied, and developed into a class book that was given to each teacher candidate. Rosaen described teacher candidates' perceptions of the poetry-writing activity and their learning in four areas: curriculum, pedagogy, multicultural competence, and social justice.

As part of poetry pedagogy and performance, Apol (2002), Apol and Harris (1999), and Certo (2004) explored authentic environments and strategies to encourage preservice teachers to (a) read diverse poetry, (b) write poetry, and (c) discover ways to perform poetry—from recitation to reading to slam—so that they would be more inclined to create such environments for students.

THE STRUGGLE CONTINUES

As researchers, we have tried to "change" the teachers, "fix" the students, utilize new literature, and implement innovative classroom strategies and teaching techniques. Although many of the theories and practices have proven to be quite successful for the teachers and students who have been fortunate enough to utilize them, these strategies and techniques need more work and wider adoption. Educators must be willing to try something different to get different results.

Additionally, if we want the academic achievement of African American students to improve, we must develop a "team" approach. The following chapter emphasizes the importance of the most important team members—parents.

CHAPTER FOUR

Village or Villain: The Role of African American Families

> With some shared understanding of their commonalities and differences, schools and homes should be able to work together to support each other in the development of a literate populace.
> —Lyn Corno, "What It Means to Be Literate About Classrooms," p. 41

Lyn Corno's quote reminds us of the importance of the connectedness between home and school. Pat shared with us the fact before school desegregation African American parents had a place in the school. Pat's mother was Parent–Teacher Association (PTA) president and she and other parents felt comfortable coming and going to the school at their leisure. The faces of teachers and administrators were familiar to them because, in many instances, the teachers and administrators were their friends, neighbors, and fellow church members. Parents could voice their concerns, opinions, and fears about their children's educational achievement, and teachers and administrators listened and responded. Unfortunately, many of today's African American parents do not feel that same connectedness. In this chapter, we explore issues of parent responsibility, poverty, and the changing American family, and we point out that not all African American families are the same. In her personal narrative, Pat shares stories about her parents and other family members and how literacy was an integral facet in their lives.

NARRATIVE BEGINNINGS—
PATRICIA A. EDWARDS: "A FAMILY THAT VALUES EDUCATION"

I was born in Albany, Georgia, to John and Annie Kate Edwards, an African American working-class couple, who were determined that their three daughters would receive the college education that they were not afforded. Growing up in the Deep South during segregation was difficult. Overcoming obstacles designed to block my success was a daily task. At times, the terrain was mountainous, but I refused to give up. My parents taught me to prepare myself; when the door of opportunity opened, I needed to be ready to walk through.

I was told that the African American community chose their best and brightest to represent them. My parents encouraged me to embrace the opportunity to gain access to educational resources that were not normally offered to African Americans; but they shared words of wisdom—candidly telling me that everyone was not going to be pleased with my presence at the all-White school. Regardless of others' prejudices, they told me to stand tall, with my head up, displaying the pride that had been instilled in me since childhood.

When my peers and I arrived at Albany High School, we were faced with racism on many levels. In my Spanish class, students were required to converse during presentations with a partner. I watched as all of the students found a partner, leaving me alone to decide how I should "appropriately" respond. I hoped that the teacher would advocate for me, but she did not. I'm sure she knew that I needed help, but why should she put her teaching career in jeopardy for the lonely African American girl who might not have the intellectual capacity to learn a foreign language anyway? The teacher ignored the situation, continuing with the instructions as if everyone had a partner . . . as if I were invisible. My mother made me the best student in that class by teaching me to learn both sides of every conversation, and make my presentations alone. Mama could have allowed me to become oppressed by the students' and teacher's actions, but instead she reassured me that learning both sides of the conversation would increase my Spanish knowledge exponentially. During presentations I would ask myself several questions in Spanish, and respond to the questions. Students would snicker softly; they were quite amused. However, after several months of this, I decided to take a calculated risk. Appealing to my classmates after having had yet another Spanish conversation with myself, I explained, "I understand that I'm Black and that's not going to change, but I sure wish that someone would volunteer to work with me, because I'm getting bored with being the top student in this class." The students laughed, and that day several volunteered to be my partner. I began to develop many friendships in the school. In a school with a population of 2,500 students, only 24 of whom were African American, I became the first female African American school president.

I was also the first African American on the Albany High School Debate Team. My team won the chance to compete in the Georgia State Championship in Atlanta. My coach, teammates, and their parents spent the night before the competition in Atlanta. I could not go with them because the hotel was "for Whites only." So my neighbor agreed to drive my parents and me to Atlanta the day of the competition. When I arrived at the hotel, I was stopped in my tracks and sent to the back door. I had to kiss my parents and neighbor good-bye at the entrance to the kitchen. They had to sit in the car all day waiting, hoping and praying, because they were not allowed in the room where the competition would take place. As I passed through the kitchen, Black cooks, waitresses, and waiters cheered for me, shouting out words of encouragement, and giving me gentle taps on my back. The debate question for the competition was: Should Black students be allowed to attend White schools? Of course, I thought that Black students had the right to attend White schools and so did the debate committee and/or judges.

I continued overcoming obstacles, gaining momentum as I went along. I graduated with honors from Albany High School, and finished my B.S. at Albany State University (Georgia) in just 3 years. I received my master's degree from North Carolina A & T (Greensboro); attended Duke for 2 years, attaining an educational specialist degree, and transferred to the University of Wisconsin–Madison, where I was told that many Blacks had struggled to finish the program. But I finished with honors.

My mother and father had great influence on my decision making throughout my years of education. They were wise enough to encourage me to develop relationships with others (i.e., neighbors, teachers, students, church members, ministers, Brownie/Girl Scout leaders, music teachers, elders, etc.) who could help me. I was careful to choose mentors who were exceptionally knowledgeable, but who had characteristics similar to those of my parents. Such mentors were wise and caring, but frank and honest. In many ways my mentors have been like family to me. Like my family, they have supported me when I needed assistance, provided scaffolding during the learning process, encouraged me during tough times, and celebrated my victories with me.

In my second year at Louisiana Tech University, I became a Kellogg Fellow and was given a chance to spend an entire summer with Shirley Brice Heath, who took me under her wing, gave me a place to stay, and mentored me daily. After this intense training period, I authored in 1990 two nationally acclaimed programs—*Parents as Partners in Reading: A Family Literacy Training Program* and *Talking Your Way to Literacy: A Program to Help Nonreading Parents Prepare Their Children for Reading* (Edwards, 1990a, 1990b).

My affiliation with the International Reading Association brought me into close contact with another mentor, Dorothy Strickland, who in 1978-1979 served as the first Black president of the International Reading Association. In 1978, while a graduate student at the University of Wisconsin–Madison I had the opportunity to attend the Great Lakes Regional Conference in Indianapolis, Indiana. I had never seen a person of color on the big stage. When I first saw Dorothy on the center stage, I decided that I wanted to follow in her footsteps by becoming a leader in the organizations that focused on literacy. I became the first Black president of the National Reading Conference in 2006. Dorothy was there to cheer me on. In 2008, I was elected vice-president of the International Reading Association and will become president in May 2010. In my role as president-elect of IRA, I will take center stage at the IRA 2009 Great Lakes Regional Conference in Grand Rapids, Michigan.

My parents, John and Annie Kate Edwards, played a key role in my success by making education a top priority in my family. My grandfather (Tate Plummer) organized a school for African Americans in the early 1900s, and his brother, Elzee, was the first teacher at the Plummer School. My grandmother Callie "Robinson" Plummer's brother "Bailey Robinson" was Ray Charles's father. Ray Charles's mother, Aretha, sent him to the state-supported school for the deaf and blind in St. Augustine, Florida. Although he was heartbroken to be leaving home, it was at school where he received a formal music education, and learned to read, write, and arrange music in Braille. My uncle, Joseph Plummer, was the first in my family to graduate from college (Albany State University) and the first Black principal in Milwaukee, Wisconsin. Albany State University, my undergraduate alma mater, is where Ray Charles made a sizable contribution.

For a 1993 *Educational Policy* article, "Before and After School Desegregation: African American Parents' Involvement in Schools" (see Edwards, 1993), I had the opportunity to interview my mother, a first-grade teacher, and an elementary school principal, Mr. Erasmus Dent. My mother was president of the Parent–Teacher Association throughout my entire 6 years of elementary school. When she was asked by Mr. Dent, the teachers, and other PTA parents to run for PTA president, she felt that she did not have enough education to be a good president. She said, "I only finished high school, and I don't know how to conduct a meeting." But Mr. Dent and the teachers convinced my mother to run for president of the PTA.

I remember the night that she was elected. She was so excited! You would have thought that she was elected president of the National Council of Negro Women or the President of the United States. When I asked my mother to talk with me about her role as PTA president, I was astonished to find that she had actually saved a copy of her opening address as PTA president. In her opening address my mother said:

> Education is the key. Our children have to go further than we did in school. We don't want our children working hard for nothing. Times are tough and we want our children to have the education to get a good job. We want them to make something out of themselves. We want them to be strong men and women. We want them to not have to put up with what we have to put up with on our jobs. We don't want them to be treated unfairly and feel that they cannot do anything about it.

My mother's words really resonated with teachers, parents, and students. Her words also communicated the need for parents to make a commitment to help their children.

A CONTEMPORARY NARRATIVE:
LITERACY LEARNING ACROSS GENERATIONS

An important aspect of Pat's family life has always been sharing the value of acquiring a good education. Her uncle, Joseph Plummer, was the first person in the family to receive a college degree. After getting out of the military he pursued a master's degree in educational leadership at Indiana University, because southern colleges did not allow Blacks to attain graduate degrees. After Joseph completed his master's degree, he and Pat's Aunt Minnie moved to Chicago. Pat's mother often told her daughters that it was important for some family members to move away from home so that others could be exposed to cultural and educational activities in other parts of the United States. She encouraged them to think beyond their immediate environment and circumstances. Although they were not allowed to visit certain places in their segregated Georgia community, they spent many summers visiting Joseph in Chicago, where they would go to museums, parks, stores, and numerous events that gave them an expanded view of the world in which they lived.

Joseph and Minnie, who are still alive, and Pat's parents, who have passed away, are still important voices of wisdom whose educational values Pat has continued to rely on. Pat's niece Dee shared with Pat her thoughts about what family has meant to her and her sister, especially after their mother, Pat's younger sister, was involved in an unhealthy marriage. Dee said:

> As a child I always wanted normal parents. I love my parents very much, but I never understood why my sister and I weren't their first priority. Growing up, I felt my needs and wants were not very important to them. Now I am a mother of four children, and I try to listen to my children and love them unconditionally. Fortunately, God gave my sister and me awesome grandparents and two wonderful aunts. The old saying, "It takes a village to raise a child," is very true. My grandparents gave me the foundation, and my two aunts encouraged us to grow into responsible, strong adults. Without them I would have probably been on the streets living a life of crime and self-destruction. My parents divorced when I was 5 and my sister was 1-1/2. After that, our lives took a turn for the worse.
>
> I am happy, blessed, and fortunate that my two aunts and grandparents stepped up and gave my sister and me structure and stability. Aunt

Pat exposed us to a different world, a world of promise and hope, which Aunt Pat said my grandmother, Annie Kate Edwards, promised her when she was growing up. Aunt Pat also showed us that a Black person can have a great lifestyle with hard work and a good education. Aunt Pat provided a lot of love and financial support for my sister and me whenever we needed it. She took us on many wonderful trips throughout the United States and Canada. She treated us like we were her own children. Our other aunt, Aunt Callie, was very loving and nurturing. She gave us the hands-on support we needed from her experience as an awesome kindergarten teacher. She instilled moral and family values in us when she opened up her home.

My sister and I had a gray past, but we now have a bright future. We both graduated from Albany State University. In 2010, my sister will receive her master's in accounting and finance. She recently closed on her first home. I am happily married to a supportive husband with four beautiful children. I have a great job, and we are planning to buy our first home. My sister and I have proved that no matter how bad your life may be, with the right support, you have the opportunity for a brighter tomorrow and future.

Pat shared some personal insights about her family, especially the role her family played in her educational success. Also, Pat gave us a close-up look at the role her family continues to play in the educational success of her nephew, two nieces, and Dee's four children. Even though Pat's family story is inspiring and the researcher and practitioner communities could learn from it, she recognized that the story of one successful African American was simply not enough. Another point Pat recognized is many of the readers of this book might not have encountered families like hers and have struggled to develop positive relationships with African American families. With that thought in mind, Pat decided to devote the discussion in this chapter to the following issues: (1) the beginning of parent involvement in the United States, (2) African American parents' responsibilities for their children, (3) how the American family is a changing institution, (4) poverty and the changing American family, (5) struggling with children and parents, (6) the double standard in dealing with families, (7) the reality that parents are not all the same, (8) learning about cultural issues involving families and communities, and (9) continuing to struggle to build teams and networks.

LOOKING BACK TO GO FORWARD:
THE BEGINNING OF PARENT INVOLVEMENT IN THE UNITED STATES

For more than 4 decades in the United States, there have been federal programs and legislation supporting parent involvement (Head Start, 1965; Head

Start Planned Variations, 1967–1971; Educational of All Handicapped Children Act, 1975; Title I, 1981, and its successor, Chapter I, now reverted to Title I, 1974–1975). A major focus in all of these federal initiatives was recognition of parents as those who have principal influence on their children's development, and the importance of close cooperation between home and school. Edward Ziegler's (1979) remarks provide an excellent rationale for federal, state, and local support of parent involvement.

> Parent education is not one of the subject areas traditionally included in school curricula. It has, nevertheless, been appearing with greater frequency in recent years, either as an element woven into other subject areas or as a discrete course on its own. The message appears to be that parent education is no passing fad. It is here to stay, and it is challenging public schools to reassess the scope of their educational mission. In view of the growing interest and the profound social values at stake, the time has come for serious consideration of the feasibility of implementing parent education in the public schools. (p. ix)

The 1979 Conference of the Education Commission of the States in Denver, where Ziegler made these remarks, set in motion the action schools needed to take on parent involvement. Even though many schools have been slow to develop these initiatives, the research is clear that school practices and policies need to be related to family involvement (Epstein, 2001; Henderson, 1987; Henderson & Berla, 1994). The research overwhelmingly demonstrates that parent involvement in children's learning is positively related to achievement. Further, the research shows that the more intensively parents are involved in their children's learning, the more beneficial are the achievement *effects*. This holds true for all types of parent involvement in children's learning and for all types and ages of students. Looking more closely, there are strong indications that the most effective forms of parent involvement are those which engage parents in working directly with their children on learning activities in the home. Programs that involve parents in working with their children, supporting their work on homework assignments, or tutoring them using materials and instructions provided by teachers show particularly impressive results. The research also shows that the earlier in a child's educational process parent involvement begins, the more powerful the effects will be. Educators frequently point out the critical role of the home and family environment in determining children's school success, and it appears that the earlier this influence is harnessed, the greater the likelihood of higher student achievement.

This reality has been clearly highlighted and supported in federal policies such as the 1988 Elementary Secondary Education Amendment (ESEA) and the Goals 2000 Educate America Act. Moles (1993) found that in the 1988 ESEA, then-Secretary of Education Lauro Cavazos supported different varieties of parent participation, and recommended a number of steps that should be taken by the federal government, schools, and parents to help children learn and parents select a quality education for them. More specifically, Moles stated:

> Three tangible results of this renewed interest at the federal level are incorporated in the 1988 ESEA amendments: new parent involvement requirements for all Chapter I projects, a special grant program on family–school partnerships, and Even Start. Chapter I aid to low-income-area schools now requires a parent-involvement program in each participating school district, although no additional federal funds were added for this purpose. Parents are to provide "meaningful consultation" on the planning and implementation in this program. . . . Thus the confrontations of earlier years between parents and schools seem to be giving way to a new spirit of cooperation centered on helping disadvantaged parents prepare their children more effectively for school learning. It is significant that the training for this is directed at helping parents and school staff to work together. Without reestablishing parent advisory councils, the 1988 federal legislation calls for significant consultation with parents on parent-involvement-program design and operation. (pp. 25–26)

More than 20 years later, the federal government proposed Goal Eight of the Goals 2000 Educate Act, which states, "By the year 2000, every school will promote partnerships that will increase parental involvement and participation in promoting the social, emotional, and academic growth of children" (National Education Goals Panel, 1998, p. 6). The National PTA's publication *Building Successful Partnerships: A Guide for Developing Parent and Family Involvement Programs* (2000) explains why Congress added Goal Eight:

> Congress added this voluntary goal to encourage and increase parent participation in schools across America. It calls upon schools to adopt policies and practices that actively engage parents and families in partnerships that support the academic work of children at home and share decision making at school. Therefore, it prompts schools to examine how their policies, practices, and program designs affect parent involvement. (p. 16)

Family involvement, writes Ziegler (1979), "is no passing fad." That's why there is a continuing interest in family–school partnerships and schools must begin to examine their policies and practices. The federal government has provided and continues to provide funding to encourage states and communities to voluntarily form partnerships at the local level with parents, educators, and business and community groups to meet the challenges of educating children for the 21st century.

A good parent involvement program, according to the National PTA, would entail six factors: (1) regular, two-way, meaningful communication between home and school, (2) promotion and support of parenting skills, (3)

active parent participation in student learning, (4) parents as welcome volunteers partners in schools, (5) parents as full partners in school decisions that affect children and families, and (6) outreach to the community for resources to strengthen schools. Even though PTA is one of the largest programs for parents, very few African American parents are active members of this organization. In conversations with poor African American parents in many schools around the country, Pat has asked them why they aren't members. Many of them shared with her that they view PTA as a suburban, middle-class, White women's organization.

AFRICAN AMERICAN PARENTS' RESPONSIBILITIES FOR THEIR CHILDREN

After almost 50 years of Head Start, compensatory programs, Title I, II, III, IV—not to mention the outpouring of millions upon millions of hard-earned and hard-paid tax dollars—many teachers are concerned. We often hear them ask, "What are the roles, relationships, and responsibilities that should be assumed by poor parents, especially poor African American parents, in less privileged neighborhoods for their children's reading and overall achievement?" While many teachers and administrators agree that children from different family backgrounds can acquire basic school skills, the general consensus among them is that in order to master these skills children must receive some minimal assistance from their families. One teacher shared with Pat concerns about parent responsibility. She stated:

> My concerns are that parents are beginning to give me their parental responsibility. I have notes in my room on homework that parents have written. . . . "Please talk to Ebony about completing her homework and not talking back to me and not doing those things." So then I become the parent, so to speak. Which tells me again that the parents don't have a lot of parenting skills. I'm feeling somewhat perplexed by the limited skills that some of the parents have in parenting.

Many teachers believe, and we agree, that families who cannot help their children with their homework, for example, can at least encourage them to do their best in school and support their efforts to do so. Epstein (1986) suggested that teachers could increase the amount of involvement of parents (including minority parents) who have little education. Epstein compared teachers who were active in seeking parental support with those who were not. Differences between less educated parents' reports of their involvement in learning activities and those of more educated parents were significant only in classrooms of teachers who failed to show leadership in parental involvement. Epstein concluded that teachers who got parents involved "mitigated the disadvantages typically associated with race, social class, and level of education" (p. 279). This is encouraging because the parents highlighted that the teachers who were leaders in parent involvement practices asked them to (1) read aloud to the child or listen to the child read, (2) sign the child's homework, (3) give spelling or math drills, (4) help with worksheet or workbook lessons, (5) ask the child about the school day, (6) use things at home to teach the child, (7) play games that help the child learn, (8) visit the classroom to watch how the child is taught, (9) take the child to the library, (10) borrow books from the teacher to give extra help, (11) make a formal contract with the teacher to supervise homework or projects, and (12) watch and discuss TV shows with the child.

Despite this encouraging news, a legitimate question remains: "Can all parents teach their own children?" Also, questions have arisen about the extent to which schools can and should expect parents to serve as instructional models and supports for children. Morrison (1978) believes that:

> The answer to this question is deceptively obvious; yes, they can teach their own children. This answer is obvious because all parents, whether they realize it or not, do teach their children. . . . However, many parents don't consider themselves to be teachers and conceive of learning as something which occurs only when the child enters school. For the most part, society in general and professional educators in particular have done a good job of reinforcing the idea that "real" education begins when school begins. In this sense, many parents feel that their role is that of caregiver and caretaker. (p. 119)

At the International Reading Association's 1978 convention, John R. Rogers gave a no-holds-barred address. He lamented that "too many [poor parents] have been perfectly willing to turn as much responsibility for their children as possible over to the school" (p. 6). He went on to say that "many parents wanting to do what is best for their children—and knowing that they are not professionally trained as teachers—have come to somehow become vaguely uneasy and confused as to what should be their roles and what exactly are their responsibilities as conscientious parents" (p. 8). Then, Rogers provided a frank word of advice to poor parents: "It is your business to know what is being done to and for your children by the school. You are not a reading teacher, true enough; but you do have inescapable responsibilities for your child's reading development" (p. 8). He outlined in his address a set of responsibilities for poor parents, and some might conclude that he was referring to poor African American parents. He emphatically stated that:

> Parents *are* responsible for their children . . . Responsible for *knowing*: (a) What reading–good reading–is, (b) How well his child reads, [and] (c) Enough about what a good reading program is and what his children's school is trying to do in

order to have an informed, intelligent opinion about it. [Parents are] responsible for *action* [and must take the following] four actions (a) Providing a literate example, (b) Providing a place and a time for reading, (c) Providing something to read, [and] (d) Acting in accord with child's reading needs. (p. 8, emphasis in original)

Since Rogers's speech, we have learned a great deal about how parent involvement is linked to children's school readiness. Research shows that greater parent involvement in children's literacy learning positively affects children's school performance, including higher academic achievement and literacy development (McNeal, 1999; Snow, Burns, & Griffin, 1998; Turner & Edwards, 2009). However, the literature on parent involvement shows that African American parents exhibit a pattern of relatively low participation and that teachers often interpret this pattern to mean that such parents are uninterested in their children's literacy achievement (Edwards, 2004; Edwards & Turner, in press). But the belief that many parents do not care what happens to their children in school runs contrary to what is known about African American family life and the values placed on education (Billingsley, 1968; R. Clark, 1983; Gadsden, 1993; Gutman & McLoyd, 2000; Sampson, 2002).

No matter how minuscule the research, it is well known that many African American children's parents are unable to successfully participate in literacy interactions valued in schools. These interactions include reading to young children or talking to children in ways that expand their vocabulary (Edwards, 1989, 1995; Edwards, Paratore, & Roser, 2009). In the sections below, we highlight what researchers have had to say about these two critical areas.

Parent–Child Book Reading

While it is well documented that parent–child book reading is an important literacy event, it appears that some lower-income "parents are not sufficiently aware of their impact on their child's reading" (Pflaum, 1986, p. 10). Over the years, there has been a proliferation of research on early reading interactions, but one limitation is that almost all of the research focuses on mainstream middle-class parents and children. The few studies on parent–child book-reading interactions in low-income families have shown that low-income parents seldom ask questions or encourage their children to talk (Heath & Thomas, 1984; Ninio, 1980), do not view their young children as appropriate conversational partners (Heath, 1982a, 1982b), and do not tend to adjust their language to their child's level of understanding (Snow & Ninio, 1986). Ninio (1980) found that low-income mothers used significantly fewer object names and action words, and asked very few questions. Middle-class mothers, on the other hand, were more adept at using questions that elicited talk from the child. According to Farran (1982), middle-class mothers engaged their children in elaborate verbal dialogues. Snow and Ninio (1986) reported that poor Black mothers did not seem to adjust their language to their children's actions, as did more advantaged Black parents. Instead, poor mothers repeated their own speech. McCormick and Mason (1986) revealed that low-income parents did not foster or support acquisition of prereading skills to the same degree as parents at higher income levels.

The most extensive body of research describing parent–child book-reading interactions in poor Black families is the research reported by Heath and her colleagues (Heath, 1982a, 1986; Heath, Branscombe, & Thomas, 1985; Heath & Thomas, 1984). Her research has demonstrated that parent–child interaction patterns in Trackton, a poor Black community, were different from those found in Roadville, a poor White community, and Maintown, a middle-class White and Black community. In Trackton, parents did not see young preschoolers as appropriate conversation partners, and occasions in which they engaged these children in sustained talk were rare. Although talk was directed to young children in Trackton, this talk seldom was simplified and children often were expected to understand large spurts of speech. Heath found similar behavior patterns of interaction between a Black teenage mother and her preschool child (Heath & Thomas, 1984). This mother seldom asked her preschooler questions such, "What is this?" or interpreted any of his self-initiated utterances as labels of objects. On the other hand, the parents of Roadville and Maintown children often asked questions and engaged their children in sustained talk.

Heath (1986) found that Trackton children were encouraged to tell stories, but only after adults opened narrative episodes by questioning children. One adult would ask a question of a child, but instead of letting the child answer it, another adult would answer the question. According to Heath, "This adult-question-and-answer routine provides preschoolers with the basic components of a narrative, which preschoolers reiterate through performance after the adults have hesitated or fully stopped their question-and-answer routines" (p. 166). She further pointed out that "requests for 'sticking to the story' or telling 'what happened' [are] inappropriate during a telling [of a narrative]. Questions asked about particulars of a story, assessments of how actors played their roles, or 'what would have happened if . . . ?' [do] not occur" (p. 168). As a result, Heath explains, "Trackton children learn to use common experiences in their narratives, but they [are] not asked to explain how they [vary] either the genre from or the content from an expected organizational schema or a predicted sequence of events, requests that are made by teachers" (p. 168).

In addition, Heath (1983) found that questions Trackton children heard at home were different from the questions teachers asked at school. As a result,

Trackton children had a difficult time responding to and/or answering questions asked by teachers at school. Even though Trackton parents accepted children's stories and talked about children's experiences, they were less likely to relate these experiences to books or other literate events.

Since the time of Heath's seminal work, research has continued and researchers have contributed much to the collective knowledge of how the family environment fosters children's literacy development.

The next significant study, which occurred during the same time frame as Heath's, was the work of Denny Taylor. Taylor (1983) followed six middle-class families that each had a successful reader over the course of 3 years. Her ethnographic work, *Family Literacy: Young Children Learning to Read and Write*, provides insight into the ways in which children successfully learn to read and write through their participation in the everyday experiences of family life. The last chapter of the book explains the importance of using ethnographic methodology in the study of child literacy outcomes. Unlike Heath's (1982a, 1982b, 1983) studies, Taylor's (1983) study focused on middle-class families and found a plethora of reading and writing of complex texts such as storybooks, magazines, encyclopedias, and word-related texts in the homes she observed.

In *Growing Up Literate: Learning from Inner-City Families*, D. Taylor and Dorsey-Gaines (1988) follow four inner-city African American families. In this qualitative study, Taylor and Dorsey-Gaines observed that children from these families can be successful readers, even in the face of overwhelming poverty and unfortunate circumstances. Like the six middle-class families from Taylor's 1983 study, these inner-city African American families provided literacy experiences for their children as part of their everyday lives. However, unlike the middle-class families, the inner-city families most often used literacy activities to "get things done" (e.g., applications for food stamps, AFDC, WIC, and student financial aid). The inner-city children were successful in their home and neighborhood literacy activities, but struggled with school-based literacy activities. The children also struggled to recognize the connections between their out-of-school and in-school literacy experiences.

Following the same trend as Heath's (1982a, 1982b, 1983), Taylor's (1983), and Taylor and Dorsey-Gaines's (1988) work, Teale's (1986) descriptive study documented the many ways in which low-SES families in San Diego used print. Teale conducted an ethnography of the family lives of five low-SES families whose children were successful in school. He described the ways in which the young children in these homes participated in story- and Bible-reading events, and observed their parents writing in journals, reading newspapers and magazines, and communicating in writing with various social service agencies and with their children's schools. He concluded that his findings "should prompt a reconsideration of traditional wisdom which has it that children from low SES backgrounds come to school with a dearth of literacy experience" (Teale, 1986, p. 192). He found that some children in the homes studied had a great deal of contact with literacy before they began school, while others had relatively little. Similar to the findings of Taylor and Dorsey-Gaines (1988), Teale found that the low-SES parents in his study read and wrote mainly as part of their daily living routines (i.e., "to get things done") and did relatively little storybook reading. Teale found that what he called "social domains" in low-SES families included entertainment and daily living routines.

A study by Purcell-Gates (1996) examined the relationships between types of home literacy practices and the different written language knowledges that young children brought to school. To examine this relationship, Purcell-Gates pursued several research questions: (1) What are the different ways in which people in these homes use print and how frequently do they do so? (2) What knowledges of written language do the young children in these homes hold? (3) What is the relationship between home literacy practices (in both type and frequency) and types and degrees of written language knowledge held by the children?

To address these research questions Purcell-Gates (1996) conducted a 1-year descriptive study of in-home uses of print and their relation to emergent literacy knowledge of young children. The study participants were 20 low-income families (10 African American, 7 White, 2 Hispanic, 1 Asian) including 24 children. The literacy levels of the parents ranged from low literate to functionally literate. Children's ages ranged from 4 to 6 during the course of the study.

Purcell-Gates's (1996) study had three main findings. First, children's understanding of print was related to the frequency of in-home literacy events as well as children's personal focus and engagement with the literacy events. Second, in homes where literate adults read and wrote at more complex levels for entertainment and leisure, children knew more about the alphabetic principle and specific forms of written language. Finally, Purcell-Gates found that many parents became more involved with their children's literacy learning (especially in the form of intentional instruction or scaffolding) once their children began formal schooling.

Parent–Child Talk

Similar to the discussions in Heath's work, several more recent studies also have reported on parent–child talk. For example, Baker, Mackler, Sonnenschein, and Serpell (2001) showed that parent–child talk during book reading differed in both amount and content. Talk content included talk about illustrations, meaning, word recognition, immediate book content, and content that went beyond the immediate book content. Talk about illustrations was the most common type of meaning-related talk, and parental word provision was the most common type of talk involving word recognition (which occurred only when children took a turn at reading).

Earlier, Neuman (1996) had noted that different types of texts tended to create different patterns of interactions between parents and children. For example, interactions around highly predictable repetitive texts made it easy for children to follow along and guess what would come next. Because predictable repetitive texts have very simplistic storylines, these texts also provided the opportunity for children to chime in with a word or phrase and for the adult to provide feedback. In contrast, reading narrative texts involved more bridging and recalling of text. Narrative texts have more complex characters, storylines, and language; thus, when parents and children read these texts, the interactions involved greater emphasis on reconstructing certain events in the story, then moving outside the text to take into account children's life experiences.

A study by Saint-Laurent and Gaisson (2005) included an intervention that helped parents develop scaffolding skills in parent–child reading that would help facilitate their children's school performance in reading. Parents were shown how to support their children as emergent readers, beginning readers, and developing readers (i.e., not-yet-fluent or moderately fluent), by providing their scaffolding in three phases: (1) book reading that adapts parental intervention to the child's gradually increasing skills in reading during the school year, (2) support for writing activities, and (3) enjoyable home activities complementing in-class teaching.

What do these studies by Heath and others tell us? How do they point us toward solutions? We believe that they point to the continued need to encourage parents to participate in book-reading interactions with their children. They also focus attention on the need to show parents how to share books with their children. More than 20 years ago, Pat drew the same conclusion. Specifically, she argued for the need to "go beyond *telling* lower SES parents to help their children with reading. We must *show* them how to participate in parent–child book reading and support their attempts to do; we must help them become confident readers simultaneously" (see Edwards, 1989, p. 248, emphasis in original).

We believe that it is crucial that the parents of children who live outside the mainstream of American life understand the importance of engaging in successful book-reading interactions. They are precious human cargo and do not have time to wait until researchers find out how to accommodate and incorporate their families' literacy practices into the curriculum of schools. While we patiently wait for answers from the research community, these families and children have to develop a "double consciousness" of how to negotiate the borders between home and school. In Pat's journey of developing a double consciousness, she did not perceive that her home was lacking literacy. She did not feel inferior. In fact, she felt empowered moving successfully between the Black and White worlds. She was already succeeding in her home, but her parents wanted her to succeed in school, too.

Vocabulary Development

Another widely cited study regarding the performance of African American children was conducted by Hart and Risley in 1995. They began their research against the background of the apparent failure of Head Start to raise IQ scores and the general failure of the War on Poverty to overcome the transmission of poverty across generations. They directed a Head Start program at Turner House in Kansas City, Kansas. Observation and information about the children's families suggested that the children were not dissimilar from their parents and siblings (Hart & Risley, 1995). The research effort then centered on how children living in poverty continued to develop at one rate (despite intensive intervention efforts from many different approaches), while middle-class children were developing at a different rate. The importance of their book, *Meaningful Differences in the Everyday Experience of Young American Children,* stems from Hart and Risley's refusal to merely accept these differences, or to attribute them to socioeconomic or intellectual variables. They sought to learn how these differences between groups developed.

Vocabulary growth rate was chosen as a directly observable criterion measure, rather than IQ, an indirect measure. Hart and Risley (1995) state:

> We wanted the children to know more, but we also wanted to see them applying that knowledge, using language to elicit information and learning opportunities from their teachers in preschool. We watched what the children were doing to guide what we were doing. (p. 5)

Hart and Risley's longitudinal study of parent–child talk in 42 families in Kansas was conducted over a decade. Specifically, they looked at household language use in three different settings: (1) professional families, (2) working-class, and (3) welfare families. Hart and Risley gathered an enormous amount of data during the study and subsequent longitudinal follow-ups to come up with an often-cited, 30-million-word gap between the vocabularies of welfare and professional families. This number came from data that showed welfare children heard, on average, 616 words per hour, while children from professional families (essentially children with college-educated parents) heard 2,153 words per hour. The longitudinal research in the following years demonstrated a high correlation between vocabulary size at age 3 and language test scores at ages 9 and 10 in areas of vocabulary, listening, syntax, and reading comprehension. Hart and Risley's three key findings were: (1) the variation in children's IQs and language abilities is relative to the amount parents speak to their children, (2) children's academic successes at ages 9 and 10 are attributable to the amount of talk they heard from birth to age 3, and (3) parents of advanced children talk significantly more to their children than parents of children who are not as advanced.

Before the Hart and Risley study, A. Anderson and Stokes (1984) observed families from Anglo-American, African American, and Mexican American populations to determine the average frequency of literacy events per hour of observation. They found a wide range of language-learning activities in the homes, most of which were unrelated to schoolwork. They identified nine "domains of literacy activity": (1) religion, (2) daily living, (3) entertainment (source, instrumental, media), (4) school-related activity, (5) general information, (6) work, (7) literacy techniques and skills (adult-initiated, child-initiated), (8) interpersonal communication, and (9) storybook time. In contrast to the belief that many minority children do not begin school with rich literacy backgrounds, Anderson and Stokes found that minority children in their study had varied literacy experiences in several domains of literacy activity, with entertainment (30.2%) and religion (26.5%) being the most prominent. Unfortunately, most teachers of African American students do not know how to build on the funds of knowledge that their students bring from their home and community cultures. Thus, many African American students experience a noticeable disconnect between their primary discourse environment and their secondary discourse environment at school. As a result, many African American children are still struggling to bridge the gap between their home and school discourse.

THE AMERICAN FAMILY: A CHANGING INSTITUTION

You just finished reading about African American parents' responsibilities for helping their children. But you might be scratching you head and saying to yourself, "Many of the students in my school are not living with their biological parents, and I honestly don't know who is serving as the parent. That's why I don't know whom to hold responsible." One teacher shared the following comment with Pat: "We have so many children that aren't being raised by their mother and father, they are being raised by an aunt, uncle, or a grandmother, because the father is in jail and the mother is on drugs. . . . I really feel sorry for some of the children we have now." These changing patterns of who is a parent have important implications for today's schools and teachers.

What constitutes a family and/or parent has undergone a radical change over the years. An observation by Footlick (1990) confirmed that a radical change has occurred in family situations in America. He stated:

> The American family does not exist. Rather, we are creating many American families, of diverse styles and shapes. In unprecedented numbers, our families are unalike: we have mothers working while fathers keep house; fathers and mothers both working away from home; single parents; second marriages bringing children together from unrelated backgrounds; childless couples; unmarried couples, with and without children; gay and lesbian parents. We are living through a period of historic change in American life. (p. 15)

The family as a social institution has experienced many transformations that have profoundly influenced not only the ways in which we understand what constitutes "family" but also the function of the family unit as well (Tutwiler, 1998). Children are born into many different kinds of families, and parents create for children a wide variety of living arrangements. These family structures affect, in obvious and subtle ways, children's development and how teachers relate to them. Since families have changed dramatically, so, too, should schools. Yet schools have been more resistant to change than any other of our institutions.

Teachers must understand that cultural and ethnic diversity can be a key to identifying and respecting changes in American family life. Tutwiler (1998) believes that "school and home connections are likely to be enhanced when teachers and other school personnel are respectful of a family's living circumstances, as well as the unique ways a family might support the education of their children" (p. 41). Houston and Houston (1992) see a need to acknowledge the changing structures and culture of the family, the "new reality" that teachers find in today's schools. Evans and Nelson (1992) aptly describe these changes as the "urbanization of 'Dick and Jane'" (p. 236). Communication with students and their parents is essential to acknowledging and dealing with these changes. If family involvement is to become a reality in schools and classrooms rather than simply a professional dream, close attention must be paid to how the family has changed. Johnson's (1990) warning that "somebody had better wake up and realize" that American society is changing and becoming more complex should communicate to educators that we also must acknowledge that the cultural makeup of classrooms is changing in conjunction with the ethnic, cultural, and economic changes occurring in families.

These changes are encroaching on the school and on the lives of the families we serve. The recurring message is that "families today are just not like we used to know them. . . . Time and people have changed" (Leitch & Tangri, 1988, p. 73). Nieto (1992) warned that:

In a society increasingly characterized by either one-parent families or two-parent families in which both work outside the home, traditional kinds of parent involvement become more problematic. PTA meetings, help during the day, parent–teacher conferences during school hours, and the ubiquitous cake sales are becoming remnants of the past. Most parents nowadays, regardless of cultural or economic background, find it difficult to attend meetings or otherwise to be involved in the governance of the school. (p. 82)

The comments by Leitch and Tangri and Nieto are still relevant. Today's families are different and schools must address these differences. Edwards (2009) argues that most parents want to be supportive of their children and to participate in their children's educational success. Participation will mean different things to different parents, but may include:

- Establishing a comfortable relationship with their children's teacher.
- Knowing when and how they can get in touch with the teacher, especially if their child is having a problem.
- Understanding the teacher's program and her academic and behavioral expectations.
- Acknowledging the school and district standards and curricular guidelines.
- Understanding how and when they might volunteer in the classroom or help with special school events.
- Working with their children at home, monitoring their homework, and helping as needed in appropriate ways. (p. 17)

POVERTY AND THE CHANGING AMERICAN FAMILY

Twenty years ago the authors of the Holmes Group Report, *Tomorrow's Schools*, predicted: "More [children] will be raised by single parents. More will come from families different from the mainstream culture. More will speak languages other than English. . . . The biggest shadow falling over tomorrow's children will be the scourge of deep poverty" (Young, Sykes, Featherstone, Elmore, & Devaney, 1990, p. 29). This prediction has become a reality.

Perhaps it comes as no surprise to you that a large and growing concentration of persons in poverty live in the nation's large cities. This reflects changes in the inner-city class structure and has been accompanied by increasing rates of joblessness, families headed by women as breadwinners or families with one female parent, and welfare dependency. Many inner-city neighborhoods today include almost exclusively the most disadvantaged segments of the urban minority population, families plagued by persistent poverty and welfare dependency, workers who experience long spells of joblessness, and individuals who are pushed into street crime and other forms of aberrant behavior because of limited opportunities (Hays, 2004; Iceland, 2006; Shipler, 2005).

Added to this bleak outlook for urban families is a problem that research-ers and educators face: Many school professionals do not fully understand the interaction of these different factors and how to make the necessary ad-justments in school to sufficiently address the needs of urban families. Kozol (1994) describes a chilling reality for many urban Black children and their families. He states:

> On an average morning in Chicago, about 5,700 children in 190 classrooms come to school only to find they have no teacher. Victimized by endemic funding short-ages, the system can't afford sufficient substitutes to take the place of missing teach-ers. "We've been in this typing class a whole semester," says a 15-year-old at Du Sable High, "and they still can't find us a teacher.". . . In a class of 39 children at Chi-cago's Goudy Elementary School, an adult is screaming at a child: "Keisha, look at me . . . Look me in the eye!" Keisha is fighting with a classmate. Over what? It turns out: over a crayon, said *The Chicago Tribune* in 1988. Last January the underfunded school began rationing supplies. . . . The odds these black kids in Chicago face are only slightly worse than those faced by low-income children all over America. Children like these will be the parents of the year 2000. Many of them will be un-able to earn a living and fulfill the obligations of adults; they will see their families disintegrate, their children lost to drugs and destitution. When we later condemn them for "parental failings," as we inevitably will do, we may be forced to stop and remember how we also failed them in the first years of their lives. (p. 75)

Poverty, homelessness, drugs, and teen pregnancy are among the many social and economic problems that have been highlighted in the media to underscore the decline of urban America. However, these problems that ur-ban families face are similar to those faced by families all across the country. For example, poverty is not just an "urban issue." DeNavas-Walt, Proctor, and Smith (2009) revealed that 19% of children under age 18 live in poverty. They noted that in urban areas, it is 12.9% and in rural areas, 15.1%. The rea-sons given by Fuller and Tutwiler (1998) were confirmed by DeNavas-Walt and colleagues (2009). The continued rise in child poverty can be attributed to: (1) the failure of hourly wages to keep pace with inflation, particularly for young workers and those with less than a college education, and (2) the increase in the number of families headed by a single parent—usually the mother. Mother-only families are at high risk for poverty due to the absence of a second adult earner and the historically lower earning power of women. Poverty has always been a part of American life. Kozol (1994) describes the grim situation as he portrays the children of the poor as social outcasts. He warns us of the gulf that is being perpetuated between the haves and have-nots and wonders what kinds of adults the latter will become. He cites differ-ences in school expenditure, infant mortality rates, homelessness, and school standards, all of which compound the problems of the poor.

Poverty affects children in devastating ways. Kozol (1994) poignantly describes the lives of homeless children, and explains what they tell us about the disregard our society has shown for vulnerable people. He points out:

> Many of these kids grow up surrounded by infectious illnesses no longer seen in most developed nations. Whooping cough and tuberculosis, once regarded as archaic illness, are now familiar in the shelters. Shocking numbers of these children have not been inoculated and for this reason cannot go to school. Those who do are likely to be two years behind grade level . . . many get to class so tired and hungry that they cannot concentrate. Others are ashamed to go to school because of shunning by their peers. Classmates label them "the hotel children" and don't want to sit beside them. Even their teachers sometimes keep their distance. The children look diseased and dirty. Many times they are. Often unable to bathe, they bring the smell of destitution with them into school. There *is* a smell of destitution, I may add. It is the smell of sweat and filth and urine. . . . Their parents—themselves too frequently the products of dysfunctional and under-funded urban schools—have nonetheless been lectured on their "lack of values." (p. 77)

Kozol's words might be shocking, but there are teachers who work with these children each day. Fuller and Tutwiler (1998) provided some "reality" about the myths that teachers, and most people, have about poverty. Educators should pay close attention to these myths, and the actual realities, so that they will better understand how to respond to children who are living in deplorable conditions. Paying attention to these myths does not mean "rushing to judgment" by making the assumption that these myths are representative of all children from impoverished backgrounds. Further, teachers should be aware of the fact that their preconceived notions about poor children could cause them to neglect or to provide less effective instruction to them (Rist, 1970; Rosenthal & Jackson, 1968). For example, we have had conversations with teachers who have made comments that would lead one to believe that "poverty is a minority issue." This is a myth. Look at the statistics. In 2008, the overall poverty rate was 13.2%; 24.7% of Blacks, 22% of Hispanics, 11% of Asians, and 8.2% of Whites were categorized as poor. Another myth that we have heard from some teachers is that poor people have babies to get more welfare (the Welfare Mamas). Having more children does not mean receiving more aid. The average welfare increase is around $60 per month for a baby. There are some states where one doesn't qualify for any additional aid after a second child is born. Other states only allow slight increases (like $25) for a new child.

Many of you may be asking yourselves, "Why do teachers believe these myths?" It may be more comfortable for teachers to create myths about children and families that they do not know than to pursue the kind of deep relationships necessary to develop accurate portrayals of the family lives of their students. Most of the prejudices that people have about poor people, especially poor African Americans, seem connected to the American myth that anyone can be successful if willing to work hard. Consequently, economic failure is perceived to be a personal rather than a social problem. The impoverishment of inner-city neighborhoods and the flight to the suburbs by middle- and working-class residents have significantly altered the families in which children grow up (Neckerman & Wilson, 1988). Therefore, many teachers believe that among the possible consequences for education are a deterioration of the ability of families and neighborhoods to supervise children and support schools. So many teachers don't even attempt to reach out to these parents. In addition, class or ethnic tension between middle-class teachers and lower-income parents discourages parental involvement in school (Edwards, 2004, 2009; Epstein, 2001; Lightfoot, 2004).

Fuller and Tutwiler (1998) were quick to point out that "parents in poverty, like parents of all other socioeconomic groups, love their children, but may feel uncomfortable in their children's school. They frequently feel helpless in their relationships with schools and teachers" (p. 260). Haberman, in his book *Star Teachers of Children in Poverty* (1995), discusses the difference between "star" teachers' perceptions of parents of poverty and those of other teachers. Haberman says, "Star teachers do not blame parents. As much as they may find out about the child and/or the family, they use the information as a basis for helping children learn more or want to learn more" (pp. 11–12).

STRUGGLING WITH CHILDREN AND PARENTS

We recognize, and many of you might share our views, that the general public believes teachers should create an equitable learning environment for all of the students who enter their classroom. We also know that many of the teachers reading this book might be really struggling to work with poor African American children and their families. We can hear some of you saying, "I want some answers. I heard that these students learn differently. Tell me what to do. Tell me about the cultures of these students."

Let us begin by pointing out that school is a microcosm of society, and whatever exists in the larger community (e.g., drug abuse, child abuse, teen pregnancy, alcoholism, poverty, illiteracy, etc.) can come to school and influence classroom learning. As a teacher in a public school, you have no control over what kinds of children you will teach, because everyone has the right to attend public schools. As Edwards, Pleasants, and Franklin (1999) noted, "Schools and teachers must realize that children do not live in a utopia free of the problems that plague adults. Children are a part of society, and what happens in their family, community, and school affects them and all aspects of their development" (p. xix).

Consequently, many teachers are slowly beginning to recognize that they have to work with children who live in difficult situations. In fact, a number of teachers have shared with us comments like the ones below:

It's not like I want to pry, but I think it is very important to know what kind of home situation the child is coming from. If you teach in a low-income school you might hear parents admitting that there drugs in their home. If fact, I've had parents come right out and tell me that there are drugs in the home and at the time that they were pregnant they were on a certain drug.

One parent told me that she and her family were living in two rooms, and four children were sleeping in one bed. . . . Things like that are what we need to be paying attention to.

I'm now dealing with children who have emotional problems, drug problems, physical abuse, sexual abuse, the children are so far behind in grade level that I didn't know what to go for first. Do I try to get them up to grade level? . . . Do I try to get their home more stable? . . . Sometimes I feel at a loss.

Over the past 25 years, Pat has had many conversations with teachers about their struggles with children and parents. In addition to the above comments, many teachers have shared with Pat that they teach children who live in poverty and come from homes or neighborhoods where they fear for their lives. One teacher admitted, "Some of the neighborhoods that the students live in are frightening to go into for me. Sometimes parents are embarrassed of their surroundings and how they live. I have one parent I knew was in the house and didn't open the door." In particular, one teacher shared a story about one of her sixth-grade students that brought tears to Pat's eyes. The teacher said that she noticed that the student had been doing well in school, but appeared sad and distracted, so she decided to ask her what was wrong. As the teacher tells it, the student said:

Our lives [the student's and her sister's] soon changed after my mother remarried. I didn't have a problem with him until he changed into a mad man and has destroyed the bond my sister, mother, and myself once had. He is very controlling and angry most of the time and his anger progressed into abuse. At the beginning, he verbally abused my sister and me for just being there. The verbal abuse is not enough for him, so he decided to physically abuse us also. One afternoon my sister and I were playing in our room and he came in and told us we were the devil's children and we deserved to be punished. We never understood why he made those comments. We thought we were good kids because we didn't like to worry our mother.

One day he told me that every night he was going to beat us in the middle of the night for no reason because we were evil children. There was another incident when my sister was at the table eating and he told her to get up from the table. I knew something bad was going to happen by the tone of his voice. I saw him put his hand under running hot water and slapped my sister in the face with a strong force. This was the last straw for me. As the days go by and the abuse gets worse, my hate for him has grown into deep depression. I hate coming home from school. I hate my life right now. I want to cry myself to sleep some nights, but I know I have to be strong for my sister.

My mother works really long hours and she is never at home to protect us. I eventually got up the nerve to tell my mother to leave her husband (my stepfather) because he was ruining our lives. My mother never responded to my request. Our household remains a living hell. My sister has begun acting out at school. Her grades have dropped and she has started getting into trouble. I try my best to protect her. I have started taking all the heat from my stepfather, so he won't hurt my sister. I feel it is my obligation because I am the oldest. I am only 11 years old and my sister is 7.

I have begun to rebel against him and fight back, but I am too weak mentally and physically. He gets into my head and makes me feel worthless. One morning I was putting my socks together to put them in the dresser drawer. He yelled at me and said I wasn't supposed to sit on the floor to put up clothes. He made get into the closet and he locked the door. He left me in there for few hours. I was actually relieved because I didn't have to be in his presence.

When my stepfather would allow us to see our father without a big fight, I thought it was an opportunity for me and sister to escape. Unfortunately, my father had issues of his own. He is a loving father, but he is an alcoholic. My father has never abused my sister and me. However, his alcoholism has ruined our chances of living with him and having a stable life. Being with my father was like a breath of fresh air compared to our lives with our stepfather.

On the other hand, I have had to carry myself like an adult with my father. He has trust issues with his parents and family. So, after my mother left him he was never the same. He tried to drink his insecurities and problems away. I am the only one he trusts. I am only 11 years old, but my father comes to me with all of his problems. I talk to my father and try to console him every chance I can get. When he is drinking, he often talks to me about his relationships with his girlfriends. Believe it or not I can answer some of his questions just by observing my mother's marriage to my angry and controlling stepfather. I will never forget when one of my father's girlfriends pulled a knife on him. He is usually very abusive to his girlfriends when he is drinking. This woman had enough of his bad treatment. They were arguing about something and she decided to get him before he got her. I saw her pull a butcher's knife out of the kitchen drawer and put it to his throat. I had to talk to her calmly and beg her to put the knife down. I had to become an adult and think for adults. I blame my parents for allowing me and my sister to have a bad childhood. My father's alcoholism and my mother's dependency on men like my stepfather, for financial support, I feel is costing me my childhood. You are only a child once.

The teacher was so touched by this child's story that she requested a meeting with the child's mother and during the meeting she planned to ask whether the mother would allow her daughters to participate in Big Sisters. Even though the teacher previously had requested several meetings with the mother, and she had failed to show up, the teacher prayed that she would show up this time, and she did. The teacher was very careful not to mention that this 11-year-old girl had shared with her the problems she was experiencing at home. Luckily, the mother did not ask why the teacher was suggesting her daughters a needed "big sister." Of course, the teacher felt that if the two girls participated in Big Sisters, this would give them a safe haven for a few days a week and make them feel like children instead of miniature adults. The teacher also met with the school's counselor about having the girls meet with her.

In addition to teachers sharing stories about students that concerned them, they have talked about parents who are illiterate and simply can't or won't even attempt to help their children in school. One teacher admitted: "I have seen a sharp decline in the literacy levels of the parents of the children I teach. I have a parent who said to me that her husband is a 'non-reader.'" This mother said that her husband is getting concerned now because their son is starting to read and he doesn't know how he is going to be able to hide from the child his own inability to read. Teachers also have shared the belief that "some parents are never going to come to school because they feel so disenfranchised from the school community that they would never model or suggest that school matters."

Pat has cautioned teachers and administrators that it is important for them to talk in specifics when they are dealing with African American children and parents so that they don't begin to generalize based on cultural, class, or linguistic differences. As a result, teachers and administrators came up with these four specific cases that further highlighted their concerns about the social and physical well-being of their families and children.

Case # 1: The drug bust. A first-grade student was absent for 16 consecutive days. The student's concerned teacher did what most teachers would do: She attempted to contact the child's parent. She sent several letters home and telephoned the parent. The teacher even called one of the parent's neighbors to inquire if the neighbor would inform the parent of the need to arrange a conference. None of these efforts to reach the parent proved successful.

Sharing her concerns with the principal, the teacher learned that the mother previously had been arrested for drug use. The principal's fear that the mother might have resumed her involvement with drugs was borne out when the mother was arrested a few days later. The children were placed in foster homes; the mother faces a 20-year prison sentence.

Case # 2: My sister's children. A teacher's attempt to contact a third-grader's parent led to the discovery that the parent was missing. The child's 17-year-old aunt stated that she had not heard from her 22-year-old sister and did not know where she was.

Case # 3: Caught in the middle. A mother who has custody of her 5-year-old son suspected that her former husband had been sexually abusing the boy. Consequently, the mother did not want the school to contact her former husband about their son's performance in school. The father, however, demanded that he be kept informed by receiving the same communications from the school that were sent to his former wife. He further charged that the mother was an alcoholic and that he was in a better situation to respond to the child's needs.

Case # 4: Bewildered in kindergarten. A kindergarten teacher with more than 20 years of experience was at a loss as to how to develop a workable instructional program for a child who was acting, according to the teacher, "strange." The child's learning style did not fit any pattern that the teacher had observed in all her years of teaching. She arranged a conference with the parent to better understand how best to work with this child. During the course of that conversation, the parent revealed that her daughter had tested positive for the virus that causes AIDS. The mother added, "I want the best for my child, but I just don't know what is going to happen to her school-wise." While the teacher did not verbalize her feelings at the time, she later confided to a colleague that she did not know the best way to develop the child's learning potential (see Edwards & Young, 1992, p. 76).

From these voices of concerned school professionals, we get a glimpse of what it is like to be a teacher in a classroom with children whose home lives are complicated and whose parents, in the opinions of many teachers, "simply don't care." In these situations, teachers have legitimate questions and issues: How do they reach these children? How can they take on the role of being parents in light of the many responsibilities that they have? In Chapter 5, we provide some possible answers/solutions to these questions.

DEALING WITH FAMILIES: A DOUBLE STANDARD

In 1988, the American Council on Education's Commission on Minority Participation in Education and American Life issued its report, *One-Third of a Nation* (American Council on Education & Education Commission of the States, 1988). In that report the Commission stated: "America is moving backward—not forward—in its efforts to achieve the full participation of minority citizens in the life and prosperity of the nation" (p. 3). The commission members recommended a call for action.

> Minority Americans are burdened not by a sudden, universal, yet temporary economic calamity, but by a long history of oppression and discrimination. They remain largely segregated in minority neighborhoods and minority schools. For many, full participation in the dominant culture imposes a painful choice: to dilute or abandon a rich and distinctive heritage. Above all, they are marked by the color of their skin as different, and therefore more vulnerable . . . yet, minority citizens are not separate. They are, in a real sense, the new America. In a few years they will comprise one-third of the nation's children; soon afterward they will be one-third of the nation's adults . . . they are not other; they are us. How well and under what conditions minority groups are integrated into American life—and the extent to which they participate in and contribute to our educational system and the economy—will determine the continuing strength and vitality of the nation as a whole. (p. 6)

Recognizing the fact that schools are dealing with people rather than technical information, the National Education Association formed four subcommittees to address the special needs and concerns of ethnic minorities—African Americans, Hispanics, Asians/Pacific Islanders, and Native Americans/Alaska Natives. One of the major findings was that educators tend to use a double-standard approach in dealing with African American parents. Pat has worked with several schools and has had numerous conversations with low-income African American parents about their involvement or lack of involvement in school. Many of these parents have shared with Pat that they often feel singled out about every little thing. For example, if their child is late or misses school one day, instead of the school believing that they actually might have a legitimate excuse, the school automatically thinks the worst of them—quickly rushing to judgment about them and their children. However, it is of critical importance that schools recognize that all parents can make significant contributions. It is of equal importance that teachers and administrators not prejudge parents and children from certain groups. Among the biggest barriers to successful parent involvement is the false labeling of African American parents as not interested in supporting, and as unwilling to support, their children's education.

Many public school administrators and teachers have viewed African American parents negatively. In most instances, a number of problems have been pinpointed that administrators and teachers tend to have with African American parents—not caring, poor literacy skills, language deficits, inability to implement suggestions, cultural distance between school and community, unwillingness or inability to attend meetings and support their children's academic development, and inability to recognize their importance to their children's achievement. However, Stevenson and Baker (1987) stated that although it is true that parental involvement through activities such as attendance at parent–teacher conferences, participation in parent–teacher association, and influence over their child's selection of courses predicts student achievement, such parental involvement is becoming more and more scarce.

Preservice teachers as well as experienced teachers working in diverse school settings must look beyond the idea of a single, model child. Haberman (1993) warned of the danger in supposing that child development proceeds "in the same way and at the same year-by-year rate in all groups and cultures and under all life conditions," calling such an assumption "dangerously naïve" (p. 2). Specifically in regard to urban or inner-city communities, Haberman (1993) wrote:

> Children develop by interacting with specific people in particular environments. What is "normal" in one set of circumstances will not be "normal" in another. In fact, given the facts of life in growing up in urban poverty today it is clearly unreasonable to expect children to resemble the textbook models future teachers are trained to regard as normal. The important point is that the urban poor are quite normal. They are making perfectly reasonable responses to those who raise them and to the life conditions under which they live and grow. (p. 2)

A similar observation was made by Tutwiler (1998), who stated:

> The relationship between parents and schools may be affected by faulty perceptions schools hold of given groups. Typically, school expectations of families reflect behaviors, value orientations, and capabilities of middle-class nuclear families. In this way, uniform standards for measuring familial competency exist that

often ignore or negate the diversity among families as well as the contributions families bring to the educational settings. . . . While traditional bonds between white middle-class families and schools must be maintained, a need exists for recognition of the variety of ways in which families not fitting this form conceive of their roles in the educational lives of their children. (pp. 41–42)

Even though Haberman (1995) and Tutwiler (1998) have built a strong case for rethinking normalcy and challenging faulty perceptions schools hold of given groups, it is still not surprising that many teachers and administrators often become angry and complain that the very parents who most need to come to school fail to become involved, making their job even tougher. Some school personnel, including some African American teachers and administrators, in disgust even come to the conclusion that nothing can be done with these children, since their parents do not support and reinforce their school achievement. Nearly 35 years ago, White (1975) expressed a similar opinion about the impact that families have upon their children's educational lives. He stated that:

> the informal education that families provide for their children makes more of an impact on a child's educational development than the formal educational system. If the family does its job well, the professional can provide effective training. If not, there may be little the professional can do to save the child from mediocrity. (p. 4)

Ron Edmonds, a strong advocate in the school effectiveness movement, vehemently disagreed with White's position. Ulric Neisser (1986) summarized the remarks Edmonds made at a Cornell conference prior to his death on July 15, 1983. Edmonds argued:

> Minority children's failure to learn can just as easily be seen as the school's failure to teach them. The fact that many poor and minority children fail to master the school curriculum does not reflect deficiencies in the children, but rather inadequacies in the schools themselves. Variability in the distribution of achievement among school-age children in the United States derives from variability in the nature of the schools to which they go. Achievement is therefore relatively independent of family background, at least if achievement is defined as pupil acquisition of basic school skills. (p. 6)

We disagree with Edmonds's assessment that educating students should be left to schools alone. However, we don't agree that teachers and administrators should develop a blaming attitude toward parents for the underachievement of their children.

Taking a page from Bruner (1996), we assume that teachers and administrators have "folk theories" about students and their families, and that these folk theories influence the teaching and learning process (see Edwards, Mc-Millon, Turner, & Laier, 2001). Folk theories are expectations, beliefs, and assumptions formed over time through personal and professional school experience; their gradual formation gives them a durable quality. Teachers' folk theories tend to place responsibility for students' problems in school on the students and their families. For example, we all know that violence, drugs, and teen pregnancy can happen in a suburban affluent school as well as in schools located in the inner city. However, there is a double standard. When violent acts occur in inner-city schools, it is no surprise. Many will say, "Those people are prone to act violently." On the other hand, when violent acts occur in suburban affluent schools, many teachers, and the general public, are shocked and tend to make up excuses or justifications for these violent acts. In the past, people, including teachers and administrators, have suggested that these violent acts in suburban schools are not the acts of students who attend these schools. Instead, students from inner-city schools often are assumed to be the perpetrators of these violent acts on the families who live in the suburban affluent communities (Casella, 2001; Parker, 2008). Yet, many of these violent acts have occurred in suburban communities (e.g., school shootings in Oliverhurst, California, in 1992; Richard, Virginia, in 1995; Pearl, Mississippi, in 1997; Paducah, Kentucky, in 1997; Fort Gibson, Oklahoma, in 1999; Edinboro, Pennsylvania, in 1998; Littleton, Colorado, in 1999; and Mount Morris Township, Michigan, in 2000), revealing that White children in both affluent suburban and isolated rural schools bring hatred and violence into their schools as well. In this day and time, many schools, whether located in inner-city or suburban affluent communities, are struggling with violent acts by students.

Over the years, we have heard other folk theories about African American parents and children from teachers and administrators. Some of them have included comments like the ones below:

> At my school, we are dealing with a lot of problems where the children have had years of issues from home. I want to teach these children at the appropriate grade level in reading, but I can't because they appear so preoccupied. Even though they come to school, oftentimes their mind is at home. So, in my classroom, I see children dealing with complicated home issues that I didn't see when I began teaching 20 years ago. And I'm sure before I retire in 10 years, I will see more children living in difficult conditions than I am seeing right now.

> I have a lot of young 5-year-olds who have not had previous academic exposure prior to coming to school. They tend to be more timid, shyer. I have several children that are violent.

I've noticed that a lot of the parents are younger. I had one parent who told me that a lot of the work was hard for her to do and she is a very young woman. Her child would bring her work that she's unable to do; she has to get her sister to help. A lot of the parents now, I wonder if they even get through high school. It seems like they don't know a lot about second grade.

A lot of kids come to school now that don't even know what a rule is and they are not under any adult rules at home.

I challenge you to ask yourselves whether you have folk theories like the ones you just read. You might feel that what we are referring to as "folk theories" are the realities of what you as a teacher have observed about African American students. To assume that all of your students come from violent neighborhoods, have unstable homes, and arrive at school lacking basic literacy skills, and use these assumptions as justification for why it is useless for you to even try to work with your students and their parents, is both sad and scary. You wouldn't want your child's teacher, if you had children, to draw these bleak conclusions about him or her.

PARENTS ARE NOT ALL THE SAME

We, as educators, must understand that parents are not all the same. Parents are people, too. They have their own strengths and weaknesses, complexities, problems, and questions, and we must work with them and see them as more than "just parents." In Pat's work with parents, she coined two terms, *differentiated parenting* and *parentally appropriate*, to help teachers find new ways to think about whom parents are. *Differentiated parenting* means recognizing that parents are different from one another in their perspectives, beliefs, and abilities to negotiate school. While parents might have the same goals for their children (i.e., to read, write, and spell well), they might have different ideas about how they can help their children accomplish these goals. *Parentally appropriate* means that, because parents are different, tasks and activities must be compatible with their capabilities. For example, parents who don't read well might be very intimidated and frustrated by teachers who expect them to read to their children every night, and teachers might need to select other activities to support these children in developing reading fluency. As mentioned earlier, parents who work multiple jobs or who are raising their children by themselves might not be able to attend parent conferences after school or in the early evenings, and teachers might need to make other arrangements to accommodate them. When we as teachers plan these activities and tasks, we must remember that parents want to successfully accomplish them and we need to provide as much support to them as possible. When we as teachers ask parents, for example, to "read to their child," more times than not, we assume that parents know what we mean. Unfortunately, many do not. Pat found this to be true in her study of the book-reading practices of poor and minority parents at Donaldsonville Elementary School. The following anecdote illustrates this point:

> Donaldsonville Elementary School had been recognized for its "good curriculum," even though teachers were disappointed with the progress of their students. Eighty percent of the student population was African-American children, and 20% was white children; most were members of low-income families. Teachers felt that they were doing all they could to help these children at school. Without parental assistance at home, the children at Donaldsonville were going to fail. The teachers' solution was to expect and demand that parents be involved in their children's education by reading to them at home.
>
> The teachers felt that this was not an unreasonable request. There is good evidence of positive gains made by "disadvantaged" elementary students when parents and children work together at home on homework and learning packets. What the teachers did not take into account was that 40% of the school's parents were illiterate or semi-literate. When the parents didn't seem willing to do as the teachers asked, teachers mistook parents' unfamiliarity with the task being asked of them, coupled with low literacy skills, for lack of interest in their children's education. The continued demand that parents read to their children at home, which had a particular meaning in teachers' minds, sparked hostility and racial tensions between teachers and parents. Each group blamed the other for the children's failures; each felt victimized by the interactions. Children were caught between their two most important teachers—their classroom teacher and their parent. (Edwards & Young, 1992, p. 76)

In another instance, Angela, a 32-year-old African American mother with five children ranging in ages from 22 months to 16 years, becomes fearful and sometimes defensive when her child's teacher requests that she read to the child. The mother quietly admitted to Pat a secret that mirrors the reality of some other parents:

> I'm embarrassed, scared, angry, and feel completely helpless because I can't read. I do care 'bout my children and I want them to do well in school. Why don't them teachers believe me when I say I want the best for my children? I know that my children ain't done well in kindergarten and first grade and had to repeat them grades. My older children are in the lowest sections, and are struggling in their subjects. My children are frustrated, and I am frustrated, too. I don't know how to help them, especially when the teacher wants me to read to them. These teachers think that reading to children is so easy and simple, but it is very difficult if you don't know how to read. (Edwards, 1995, p. 54)

Mrs. Colvin, a first-grade teacher at Donaldsonville Elementary School, expressed her frustration with parents or other caregivers like Angela:

> Year in and year out these parents who are mostly low-income African American and white send their children to school with serious literacy problems. It seems as if the children have no chance of passing. They don't recognize letters of the alphabet, numbers, and they can't even recognize the letters in their own name. Consequently, it is not surprising that most of them have had to repeat kindergarten and first grade. All of the kindergarten and first grade teachers have seen similar behaviors in these children. These behaviors include limited language skills and the inability to interact with adults. We feel that these children have not been read to and have rarely engaged in adult–child conversations. Each year when we see parents at the beginning of the school year we tell them the same old thing, "Please read to your child at least two to three times per week. It will make a world of difference in how well your child does in school." We know the parents hear what we are saying, but we don't think they have read or plan to read one single book to their children. We, as kindergarten and first grade teachers, cannot solve all of these children's literacy problems by ourselves. The parents must help us. (Edwards, 1995, p. 55)

Unfortunately, many teachers haven't created the structure to involve mothers like Angela. Despite the continued low academic performance of poor Black students, for the most part, scholars and policymakers concerned with this situation continue to look for school-based solutions. However, they fail to pay sufficient attention to the family as a possible source of help.

At the same time that most schools do not look to parents for help and support, few would disagree with Epstein (2001) and Lightfoot (2004) that parent involvement is important. The involvement of parents in their children's education is considered a cornerstone to children's success in school. Irvine (1990) argues that for Black parents, their role as teachers in the home is "crucial," and is the one role directly related to the achievement of Black students. Ogbu (2003) wrote that, according to Black students he studied who were doing well in school, "parents' supervision of their schoolwork and homework was an important reason for their academic success" (p. 241). Yet, the teachers of these students tend to believe that poor working-class Black parents fail to supervise the homework of their children. We also know that Black children living in poverty are far more likely than others to have academic difficulties, "including low performance on cognitive tests, low school performance, and higher rates of school drop-out than their non-poor European-American peers" (Gutman & McLoyd, 2000, p. 2).

The school, according to Comer (1993), is an instrument of the mainstream culture. Indeed, schools not only inculcate the middle-class/middle-income culture into our children, but also are designed to shape and mold students to fit into that culture. Yet, many poor families are not really a part of that culture; as a result, they send children to school ill prepared to learn. The children lack the values, attitudes, beliefs, and communicative styles upon which the school is built, and that the school uses to teach the child. Such children are often hopelessly behind when they start school. If parents fail to work to boost the self-esteem of the child, fail to teach the child to delay gratification, and fail to teach the child discipline or the moral and intellectual-cognitive lessons so important to the school, not only does that child begin the educational experience behind, but he or she is likely to fall even farther behind as the school experience becomes increasingly negative (Lightfoot, 1978). However, this is not the experience of all poor Black schoolchildren. Sampson (2004) is quick to point out that "some poor blacks . . . appear to be middle class and do many of the things that seem to be important for good academic performance for their children, while others are not and do not" (p. 12). Epstein (1985) reinforces the importance of parent involvement by discussing the positive effects that it has on parents' abilities to help their children learn.

R. Clark (1983) made detailed observations on the quality of African American students' home life, noting how family habits and interactions affect school success and what characteristics of family life provide children with school survival skills, a complex set of behaviors, attitudes, and knowledge that are the essential elements in academic success. Clark reported that high-achieving Black students had parents who (1) were assertive in their parent involvement efforts; (2) kept abreast of their children's school progress; (3) were optimistic and tended to perceive themselves as having effective coping mechanisms and strategies; (4) set high and realistic expectations for their children; (5) held positive achievement orientations and supported tenets of the achievement ideology; (6) set clear, explicit achievement-oriented norms; (7) established clear, specific role boundaries; (8) deliberately engaged in experiences and behaviors designed to promote achievement; and (9) had positive parent–child relations characterized by nurturance, support, respect, trust, and open communication. Conversely, underachieving Black students had parents who: (1) were less optimistic and expressed feelings of helplessness and hopelessness; (2) were less assertive and involved in their children's education; (3) set unrealistic and unclear expectations for their children, and (4) were less confident in terms of their parenting skills.

Sampson (2002) concurs with R. Clark (1983), writing that "differences in family dynamics and/or home environment account for the differences in school performance" (p. vii). Sampson (2004) also argues that it is important to remember that Blacks are not a monolithic group. Sampson (2004) laments that "all too often, scholars, teachers, and educational administrators look at all Blacks as though they are the same: disinterested, undisciplined, with no ability to delay gratification, and little sense of responsibility" (p. 5). Taylor, Pearson, Clark, and Walpole (2000) reported in their work with low-income schools that beat the odds that a large number of African American parents were involved in their children's literacy lives. They further reported that teachers in the most effective schools realized that good communication and collaboration, found among the staff, must extend also to the parents of the children in their schools.

Most educators agree that parent involvement is important; however, few actually know how to implement successful home–school connection initiatives. Rodriguez (1981) warned, "The failure to involve minority groups in educational policy-making activities of the school represents a tremendous loss in human resources for the parent, the child, the minority group to which he or she belongs, and the school as a whole" (p. 40). McLaughlin and Shields (1987) argued, "What's lacking, in most schools and school districts, are appropriate strategies or structures for involving minority parents" (p. 157).

How would you assess your school's record in working with poor minority families, especially poor African American families? If there are other parent groups in your school other than poor African Americans, you need to keep in mind that not all poor African American are the same, and the members of other parent groups are not all the same as well.

LEARNING ABOUT CULTURAL ISSUES INVOLVING FAMILIES AND COMMUNITIES

Viewing families from a historical and humanistic stance is important, but there is one other approach that educators must consider—the cultural approach. The cultural approach focuses specifically upon the needs of diverse families and emphasizes the fact that families' cultural differences should not be viewed as deficits. Berger (1995) revealed that:

> Two challenges face the schools as they work with culturally diverse students. One is to understand each child's abilities and actions. The other is to eliminate ethnic discrimination. The more the school and home become involved with each other in a positive relationship, the greater are the opportunities for understanding the family and reducing discrimination. (p. 105)

In addition, today's educators "cannot afford to make damaging and inaccurate judgments that families who comprise these new family structures are uncaring, incompetent, or apathetic [parents]" (McLaughlin & Shields, 1987, p. 157). Because certain families may not respond to the school's invitation to participate, that does not imply that successful partnerships cannot be developed. Even though today's teachers may not fully understand the possible differences that exist between themselves and observed families, they cannot simply conclude that these "differences" translate into a defect in families. As a preservice or experienced teacher, you can work not only to adeptly interpret these changes, but to find successful ways of making these students feel comfortable in your classroom. The differences actually can enhance the educational process.

We must keep in mind that children don't learn in a vacuum; they bring their culture, family experiences, and community experiences with them to school. It is apparent that when people talk about diversity, the discussion always comes back to where children come from culturally and geographically. At an early age, children become literate as they interact with family to meet personal needs, gain self-identity, and establish behavior patterns that reflect cultural values and beliefs (Heath, 1986; Schiefflin & Cochran-Smith, 1984; Wertsch, 1991). Berliner (1986) correctly noted that "teachers have no choice but to inquire into each student's unique culture and learning history, to determine what instructional materials might best be used, and to determine when a student's cultural and life experiences are compatible, or potentially incompatible, with instruction. To do less is to build emotional blocks to communication in an already complicated instructional situation" (p. 29).

Many teachers may be well intentioned and sensitive to different cultures. But they may lack the experiences and knowledge to understand and meaningfully teach diverse students and to successfully interact with families. Connecting home and school literacies can be difficult for teachers because it requires a deeper understanding of the lives, histories, or cultures of families and communities different from their own.

Irvine (1990) correctly points out that teachers must understand the cultures of their students, because culture is "the sum total ways of living that are shared by members of a population," consisting of "rites, rituals, legends, myths, artifacts, symbols, language, ceremonies, history, and sense-making that guide and shape behavior" (p. 83). Culture is what children bring from home to school. According to Diamond and Moore (1995), "The child's culture, home, family and community form the sociocultural backdrop for school learning. The classroom must be sensitive to these multiple histories, which are the ways of knowing and learning that students bring" (p. 18). Therefore, it is critical for educators to reexamine their classrooms to determine whether they are cognizant of the multiple histories and ways of knowing that students bring to the learning environment.

In her book *Culture in School Learning*, Etta Hollins (1996) describes several successful interventions that improve the academic achievement of groups traditionally underserved in the nation's public schools. These include:

1. Legitimizing the knowledge the children bring to school.
2. Making meaningful connections between school learning and cultural knowledge or knowledge acquired outside of school.
3. Creating a hybrid culture in school that is congruent with many of the practices and values children bring from the home and peer culture.
4. Creating a community of learners where collaboration is the norm rather than competition.
5. Balancing the rights of students and teachers.
6. Providing curriculum content and pedagogical practices that support a consistent and coherent core of identity and intergenerational continuity with the past. (p. 14)

In critically examining what Hollins has suggested, we need to look at our schools' structures or teaching practices to determine which of the six successful interventions have been addressed, which have not, and what additional information might be helpful. In particular, we might start by asking how teachers can begin to celebrate and respect students' diversity. Traditionally, some teachers have thought about addressing cultural diversity as what Derman-Sparks (1989) criticizes as a "tourist curriculum" that focuses on artifacts of other countries, such as food, traditional clothing, folk tales, and household items.

> Tourist curriculum is both patronizing, emphasizing the "exotic" differences between cultures, and trivializing, dealing not with the real-life problems and experiences of different peoples, but with surface aspects of their celebrations and modes of entertainment. Children "visit" non-White cultures and then "go home" to the daily classroom, which reflects only the dominant culture. The focus on holidays, although it provides drama and delight for both children and adults, gives impressions that is all "other" people—usually people of color—do. What it fails to communicate is real understanding. (p. 7)

So, how do teachers move from "cultural tourism" to seeing culture as an important part of our students' experiences and lives? One way is for teachers to understand how various cultures may foster specific interactive styles that differ from the teachers' expectations. Christine Bennett (1999) believes that culturally relevant teachers seek "intercultural competence—the knowledge and understanding of their students' cultural styles." Bennett further explains that these teachers

> feel comfortable and at ease with their students. Interculturally competent teachers are aware of the diversity within racial, cultural, and socioeconomic groups, they know that culture is ever changing, and they are aware of the dangers of stereotyping. At the same time, they know that if they ignore their students' cultural attributes they are likely to be guided by their own cultural lenses, unaware

of how their culturally conditioned expectations and assumptions might cause learning difficulties for some children and youth. (p. 38)

Hollins (1996) points out that "as a classroom teacher, you bring your own cultural norms into your professional practice. The extent to which your teaching behavior will become an extension of your own culture exclusively or will incorporate the cultures of the students you teach may be influenced by your perceptions of the relationship between culture and school practices, political beliefs, and conceptualization of school learning" (p. 14). Teachers, then, must seriously examine the relationship between their own cultural beliefs and practices and those of their students and their families. Specifically, teachers should consider the ways in which accomplished teachers are able to weave together their own cultural patterns with those of their students and their families.

THE NEED TO BUILD TEAMS AND NETWORKS:
THE STRUGGLE CONTINUES

In this chapter, Pat shared her personal narrative as well as stories about her parents and other family members and how literacy was an integral facet of their lives. The theme of "looking back to go forward" is especially important when examining literacy learning across generations. Just as Pat has explored her family's literacy learning across generations and how literacy has impacted their lives and outlooks, we encourage you to do the same. This chapter's discussion of parent involvement in literacy learning over the years provides a good backdrop against which to examine your own family's and previous generations' literacy practices. As we mention in this chapter, little research has been done about the specific in-home practices of African American parents and how they take responsibility for their children's literacy learning. If you are an African American parent reading this book, your experience of "looking back to go forward" can contribute to our larger story as African Americans and help our children progress in literacy and beyond. The majority of the literature reviewed in this chapter examined previous studies of parent–child book reading, starting with the seminal studies of Shirley Brice Heath and ending by looking at more recent analyses of parent–child book reading, especially those examining the types of talk parents do while reading with their child. The degree to which parents participate in book-related talk during the reading, as well as scaffolding comprehension strategies, has effects on overall literacy achievement, especially children's vocabulary development.

The next part of this chapter took a closer look at the African American family as a social institution, examining its evolution and challenges. Particularly, we directed attention to the effects of poverty on African American families and how this affects education, achievement, and literacy. We also addressed some of the myths about poverty and African Americans, and suggested ways that we can counter these stereotypes.

The final part of this chapter endeavored to expand ideas about what a poor African American family is. Just as not all parents are the same, not all African American families, or all poor African American families, are the same. In every case, it is important to examine a variety of parent dynamics that relate to and affect how parents feel about schooling generally, how they relate to their children, the values and goals they hold, and their attitudes about parent involvement. Often, these dynamics vary depending on cultural issues, intergenerational issues, and so on. We ended with a call for teachers to embrace children's and families' funds of knowledge as a foundation upon which to build, not a mountain to be scaled.

As a child growing up in the Deep South and attending segregated school for most of her schooling career, Pat witnessed her teachers developing strong home–school connections. Even though we are living in different times, we believe that today's teachers have the willpower and tenacity to weave together their own cultural patterns with those of their students. We believe that poor African American parents will play a role in their children's education. They will accept roles of responsibility, even if they feel insecure about their own personal literacy skills. Pat's mother did not complete high school and didn't know now to conduct a meeting, but with the positive support she received from the teachers and the principal, she succeeded as PTA president, and her three children succeeded in school.

It is imperative that teachers and parents build teams and networks to support students' academic pursuits. If athletic teams can have booster clubs to support basketball and football teams, we can have literacy network clubs to support African American children's literacy development. It is our hope that this chapter inspired in you the passion and desire to develop a close working relationship with your students and their families. The futures of the children you teach depend on it.

CHAPTER FIVE

The Road to Redemption: Moving from Victims to Victors

God, we have pushed so many of our children into the tumultuous sea of life
   in small and leaky boats without survival gear and compass.
   Forgive us and help them to forgive us.
   Help us now to give all our children the anchors of faith and love, the rudders
   of purpose and hope, the sails of health and education, and the paddles of
   family and community
   to keep them safe and strong when life's sea gets rough.
              —prayer by Marian Wright Edelman, 2008, p. xiii

Marian Wright Edelman, president and founder of the Children's Defense Fund, challenges us to accept our past inadequacies and move forward with renewed strength, passion, and commitment needed for the tasks ahead. The journey will be tedious, for the path will be riddled with obstacles. However, we can accomplish our goal to provide African American students, and all students, an exceptional educational experience that prepares them to successfully fulfill their dreams for a bright future. With a spirit of collaboration we can win the fight for literacy and equity in education, for all of us are smarter than one of us, and all of us are stronger than one of us. Our final narrative shares how Pat, Gwen, and Jen began their collaborative efforts to make a difference in the lives of African American students.

NARRATIVE BEGINNINGS—
PAT, GWEN, AND JEN COMMITTED TO MAKING A DIFFERENCE:
"ALL OF US ARE SMARTER THAN ONE OF US"

Jen and Gwen met Pat at Michigan State University while they were working on their doctoral degrees. Pat was the only African American professor on the literacy faculty, and after several conversations she took an interest in both students. She had not worked extensively with any Black doctoral students–the Black student population was extremely limited at MSU. Pat hired Gwen as her research assistant. The following year, Jen became a part of Pat's Center for the Improvement of Early Reading Achievement team, and a lifelong collaboration began. Pat encouraged Gwen and Jen to apply for Spencer Research Training Grant Fellowships. She demanded that they "step up to the plate" and complete literature reviews, write proposals, make presentations, and write chapters and articles at a continuous pace, explaining that she was preparing them for the "real world of academia." By the time they graduated, both had several publications, a list of professional presentations, and several job offers. Pat had the satisfaction of being able to say that she helped some "sistas" along the way.

Of course, since then, the three of us have continued to collaborate because we realize that all of us are stronger than one of us. When Gwen was up for tenure, Pat and Jen read her papers and gave feedback. When Jen was up for tenure, Pat and Gwen did the same. When Pat became the first Black president of the National Reading Conference, all three of us went to work 2 years before she had to deliver her speech—completing literature reviews, brainstorming in the "think tank" (Pat's basement), writing and revising, suggesting and calling, until it all came together. Whenever one of us succeeds, we all succeed. If one of us fails, we all consider what we could have done to make the difference. It's a competitive world out there, but we have found a way for all of us to get a piece of the pie. We have learned to accept that racism still exists in the "ivory tower," but we are determined to encourage one another, and collaborating has been one of the answers to some of our problems. It may be lonely at the top for some, but we plan to get there together, sharing our hopes and dreams.

CONTEMPORARY TEACHABLE MOMENTS: LEARNING TO SHARE

"Sharing" is a value that our families instilled in us. If African Americans are going to move from victims to victors, we will have to help one another along the way.

"Sharing" the stage is what Morgan (Gwen's son) has learned to do. Morgan, a student at Berklee College of Music (Boston), is an accomplished musician. When he received a call from Patrick Flynn, the conductor in California, asking him to be the featured soloist with the Riverside Philharmonic Orchestra, he agreed. Patrick also asked Morgan to include a jazz encore after his classical performance. Morgan requested that they provide accommodations for his brothers Joshua and David, who would accompany him on piano and drums. He could have asked someone else, but he understood the importance of giving his brothers a chance to share the stage with him. They were challenged to play the jazz standards that he chose, and he was pleased with the results. He smiled as he looked up from signing autographs and saw many of his fans running over to his brothers to get their autographs too.

When Monique was young, her Aunt Pat told her that the first group of Black girls that transferred from the segregated Black school to integrate Albany High School was not academically successful. So, when Pat and the second group of students decided to enroll in Albany High, the counselor at the Black high school (Monroe High) made two critical recommendations: (1) no student will go to Albany High who is not a B+ or A student, and (2) if a student is good in a particular subject, it is his or her duty to help a Black student who is struggling with that subject. The reason was to demonstrate that Black students can succeed in a high-pressure hostile academic setting. Pat told Monique that the counselor's recommendations paid off. All 24 of the students who decided to attend Albany High succeeded and went on to do well in college. While in college, Pat continued the practice of helping struggling students. Monique listened very carefully to her Aunt Pat's words of wisdom and decided to help struggling students, too. Monique did well in math and enthusiastically volunteered to help struggling students at her middle and high school.

Like Morgan and Monique, Isaiah (Jen's son) is already beginning to understand the importance of sharing the value of literacy with his younger brother. One Christmas, Pat sent a box of books to Isaiah and Elijah, who were then 4 and 2 years old. Isaiah explained that he would take the more difficult "big boy" books and Elijah could have the easy readers. He explained that he would learn to read the "big boy" books and read them to Elijah, and when Elijah got old enough he would give the books to him. Elijah was excited about the prospect of having his big brother read to him, and looked forward to growing up enough to get the "big boy" books. Even though Isaiah was a wonderful student at home, he struggled at school. His struggle wasn't academic, but behavioral. Jen and her husband Mike worked with Isaiah in kindergarten and were successful. They weren't going let their son fail in school.

Moving from victims to victors in the African American struggle toward achievements in literacy education is going to require the old and young to become involved with helping others in their families and in their communities. Like Morgan, we must unselfishly share our opportunities and accolades; like Pat, we must be willing to offer academic support; like Isaiah, we must provide motivation and hope for those who look to us as role models. Lastly, parents need to serve as "brokers" between teachers and their children.

Showing a concern for others is a theme throughout this book. In fact, each chapter provides examples of those who sacrificed for others. In the next section, we look back to review the debates before we move forward to discuss solutions.

LOOKING BACK TO GO FORWARD:
SUMMARY OF THE FOUR DEBATES

We have discussed four debates that have shaped the political, social, and educational landscape of African American literacy learners in K–12 schools. In Chapter 1, we described the controversies related to the fight for access to literacy that African American people have been waging for decades. In Chapter 2, we highlighted the ongoing debates about the meanings of success in the African American community, and revealed how these multiple meanings of success have important implications for the literacy lives and schooling experiences of African American students. In Chapter 3, we identified the controversies and debates related to teaching African American literacy learners, and the best practices, theories, and perspectives that have been identified within the research community as well as by "insiders" within the African American community. Finally, in Chapter 4, we discussed differing ideas about the role of African American families in the literacy development of their children.

We believe that these debates are more than just "research topics" or "intellectual exercises." They are real, and they have critical implications for African American literacy learners in U.S. classrooms. Although debates often are seen as "unsolvable" or "unwinnable," we argue that something needs to be done to help teachers, parents, researchers, and policymakers improve literacy education for African American students. We believe that there is *something* that can be done. As we embark on the road to redemption, we have seriously considered our own roles and responsibilities in (1) transforming African American students from victims to victors; (2) transforming our teachers into effective cultural mediators; and (3) transforming our own research and policies into powerful tools that bring about change in classrooms. African American people have more than their share of struggles, setbacks, and social burdens. But by doing the things we *can* do, we can make the future much brighter for African American youth (Cosby & Poussaint, 2007). As Dr. Martin Luther King Jr. (1966, as cited in Noffke, 1997), says, "As citizens . . . we ask you to focus on the fresh social issues of our day. . . . We ask you to make society's problems your laboratory. We ask you to translate your data into direction . . . direction for action" (p. 305). In this final chapter, we take up Dr. King's "call to action" by offering solutions that may help us to move forward on the road toward responsive and rigorous literacy instruction for African American students.

Given that the debates surrounding the literacy education of African American students are complex and multilayered, we believe that the strategies, activities, and perspectives that help us begin to resolve them cannot have a "one-size-fits-all" format. While there is no single "magic bullet" that researchers, teachers, parents, and policymakers can implement, we can work collectively and develop strategies and solutions that will help African American literacy learners. In this section, we offer: (1) policy-based solutions; (2) teacher education course-level solutions; (3) teacher education programmatic solutions; (4) school-based solutions; (5) community-based solutions; (6) research-based solutions; (7) family-based solutions; and (8) classroom-based solutions. While discussing possible solutions, we share ideas from "pockets of hope" that we have identified as exemplary examples.

TAKING STEPS TO BUILD AND MAINTAIN A HEALTHY VILLAGE

Building and maintaining a healthy village where African American children can thrive requires multileveled, multilayered, multifaceted solutions. We must have a spirit of collaboration. As we indicated earlier, all of us are smarter than one of us, and all of us are stronger than one of us. Policymakers, teacher educators, teachers, students, parents, community-based organizations, faith-based groups, social workers, and researchers, as well as crime prevention and intervention agencies and others, are needed to build and maintain a healthy village where our children can become educated and experience a better quality of life than previous generations. Each generation should strive to make our village healthier during their lifetime. We have chosen to share ways to build and maintain our village by discussing possible solutions at various levels. We do not propose an exhaustive list of suggestions. Instead, we share pockets of hope that will begin our dialogue, and we end our discussion with a call to action to move from rhetoric to work.

Policy-Based Solutions

Significant policy changes at the national, university, community, and school levels are needed in order for African Americans to move forward in literacy education. Currently, one of the most needed policy adjustments is for the government to ensure that every child has health care. We cannot expect unhealthy children to make academic progress. In his speech before a joint session of Congress on September 9, 2009, President Barack Obama stated, "The time for bickering is over; the time for games has passed; now is the season for action," as he presented his proposed comprehensive health care plan. It is our hope that Congress finds a way to provide coverage for everyone, but especially for children in the United States. Health care needs to be comprehensive, affordable, and accessible to every child in the country, according to Marian Wright Edelman, President and Founder of the Children's Defense Fund and renowned child advocate.

At the national level, funding for programs that attempt to "level the playing field" is needed. Programs such as Title I of the No Child Left Behind Act of 2001–the largest federally funded educational program–provide additional financial support for schools with the highest concentrations of students living in poverty. Based on the percentage of students receiving free or reduced lunch, Title I schools receive funds to promote high academic achievement, a greater focus on teaching and learning, local initiatives related to student performance, and improved school–home–community connections. Increased funding for Title I programs will ensure that more K–12 students receive benefits. Also, affirmative action programs are needed to assist African American students by providing opportunities for them to be admitted to top-notch colleges and hired for positions that otherwise might not be accessible.

Another policy-based program with potential to "level the playing field" is the American Recovery and Reinvestment Act (ARRA) of 2009, enacted by the 111th United States Congress in February and based largely on proposals by President Barack Obama. ARRA is invested heavily in education. Funds are available for early learning programs, elementary and secondary education, improving teacher effectiveness and performance, intensive support and intervention for low-performing schools, increasing access to higher education, and decreasing the achievement gap. In November, Education Secretary Arne Duncan issued rules for "Race to the Top," a $4 billion grant program aimed at encouraging innovation in education (Hart, 2009). The funds are to be used to improve student assessment and the tracking, recruitment, and retention of high-quality teachers. Monies will also be used to revitalize failing schools.

President Obama's commitment to education can also be seen by his agreement to fund several programs that would be modeled after Geoffrey Canada's Harlem Children's Zone, and by his ability to forge beneficial collaborations. Al Sharpton, a liberal Democrat, and former House Speaker Newt Gingrich, a conservative Republican, have joined Education Secretary Arne Duncan on a tour of schools to identify best practices (Chappell, 2009). Although the unlikely trio does not agree on some issues, they agree that U.S. educational reform is imperative (Miners, 2009). President Obama has a 5-year goal to turn around 5,000 failing schools and has asked the threesome to assist him in this quest.

In addition to projects directly involving White House administrators, opportunities for African American researchers to advocate for African American students are needed. We need to be offered a chance to sit on decision-making boards that determine the direction of education in the United States. Too often we are excluded from the behind-closed-doors conversations that influence the outcome of urban education and other vital issues that relate directly to African Americans.

It is imperative that policymakers ensure that our students are prepared for the 21st century by having up-to-date technology equipment in the schools, including SMART boards, mimeo boards, laptops, and other media. The digital divide is another example of the gap that remains between African American and White students, and it must be addressed. Encouraging educators to participate in grant-writing workshops will help administrators and teachers acquire the skills needed to secure grants that are available to help bridge the gap between school needs and the school budget.

Finally, policies also must be implemented that protect our young teachers. Many of these teachers are vibrant with innovative ideas and energy that is needed, especially in urban classrooms where teachers tend to experience burnout more frequently. We would like to see, for example, a federal program that supports young teachers who teach in urban areas by assisting impoverished school districts in subsidizing the pay of new teachers who show exceptional promise.

Teacher Education–Based Solutions

At the dawn of the 21st century, Gloria Ladson-Billings (2000) rendered an indictment on teacher education by writing that "teacher preparation is culpable in the failure of teachers to teach African American students effectively" (p. 208). Some might think that Ladson-Billings's indictment is too harsh. However, as teacher educators, we agree with her, because so many teachers walk into their schools and find that they are unprepared to teach the African American students in their classrooms.

In this section, we highlight solutions to the inadequate preparation of new teachers in teacher education programs. We highlight solutions that may be appropriate within teacher education coursework, as well as those that make sense at the programmatic level.

Course-Level Solutions. Traditionally, research on effective literacy teacher education practices has been situated within reading methods courses, with the studies highlighting pedagogical practices that teacher educators use to support preservice teachers' capacity to work with African American students as well as other children from diverse backgrounds (Boling, 2004; C. Clark & Medina, 2000; Florio-Ruane, 2001; Kidd, Sanchez, & Thorp, 2004; McMillon, 2009; Schmidt, 1998; Turner, 2007; Xu, 2000). A common theme across these studies is that preservice teachers need to develop an awareness of the role that culture has played in their own lives. Allen and Hermann-Wilmarth (2004), for example, designed their literacy teacher education course as a "cultural construction zone" where preservice teachers could openly discuss and (de)construct their own cultural identities. Through autobiographical

writing, and other extended activities, preservice teachers began to closely examine the home literacy practices that shaped their literacy learning
(e.g., parents read to them at bedtime) and their perceptions of diversity and
schooling (e.g., parents held negative views of minority people).

In addition, preservice teachers need to develop greater respect for and
deeper understandings of the multiple and varied cultural resources and linguistic knowledge that African American students bring into the classroom.
A variety of pedagogical practices have been identified in the research that
support the development of cultural competence in preservice teachers. *Technology case-based methods* (e.g., videos of effective classroom teachers in diverse
settings) help preservice teachers consider how students draw upon their
own cultural knowledge within the classroom (Boling, 2004). *Narrative-based
pedagogies,* including reading stories of culturally diverse people (Clark & Medina, 2000) and writing family stories of diverse students (Kidd, Sanchez,
& Thorp, 2004), frequently are mentioned as important teacher educator
practices. *Race-based pedagogies* are practices that "make race visible" (Greene
& Abt-Perkins, 2003, p. 22) in the enterprise of teacher education and help
preservice teachers to critically interrogate the ways in which race has been
constructed in schools and society; examine how racism, White privilege,
and other forms of power operate to advantage some and disadvantage
others; and learn how schools and teachers can work to disrupt powerful
structures through social justice teaching (Cochran-Smith, 2004; Greene &
Abt-Perkins, 2003; Milner, 2008). One example of a race-based pedagogy is
Patricia Schmidt's ABC's of Cultural Understanding. This instructional tool
requires teacher education students to write an autobiography, interview
someone whom they consider "different" (e.g., race/skin color, ethnicity, socioeconomic status, etc.), identify similarities and differences in the autobiography and biography, analyze the differences, and develop lesson plans that
incorporate the knowledge learned about other cultures. The ABC technique
has been utilized effectively in many teacher education classes, and its significance currently is being tested by a group of American and European professors funded by a policy grant from the United States and European Union.
Finally, *visioning pedagogies* provide spaces where teacher education students
can articulate their own conceptions of what teaching reading means (Duffy,
2002) and find their own definitions of culturally responsive literacy pedagogy within K–12 classrooms (Turner, 2007).

Some have argued that in order to teach African American students effectively, preservice teachers need to have specialized knowledge about
African American culture. Over the past decade, a number of recommendations have been made for preservice teachers to learn more about African
American culture and the lived experiences of African American children
and families in the United States, including (a) reading autobiographies by

African American writers (Florio-Ruane, 2001; McVee, 2004), (b) participating in field experiences in predominantly African American schools (Lazar, 2004), (c) gathering parent stories (Edwards, Pleasants, & Franklin, 1999), (d) taking African American history and literature courses (Flowers, 2007), (e) engaging in conversations with African American teachers as lecturers in coursework and as mentor teachers (Hollins & Guzman, 2005), (f) participating in pen pal exchanges with African American students (McMillon, 2009), and (g) learning about students' literacy experiences in the context of the African American Church (McMillon & McMillon, 2004; McMillon & Edwards, 2008). We strongly believe that preservice teachers, and teacher educators, need to be encouraged to take what Cochran-Smith and Lytle (1999) call an "inquiry stance" toward learning about African American culture. Many well-intentioned new teachers may hold negative views and assumptions about African American students, their families, and their community, and simply "learning" new information about African American culture may not break down these deficit views. Rather, when preservice teachers take an inquiry stance, they consider African American culture through a perspective that emphasizes "reflective, inquiry-based, and analytic thinking" (Darling-Hammond, Hammerness, Grossman, Rust, & Shulman, 2005, p. 440). By taking an inquiry stance toward learning about African American culture, preservice teachers are more likely to acquire the kind of "affirmative knowledge" that will help them to see African American students as "giving, kind, bright, athletic, and compassionate" (Milner, 2008, p. 134). Rather than looking at African American students from a culturally deficit model by comparing them with White students as the standard or norm, teachers learn to identify their own biases and concerns that may debilitate learning in their classroom. They learn to confront their own prejudices and discriminatory practices by becoming more aware of how their cultural values and beliefs may clash with their students' and their students' parents' beliefs.

Finally, in light of the high numbers of African American children in special education, we believe that preservice teachers need to have an understanding of special education policy, as well as particular instructional strategies and interventions (e.g., Response to Intervention) that are effective for students with disabilities. In order to develop inclusive classrooms, preservice teachers need "to be able to observe, monitor, and assess children to gain accurate feedback about their students' learning and development" (Banks et al., 2005, p. 262).

Programmatic Solutions. Strong literacy teacher preparation programs are critical because preservice teachers cannot teach African American students effectively without deep pedagogical content knowledge in literacy. Based on their study of eight exemplary teacher education programs across the country, the International Reading Association's National Commission on Excellence in Elementary Teacher Preparation for Reading Instruction (IRA, 2003) identified eight critical features of excellence in reading teacher preparation programs.

- Content, which includes a comprehensive curriculum that helps preservice teachers to develop a strong foundational knowledge base
- Apprenticeship through a variety of course-related field experiences where they have opportunities to interact with excellent models and mentors
- Vision, or a shared understanding of quality literacy teaching and learning
- Resources and mission, meaning that there are adequate resources to support the program's mission of preparing preservice teachers
- Personalized teaching, or a pedagogical approach in which teacher educators value the diversity of their students and are responsive to their learning strengths and needs
- Autonomy, meaning that teacher educators can make their own decisions
- Community, developed through active partnerships between faculty, students, and mentor teachers
- Assessment, or a continual assessment of students and the content of the program, which leads to programmatic changes

To derive these features, the Commission also studied 101 preservice teachers into their first 3 years of teaching and compared their instructional practices with those of other teachers who had graduated from programs with a reading specialty, programs that integrated literacy into their education courses, and general education programs without an emphasis on literacy. Based on their analyses, the Commission (2003) reported that teachers prepared in the eight exemplary programs (1) were more successful and confident in their first years, and were able to "hit the ground running when they started teaching—even mentoring other, more experienced teachers in reading instruction within their first three years of teaching" (p. 7); (2) were more effective in creating a rich literacy environment in their classrooms and achieved higher levels of reading engagement with students than other teachers; (3) performed at levels that met or exceeded the standard of experienced teachers rated as "excellent" by their principals; and (4) had classrooms with higher student achievement, because "high levels of engagement with quality texts are the foundation for growth in student achievement" (p. 8).

Although there is compelling evidence that the quality of teacher education programs makes a difference in new teachers' pedagogical practice, few studies have comprehensively investigated how programmatic changes in teacher education programs impact teachers' literacy teaching in K–12 schools. A notable exception is a study of programmatic change conducted by Keehn and her colleagues (2003) at the University of Texas at San Antonio. Analyses of a corpus of data, including survey data, faculty interviews, and other program-related artifacts (e.g., meeting notes), revealed substantive changes in the quality of the program. Working collaboratively, faculty created new structures to support program goals (e.g., adding more field-based literacy courses, creating common syllabi) and developed a system to support adjunct faculty. As part of these changes, Keehn and her colleagues noted that (a) the common course syllabi "specifically identify. . . activities to focus attention on issues of diversity" (p. 235); (b) a field placement coordinator was hired to facilitate placement in schools with diverse student populations; and (c) course instructors were making a more concerted effort to systematically add issues of diversity into their coursework (e.g., requiring that students complete a community literacy investigation).

Similarly, Ladson-Billings (2001) describes the kinds of substantive programmatic changes that led to the development of the Teach for Diversity (TFD) Program, an elementary master's certification program at the University of Wisconsin–Madison. Ladson-Billings noted that the faculty at Wisconsin wanted to address three complex issues within the elementary education program, and they began to have brown-bag lunch conversations to work through issues around multicultural education, social justice and equity pedagogy, and the disconnections between the university and the elementary school internship. In her book, *Crossing over to Canaan*, Ladson-Billings includes powerful vignettes of practice orchestrated by the TFD cohort that demonstrate the positive impact that this program had on the TFD teachers and their elementary students. What is powerful about both of these examples is that the theme of diversity is not confined to a one-shot course, but rather comprises a theme that facilitates strong "connection and coherence" (Darling-Hammond et al., 2005, p. 391) throughout the entire teacher education program.

Universities need to actively recruit African Americans to enroll in teacher education programs. One major deterrent to African American students entering teacher education programs is the grade point average required to get into college. For those who do get in, their freshman year often is filled with struggles that affect their grade point average. Some of the struggles may come from being unfamiliar with "college culture." First-generation college students may not have access to the cultural capital needed to negotiate the multiple issues that new college students face. Their parents may not understand how to advocate for them, or how to support their emotional struggles, such as test anxiety, homesickness, and so forth. Mentoring programs can help students make a smoother transition from high school to college and maintain an acceptable grade point average. For example, Oakland University's Student Success Program offers a limited number of scholarships to exceptional minority students who choose to pursue a teaching career. They are accepted into the teacher education program and mentored by faculty throughout their undergraduate years. In addition, many minority students are first-generation college students who may not have parents with knowledge and experience concerning how to effectively navigate college life. Offering mentoring and financial assistance to students who pursue a teaching career certainly may increase the number of students in teacher education programs. Programs such as the King–Chavez–Parks Future Fellowship Grant provide funds for minorities to pursue an education on the master's and doctoral level, with the goal of increasing the number of minority professors in higher education.

When students enroll in teacher education programs, it is very important that universities fund activities that provide opportunities to ensure that all teachers are prepared to teach in the 21st century. Students should be required to intern/student teach and observe in diverse educational environments from urban to rural and across socioeconomic levels. Our brightest and most educated teachers should be encouraged to teach at high-needs schools, and additional funding should be given to those teachers because of the challenges they face in teaching in these areas.

School-Based Solutions

The community must be involved and embrace the African proverb "it takes a whole village to educate a child" by incorporating mentorship in schools and connecting with faith-based organizations to build relationships. Collaboration is especially significant in the African American community, where our culture emphasizes the connection between relationships and learning. Mentorship is very powerful because it gives our young people a chance to listen to another person's struggle and see how that person survives. This will uplift our young people and inspire them to keep moving. The National Urban League has many programs to help African Americans improve their literacy achievement in schools, such as Read and Rise, Hip-Hop Reader, and Young Professional. We need to be aware of the ways in which these organizations are providing for our communities and assist with implementation.

In their book *Schools That Work*, Allington and Cunningham (2007) passionately argue that:

> We need schools that educate children—not schools that simply sort children into worker groups. We need schools that help children exceed their destiny—schools where *all* children are successful, not just the lucky ones who find schooling easy.

We need schools that develop in all children the knowledge, skills, and attitudes that have historically been reserved for a few. We need . . . schools that break the gridlock of low achievement that stymies later efforts to educate all children. (p. 2, emphasis in original)

We agree with Allington and Cunningham's vision of the schools we need, and we believe that African American children and youth are in desperate need of these schools. We must figure out how we can help schools to become the kinds of places where African American students, indeed all children, read, write, speak, and think thoughtfully and critically.

Transforming schools into places that work for African American students is not an easy task. Allington and Cunningham (2007) explain, "It has taken a century to develop the school traditions of today, and these traditions cannot be undone easily or quickly" (p. 14). However, change can occur and has occurred in K–12 schools across the country. In reviewing these practical examples, as well as the educational literature, we have identified four main factors that significantly contribute to school change: (1) strong principal leadership; (2) professional development; (3) cultures of resilient reading; and (4) positive home–school connections.

Strong Principal Leadership. This is one of the most crucial factors for transforming schools. In previous research, principals were viewed as "organizational managers," responsible primarily for managing classroom teachers and other staff, who were disconnected from the realities of classroom teaching (Bliss, 1991; Louis & Miles, 1991; Roberts & Pruitt, 2003). Schools were characterized as formal organizations that emphasized efficiency and control, and principals were given a substantial amount of authority, responsibility, and control within this rigid hierarchy (Danridge, Edwards, & Pleasants, 2003; Roberts & Pruitt, 2003). In recent years, however, the role of the principal has shifted from manager to builder (Polite & McClure, 1997). Principals are now responsible for building cultures in schools that (a) communicate a shared vision of teaching and learning; (b) set high expectations for staff and students; (c) promote collegiality and caring among faculty and students; and (d) express a positive attitude toward education, students, and families (Danridge et al., 2003; Roberts & Pruitt, 2003; Sergiovanni, 1994). As builders, principals may initiate the school change process, but they also encourage their faculty and other administrators (e.g., assistant principals) to assume leadership of the process (Roberts & Pruitt, 2003).

A good example of this kind of "builder" principal is Dr. Steve Perry. Dr. Perry, who was featured on CNN's *Black in America 2* (O'Brien, 2009a), is principal of Capital Preparatory Magnet School. Located in Hartford, Connecticut, Capital Preparatory Magnet School is a secondary school (Grades

6–12) with a population of over 80% Black and Latino students. While Connecticut has one of the highest achievement gaps between White and Black students in the country, Capital Prep's dropout rate is near 0%, and the school sends every one of its seniors to a 4-year college. Since it opened 4 years ago, Perry has sent about 80 seniors to college. Perry demands excellence of his students. In the segment on this extraordinary principal, Perry is seen talking to one young man about his shirt and tie (there is a dress code at Capital Prep and students are expected to adhere to it), greeting students as they got off the bus (something he does every morning), giving a senior a pep talk as she waited to go into a college interview, and picking up students in his car to ensure that they made it to school. Not only does Perry demand excellence of his students, he demands it from his faculty as well. Capital Prep is a year-round school, and teachers are expected to use engaging instructional techniques to help students grasp challenging concepts. Clearly, Dr. Perry demonstrates how effective principals serve as instructional leaders in order to promote academic achievement (Danridge et al., 2003).

Professional Development. For teachers, professional development is at the heart of school change, because school improvement occurs when teachers have sustained support to collaboratively talk about and work on their instructional practices (Elmore, Peterson, & McCarthy, 1996; Fullan & Hargreaves, 1996). According to the American Federation of Teachers (2002), "Without professional development, school reform will not happen. Professional development can no longer be viewed as a dispensable appendage that can be cut at will or an activity that can be isolated from the achievement of comprehensive or 'systemic' reform" (p. 28).

Professional development also helps to build teachers' capacity to teach literacy effectively because it develops their pedagogical expertise and content knowledge. As the National Commission on Teaching and America's Future (1997) noted:

> What teachers know and understand about content and students shape how judiciously they select from texts and other materials and how effectively they present material in class. Their skill in assessing their students' progress also depends upon how deeply they understand learning, and how well they can interpret students' discussions and written work. No other intervention can make the difference that a knowledgeable, skillful teacher can make in the learning process. (p. 8)

Clearly, high-quality professional development is necessary for cultivating expert teachers who are able to effectively teach literacy to African American students. We use the term *high-quality* purposefully, because very few teachers are receiving this kind of professional development. Traditionally, professional development has consisted of one-shot workshops where teachers listen to presentations made by outside consultants. Teachers often report that these professional development sessions are not useful for their classroom instruction because they are disconnected from daily practice (Darling-Hammond, 1997). In addition, some teachers do not have opportunities for sustained professional development. The National Commission on Teaching and America's Future (1997) found that fewer than 15% of American teachers had participated in even 9 hours of ongoing professional development activity in a single curriculum area in the previous year.

Thus, we encourage schools to offer high-quality professional development that (a) is connected to teaching and learning in literacy classrooms; (b) grows from teachers' concerns and interests; (c) is supported by modeling, coaching, problem solving, and inquiry into specific problems of practice; (d) is focused on the outcomes of student learning and development; and (e) builds collegiality and professional discourse through collaborative talk and critical reflection (Darling-Hammond, 1997; Darling-Hammond & McLaughlin, 1995). While there are a variety of approaches to creating high-quality professional development opportunities, we highlight teachers as readers groups and professional learning communities as two compelling examples.

Teachers as readers, or TAR, groups (Allington & Cunningham, 2007) are teachers and/or administrators who voluntarily meet monthly to discuss various books that they have read. Depending on the goals of the TAR group, teachers can build content expertise by reading a particular professional book in literacy such as *Strategies That Work: Teaching Comprehension for Understanding and Engagement* by Stephanie Harvey and Anne Goudvis (2007), trying out several strategies from the book in their classrooms, and discussing their experiences of implementing those strategies. Other TAR groups have read multicultural literature (e.g., *Too Many Tamales* by Gary Soto, 1993; *Everyday Use* by Alice Walker, 1994) and cultural autobiographies (e.g., Maya Angelou's *I Know Why the Caged Bird Sings*, 1983; Amy Tan's *The Kitchen God's Wife*, 2006) to help new and veteran teachers begin to understand the experiences and perspectives of diverse students and families (Florio-Ruane, 2001; Levin, Smith, & Strickland, 2003). We strongly suggest that TAR groups be formed around professional books, like this one, that specifically address the issues of educating African American literacy learners, because teachers can benefit greatly from reading texts that blend research with practice. In literature-based TAR groups, memoirs written by African Americans, like Janet McDonald's *Project Girl* (1999), children's books (e.g., *Hip Hop Speaks to Children* edited by Nikki Giovanni, 2008), and young adult literature (e.g., *Slam* by Walter Dean Myers, 1997) can be a starting point for teachers to talk about the cultural experiences and backgrounds of African American youth. Although TAR groups (or book clubs) have developed primarily in elementary schools across the country, this approach could work effectively for secondary teachers as well.

Based on her study of effective and typical middle and secondary schools, Judith Langer (2002) defines professional learning communities as a variety of groups, teams, departments, and collaborative partnerships that give teachers "ideas and [nourish] them in their daily efforts as well as in their grand plans" (p. 45). Langer's study focused on the ways that effective middle and secondary schools fostered these professional learning communities and investigated the various ways that teachers interacted within them. At one middle school, for example, professional learning communities took the form of cross-disciplinary groups that met on a daily basis to discuss students' academic progress and social well-being, and to plan collaborative efforts across content areas. As part of these professional learning communities, all language arts teachers at each grade level met at least on a weekly basis, with some opting to meet even more frequently. In contrast, the professional learning communities at one high school centered on interdisciplinary teams that met on a daily basis to plan assessments, develop curriculum, do scheduling, and discuss "big ideas." As with the teachers as readers groups, professional learning communities can and have been developed in elementary schools as well (Roberts & Pruitt, 2003). In fact, Debbie Diller (1999), a first-grade teacher, organized her own professional learning communities when she invited the African American teachers in her school to attend a study group meeting where they would talk about improving instruction, and invited African American parents to come and work with students in her classroom.

Culture of Resilient Reading. Johnston (2005) characterizes resilient literacy learners as having "the disposition to maintain a focus on learning in the face of difficulty" (p. 685). Building a culture of resilient reading means helping African American students take ownership of literacy and see it as personally meaningful to their lives. School libraries, for example, can help expose African American students to the joys of reading. When school libraries have multiple copies of current books, include culturally and linguistically diverse authors, and offer a wide selection of nonfiction and fiction texts, African American students, especially those from impoverished neighborhoods, will have access to quality reading material and are likely to increase the amount of reading that they do in and out of school (Allington & Cunningham, 2007). Other schoolwide programs, such as author visits and read-ins, will help African American students develop "literacies that are resilient, flexible, self-directed, open, and collaborative" (Johnston, 2005, p. 684).

Building a culture of resilient reading involves more than just literacy activities. As discussed in Chapter 2, some African American students may need to develop resilience in order to overcome the conflicts and tensions related to their racial and cultural identities. If African American students view literacy, and doing well in school, as "uncool" or as "acting White," they will be much less likely to pursue their educational dreams. When schools build cultures of resilient reading, they help African American students to break down those barriers to success by making achievement desirable and ubiquitous. Dr. Perry, principal of Capital Preparatory Magnet School, noted that at his school, "It's college prep for everybody; it doesn't matter if you're black or white. They can see that it's OK for them to be smart and black" (O'Brien, 2009a). The type of school environment that Dr. Perry is building can foster resilience in African American students, because it shows them that many other Black children are working hard to be successful as well. According to Breonna Arnum, 17, a senior at Capital Prep, this resilience-building approach works: "It makes a difference because everybody has the same goals as you. So it's not like anyone is there to pull you back. Everyone is going forward" (O'Brien, 2009a).

Positive Home–School Connections. Historically, schools have had a difficult time reaching out and connecting with African American parents, which in turn has caused some faculty and administrators to believe that African American parents don't value education (Edwards & Danridge, 2001). However, we believe that African American parents should be the first group that schools and teachers listen to: Their voices need to be heard because they are often marginalized, ignored, underrepresented, or forgotten (Edwards et al., 1999; Noguera, 2003). Allington and Cunningham (2007) have identified three tiers of "authentic" home–school connections that need to be fostered for all parents, but especially African American parents: (1) reaching out to families, through report cards, notes, and other forms of communication; (2) involving families, by adopting a broader view of family involvement, including traditional (e.g., volunteering in the classroom, chaperoning field trips) and alternative (e.g., maintaining a classroom website) parent activities; and (3) supporting families, by offering family education classes, creating parent–child activities, and providing basic literacy instruction for parents. Incorporating these kinds of authentic home–school activities can generate change in the school, because when teachers, administrators, and African American parents work together, they can develop new policies, programs, and practices that support African American literacy learners. For example, teachers who use the parent story approach (Edwards et al., 1999) to talk with African American parents are able to unearth rich information about children's home literacy practices that can be used to build a bridge to school literacy. At the secondary level, Noguera (2003) has advocated for high schools to hold discussion groups with African American parents, and to hear their opinions and perspectives, as a critical starting point for rethinking how disciplinary policies and curriculum negatively impact African American students, and for initiating school reform.

One example of a school experiencing the "four factors of change in action" is Houghton Elementary School in Saginaw, Michigan. Gwen has received funding to work with the principal, teachers, and students for 3 years through a Title II Improving Teacher Quality Grant funded by the Michigan Department of Education. The school experienced a major decrease in its standardized test scores, which resulted in failing to make average yearly progress. Previously, Houghton was known as one of the best schools in the district, but cutbacks forced district administrators to close several schools, and Houghton became a "melting pot" for numerous neighborhoods. The climate and culture of the school changed, teachers were switched around, and the morale of the school diminished temporarily. However, the strong principal leadership of Mrs. Peggie Hall, a doctoral candidate at Oakland University, has been the foundation for the major changes that are taking place. "The Saginaw/Oakland Literacy Project has made a difference by forcing all of us to stretch out and try things that we hadn't tried before," Mrs. Hall stated. She continued, "I have wonderful teachers, but they were so inundated with requirements until they just didn't seem to have time to develop new ideas. Dr. McMillon provided a forum for all of us to come together, receive professional development from experts in the field, and implement data-driven instruction. We know it works. Sometimes we just need help getting started." Tam Harris, a fifth-grade teacher agrees: "I appreciate the opportunity to participate in the Saginaw/Oakland Literacy Project because I have attended many professional development workshops, and the information shared sounds really good, but when I get back to my 30-plus fifth graders, it's hard to implement the ideas the way they are presented at the workshop. I am a hands-on learner. I need someone to come into my class and show me how to do what they're talking about."

Teachers from the Saginaw/Oakland Literacy Project have participated in more than 200 hours of professional development over the past 3 years. "It's a big commitment, but it's worth it," shared Rebecca Benner, who wrote her master's thesis from research collected during her shared writing lessons implemented daily by project participants. Mrs. Hall reported: "We now have a culture of reading and writing in our school, and parents are becoming more involved because they see that we are working hard to help their children. Houghton has always had high reading scores, and parents love to attend special events and programs. But things are different now. We have a schoolwide daily reading period and writing workshop period. We are on our way to becoming a blue-ribbon school. The parents are excited about our new approaches. In fact, we have scheduled several parent nights to help them learn exactly how to help their children." The Saginaw/Oakland Literacy Project is a "pocket of hope," and the success of teachers and students is largely because of collaborations with several community groups.

Community-Based Solutions

Organizations exist within the African American community that focus on keeping African American racial identity strong, but also address issues of "double consciousness" (Du Bois, 1903/1995) by teaching African American children (and adults) the importance of academic achievement and cultural enrichment. Community organizations that help African American children and youth to achieve academically while remaining connected to their Black cultural "roots" include (a) African American churches, (b) African American Greek-letter fraternities and sororities, (c) African American social organizations (e.g., NAACP, Jack and Jill), and (d) neighborhood organizations (e.g., Boys and Girls Clubs of America).

Creating school–community partnerships is a critical approach for improving the literacy education of African American students (Edwards, 2004). There are many ways that these school–community partnerships can be established and maintained, including (a) adopt-a-school (or a community organization) programs; (b) community-related literacy projects that may be sponsored by local libraries, churches, or African American fraternities and sororities; (c) Literacy Network Clubs (similar to athletic booster clubs) that support reading and writing; and (d) programs that provide assistance to parents (e.g., mentors for children from single-parent homes, parenting support groups to teach literacy and/or parenting skills). Several successful community programs are described below.

The National Sorority of Phi Delta Kappa, Inc., is a professional organization of teachers dedicated to the task of training African American youth to strive for academic excellence, good moral character, and respect for self and others, and to develop cultural awareness with a focus on community involvement. The sorority has a national scope divided into five regions: eastern (33 chapters), far western (12 chapters), midwestern (19 chapters), southeastern (28 chapters), and southwestern (23 chapters). All chapters operate under common guidelines mandated at the national level by an executive body with representatives from each region.

Gamma Kappa Kudos was chartered in 1993 under the auspices of the National Sorority of Phi Delta Kappa's Gamma Kappa Chapter, to contradict the media's claim that there were no African American males who were academically strong and productive in the community. Since 1993, the chapter has boasted a 100% graduation rate, with 100% of the members going on to attend college and become successful in the career of their choice. "All of the young men have made me very proud. The list of their pursuits is exceptionally impressive: teachers, medical doctor, investment banker, pharmacist, professional musicians, journalist, engineers, ministers, and good fathers, husbands, and community citizens," states Mrs. Currie, Midwestern Regional Kudos Chairperson and organizer of Gamma Kappa Kudos. Each year the Kudos Parent Group sponsors a winter ball where the Kudos bring their dates to a luxurious celebration, display their talents, and enjoy fine dining. Regional conferences are held across the country, with the Midwestern Regional Conference convening every April. Gamma Kappa Kudos compete with other chapters in various categories such as oratory, drama, instrumental and vocal music, science fair, art, and scrapbooks. One of the most enjoyable events is the step show. Chapters line up outside and enter the door demanding recognition for creatively choreographed step shows similar to the step shows on college campuses. "Participating in the Kudos competition helped me get prepared for ACT-SO," stated Joshua McMillon, Gwen's son. "I competed in the oratorical contest for the first time at the conference this year and won second place. After critiquing myself, I knew what I had to do to win at the local ACT-SO competition." Two weeks after the 2009 Kudos conference in Cleveland, Ohio, Joshua won a gold medal in oratory at the local competition. Participating in positive peer groups such as the Kudos and ACT-SO helps African American students stay focused on academic achievement and community service.

The NAACP ACT-SO (Academic, Cultural, Technological, and Scientific Olympics) is a year-long enrichment program designed to stimulate and encourage academic and cultural achievement among African American high school students. The program depends on volunteers from the community to serve as mentors and coaches for the participants. Competitions are held each year to determine who will represent the local chapters at the national competition in 26 categories, including the sciences, humanities, business, and performing and visual arts. More than 261,000 students have participated in the ACT-SO program nationwide from 180 local programs, with 781 national gold medalists winning more than $131,000 in monetary awards and $83,000 worth of laptops. Competing at the national level gives students an opportunity to network with successful African American role models who volunteer as judges. Gwen's son David, who won three gold and two silver medals, has two provisional patents as a result of following the advice shared by two African American ACT-SO judges from NASA. When Morgan performed with the Riverside Philharmonic Orchestra, the Riverside ACT-SO Chapter honored him with special recognition for winning the ACT-SO Gold Medal in Instrumental Classical in Washington, DC. Currently, Morgan attends Berklee College of Music with several other ACT-SO winners. ACT-SO is like a national family. Students participate throughout their high school years; they get to know one another quite well and look forward to competing the following year. ACT-SO definitely provides a "pocket of hope" for African Americans students.

Another community program that has made an indelible impact on African American children is the Children's Defense Fund Freedom Schools program, which provides summer and after-school enrichment that helps increase children's interest in reading, improves their self-esteem, and generates better attitudes toward learning (Edelman, 2009). The program focuses on five components: (1) high-quality academic enrichment, (2) parent and family involvement, (3) civic engagement and social action, (4) intergenerational leadership development, and (5) nutrition, health, and mental health. More than 70,000 children have participated in the program since 1995. The E.M. Kaufman-funded Philliber Research Associates evaluation of the Kansas City Freedom Schools program (2005–2007) found that Freedom School participants scored significantly higher on standardized tests than students who attended other summer enrichment programs, with African American middle school boys making the biggest gain of all. One of the greatest assets of the Freedom School program is that the schools are basically operated and taught by college students who are involved in their communities and campuses. Their energy and passion for the work are contagious.

One community-based program that includes a school–community partnership is the Houghton–Jones Resource Center summer program, located in Michigan across the street from Houghton Elementary School. Every summer committed collaborators work with children and youth from the neighborhood to keep them off the street. The summer of 2009 was not going to be pleasant because the funding for the program had diminished to the point that the students would not be able to have field trips and other important activities. At the same time, the Saginaw/Oakland Literacy Project needed a location to meet with teachers during the summer because the school year had been overwhelmingly hectic because of trying to complete the requirements for schools that did not make annual yearly progress. During a meeting of Principal Hall, Mrs. Ola McMillan (master teacher), Rhonda Butler (Director of Youth & Children's Services of the Public Libraries), and Gwen, Rhonda suggested contacting the Houghton–Jones Resource Center as a possible site for summer professional development workshops. The end result was phenomenal. Saginaw/Oakland Literacy Project teachers participated in professional development sessions every Tuesday and Thursday for 7 weeks. Houghton–Jones provided the building and the students for the teachers to work with. It was a win–win situation. Most of the summer program students attend Houghton School, which allowed Gwen's team to improve student–teacher–parent relationships, instructional techniques, and students' writing skills.

Another community-based literacy program that has been exceptionally successful for African American students is District Judge Thompson's Making Choices and Facing Consequences crime prevention program (Thompson & Nuckolls, 2005). Judge Thompson and Monica Nuckolls, professor at Thomas Cooley Law School, developed a program that uses real-life hypotheticals to teach students about gangs and violent crimes, drugs and alcohol, the court system, and several other important topics. The material has been utilized as a part of the English language arts–social studies curriculum, in after-school programs, at juvenile centers, in church youth meetings, and elsewhere. Statistics show that the program has had an exceptionally positive influence on students. In addition to offering the program, Judge Thompson has sponsored court-to-school sessions at several middle schools in the community as a way to help students become more literate about the judicial system. In response to an increase in gang violence, he organized a group of men from the community to offer the Boys-to-Men program for young men who were struggling in school. Boys from single-female-headed households were especially encouraged to attend. Every Saturday morning for 13 weeks, the boys spent time with African American men who cared about them. They had breakfast together and attended sessions taught by their mentors. The success of the program garnered support from retired Black educators in the community who have joined Judge Thompson to offer Boys-to-Men and How-to-Become-a-Lady programs in January 2010. More programs such as Making Choices and Facing Consequences, Boys-to-Men, and How-to-Become-a-Lady are needed to stop the cradle-to-prison pipeline.

Research-Based Solutions

We believe that members of the African American community need access to researchers who seek to improve their quality of life, not to illuminate deficiencies and disadvantages, but to help them develop the needed knowledge base and skills. For far too long, African American children have been the "subject" of research projects that have described their cultural traditions and experiences in deficit terms, without offering any practical solutions or interventions that could improve their literacy lives. How can we expect our research to make a difference for Black students and parents if we continue to know what's needed, but feel uncomfortable being honest and forthright with our own research subjects? We know there are problems. We have identified many of them. Unfortunately, some researchers focus on African American children because "diversity" is a hot topic or because studies of these children yield "interesting" data for research projects and publications. But we believe that researchers, especially those working with African American literacy learners, must ask themselves these critical questions: Am I doing research for research's sake? Am I doing this research to further my own career? What am I doing to help close the achievement gap? If your research findings are not used to improve the subjects' quality of life, do you really consider that worthwhile?

We challenge educational scholars and literacy researchers, no matter what their interests or areas of focus are, to move out of their comfort zones and engage in the following activities: (1) mentor minority graduate students; (2) mentor minority junior faculty; (3) explicitly instruct teacher education students in how race and culture impact their decisions, their classroom environment, their interactions with students and parents, and their attitudes about education; (4) develop relationships with minority colleagues and invite them to critique and challenge you concerning how your work can contribute to the war on the achievement gap; (5) make a special effort to cite minority colleagues in your work; and (6) attend presentations given by African American researchers that focus on these issues and debates. Often these presentations are given by us, about us, to us—because few others attend. Accepting a workshop proposal is not enough; attend the sessions and provide helpful feedback.

One example of a worthwhile research project designed to help African American students is Althier Lazar's project in Philadelphia. Lazar (2004, 2007) focuses on helping teacher education students acquire a "mindset" for working with African American children. Teaching at a Jesuit university within the predominantly African American community of West Philadelphia, Lazar has generated a range of university and field-based experiences that have allowed teachers to grow in their understandings and appreciation of the children and families who live there. To establish an environment conducive to learning about culture, she shares her monolingual, White, working-class roots and the ways in which Whiteness has worked to provide specific kinds of educational advantages and literacy opportunities within her family and for her children. She encourages her students to write parallel stories interrogating Whiteness and focusing on how race, class, and gender have shaped their opportunities and the opportunities of children in these urban neighborhoods. Lazar's students also examine the social, historical, political, and cultural factors that impact children's access to school-based literacies. Further, they investigate the many "classrooms of hope" that abound within the city—places that showcase excellence in literacy teaching due to the efforts of caring, knowledgeable, and culturally aware educators.

Lazar also explores with her students explanations for the Black–White achievement gap and they take African American history tours and attend lectures at the African American Museum in the city. Through these experiences, preservice teachers begin to think about techniques to draw from children's histories as a way to connect them to the school curriculum.

Another area of investigation is the relationship between language, identity, and power. Preservice teachers investigate African American Language (AAL) through readings (Delpit, 1992) and through a simulation activity (Lazar, 2007), during which they are required to master a hypercorrect form of English, or The Queen's English, in order to secure their teacher licensure in the Commonwealth of Pennsylvania. Following the simulation, teachers write about their anger and frustration during the simulation, and how they felt about the instructor and the language rules imposed on them. In the debriefing, Lazar invites teachers to discuss how it feels to be in a subordinate role and how students may feel when their home language is devalued and dismissed within the school setting. This activity sets the stage for launching investigations of AAL, its structure, historical roots, usage within literature and popular culture, and use as a tool for helping children acquire the additional code of Standard English.

Finally, there are particular field experiences within the teacher education program that complement and extend the understandings that preservice teachers construct in the university classroom. Community involvement is encouraged through faith-based programs and the Office of Campus Ministry. Most preservice teachers volunteer to spend time in local shelters, libraries, and community centers. They also work alongside experienced teachers in urban and high-poverty communities as part of their coursework. In literacy courses, individualized tutoring and small-group teaching emphasize assessment-based, culturally relevant teaching. Preservice teachers are shown how to build literacy instruction on students' existing knowledge. They also are asked to use literature that represents students' lives and heritage. Parent communication projects (Edwards, Pleasants, & Franklin, 1999) are also an integral part of the field experience.

SchoolRise is another "pocket of hope" for at-risk schools, teachers, and students. Founded by prominent literacy researchers Kathryn Au and Taffy Raphael, SchoolRise's mission is to help schools implement a system for improving student achievement through standards (Au, in press; Raphael, 2009). The standards-based change process solves four main problems typically faced by schools: (1) lasting change—a step-by-step system that helps schools stay on task, build a foundation, and sustain the changes over time; (2) moving from external to internal accountability—implementing data-driven instruction based on data collected three times a year; (3) coherent curriculum across grade levels and curriculum—teachers develop a staircase curriculum and have in-depth knowledge about the curriculum because they developed it; and (4) focused professional development—curriculum development tied to specific professional development.

Statistics show that Hawaiian fifth-grade students in Title I schools scored significantly higher than their counterparts in non–standard-based change schools, and 8 out of 11 Title I SchoolRise schools in Chicago boast improved reading scores.

More worthwhile research such as the work of Lazar (2004, 2007), Au (in press), and Raphael (2009) must be conducted that seeks to close the achievement gap between African American students and their White counterparts.

Family-Based Solutions

As African Americans, we must teach our children the value of education by providing more structured literacy activities in our homes. Scholastic and the National Urban League have teamed together in an initiative to aid parents in this critical transition between home and school by establishing the Read and Rise program, which provides a parent handbook that contains literacy activities for children (www.readandrisemag.net). The website also provides online books, magazines, and games to foster communication between parent and child. We also must monitor TV watching and help our children read more fluently by having them "read" television captions when they are allowed to watch television, rather than watching passively. We must create a learning environment in the home from cooking together while following instructions on recipes and writing grocery lists, exploring electronic devices together, and playing board games. We need to make learning a family affair by asking elders to share stories of "the way things used to be," or taking pictures of important moments and writing captions for the photos, or developing "family books" full of biographical information. Family newsletters also have become a popular way of communicating. These activities reinforce literacy skills and teach family values, while students learn their family history.

Family literacy should expand outside of our homes into our community. African American parents must take their children to the library and participate in the programs offered, such as dial a story, summer reading program, and puppet shows. Dial a story is a program that enables children and adults to call their library from any telephone and listen to taped stories. African American children also benefit from taking field trips to the zoo, museum, and planetarium with their parents. Engaging children in meaningful conversation about people, places, and things will broaden their horizons. We must take back our position and become our child's first teacher.

According to Westmoreland, Rosenberg, Lopez, and Weiss (2009), there is widespread consensus that family engagement is a critical ingredient for children's school success from "birth to work." Research suggests that family engagement promotes a range of benefits for students, including improved school readiness, higher student achievement, better social skills and behavior, and increased likelihood of high school graduation (Dearing, McCartney, Weiss, Kreider, & Simpkins, 2004). Policymakers, practitioners, and researchers also recognize family engagement as a critical intervention strategy that maximizes return on other investments in education. Early childhood programs that have demonstrated significant short- and long-term benefits for children have intensive family involvement components.

How can school districts build systemic family engagement from birth to work as a core educational reform strategy to ensure that parents, educators, and administrators share responsibility for family engagement resulting in student success? Shared responsibility requires parents to do their part to support their children's learning, from turning off the TV to communicating with teachers about their children's progress to checking (and sometimes helping with) homework. But even though parents want the best for their children, many do not receive the information and support from school and district staff that they need to understand the importance of the parental role in children's education and how best to fulfill that role. Lack of school communication to parents is linked to lower levels of involvement, particularly in lower-performing schools (Bridgeland et al., 2008), and parents are more likely to engage when school personnel value, expect, and invite them to be involved (Hoover-Dempsey et al., 2005).

Given that district leadership and capacity building play a key role in supporting strategic and systemic family engagement, it is important to better understand what leadership and capacity building looks like, how it can be developed and sustained, and how federal, state, and local policies can support it. Westmoreland and colleagues (2009) suggest that the core district-level components necessary for systemic family engagement are as follows: (1) fostering district-wide strategies, (2) building school capacity, and (3) reaching out to and engaging families (p. 2). In their study, they found six districts that showed all of the core components of a systematic family engagement strategy in place, and in the schools, implementing the core components required a commitment to a set of five best practices that ensured that family engagement efforts were interconnected and strategic across the various levels of a family engagement system. These promising practices are (1) a shared vision of family engagement, (2) purposeful connections to learning, (3) investments in high-quality programming and staff, (4) robust communication systems, and (5) evaluation for accountability and continuous learning.

Parental involvement is necessary for all students, especially African American males. Jen's story about her son Isaiah is an example of the importance of parental involvement.

> Isaiah, our oldest son, knew how to read before he entered kindergarten. He absolutely loved reading. He is the type of kid who will pull the cereal box close so that he can read the back of it. When he plays video

games, he reads the game manuals from cover to cover so that he knows all the secret moves. He takes books with him in the car, and lately, he has become very attached to my husband's Kindle.

But Isaiah had a difficult time in kindergarten. Like many kids, he did not handle transitions very well at school. If he wanted to continue playing with blocks, when it was time to line up and go to lunch, he would look at the teacher, then continue building. He would sometimes protest when he was asked to clean up and move on to a new activity. Isaiah is a very energetic boy, and so were the others in his class. So the children had a very difficult time keeping their hands to themselves, not bumping each other in line, and walking quietly in the hallways.

In our school, teachers call during the first week of school to make contact with parents and to let them know how their child is doing. When Isaiah's teacher called, I expected to hear good news about how much Isaiah already knew, or how much fun he was having in school. But his teacher called to say that she was having problems with him. "Problems? What kinds of problems?" I asked, incredulous. His teacher told me that he had some "behavior issues" and that while they were nothing serious, she wanted me to be aware that he was not behaving appropriately.

My husband, Michael, was livid. I was also upset. When I asked Isaiah how things were going in school, he said that they were fine. So Michael and I went to talk to the teacher. She told us that he had been doing things like pushing kids in line, talking when he wasn't supposed to talk, and playing around during transitions. She had to remind him several times to follow her directions. And I could tell in her voice that she was getting tired of it. I was frustrated. Isaiah knew how to read, do math, and so many other things, but here we were, talking about his behavior. And because Isaiah was one of two African American children in the class, I did not want him to be labeled as the "bad Black boy."

When I called Pat to talk with her about the situation, she encouraged me to work with Isaiah rather than getting upset with the teacher. So I bought a timer and set it to 20-minute intervals. When the timer went off, I told Isaiah that he had to switch to a new activity. When he started to complain, I reminded him that he needed to follow my directions the first time. I realized that Isaiah was used to negotiating with his dad and me, and he very often got what he wanted. But in school, he was expected to follow the rules, no questions asked. So I worked with him to recognize that when the timer went off, or when he was asked by a teacher to move to a new activity, he had to do that. Soon, he was able to handle the transitions; he had practiced so much at home, he knew what to expect at school.

I also worked with Isaiah's teacher. I wanted her to be on my side because she was with my precious boy all day long, and I didn't want his experience in kindergarten to be miserable. So I asked her to make a calendar and draw smiley faces for the days he was fine and to draw sad faces for those where he had problems. When Isaiah had sad-face days, Michael and I talked with him about them. Most often, it was an accident, or he was just being silly and playing around. But we still took it seriously, and we talked to him about controlling his behavior and keeping his hands to himself. Over the next few months, his teacher told me that she saw so many smiley faces that she didn't think we needed the calendar anymore. She had finally begun to believe that he was a good boy. Around that time, she also realized that he knew how to read. She was really impressed with that. But that led to its own issues because Isaiah would read and complete his work so quickly that he began talking to the others at his table. His teacher figured out that she needed to group him with other students who could read and began giving him some additional work to complete. At my suggestion, she also let Isaiah walk around and help some of the others who were struggling. Isaiah absolutely loved helping out, and he was proud that he could share what he knew with his friends.

We ended the kindergarten year on a high note, with glowing comments from Isaiah's teacher. He was happy, too. But the year was difficult for me. It was scary, because I realized, for the first time, that my son may not be protected in school. He was smart, he was a reader, and still his strengths went unrecognized. Was good behavior, and sheer compliance, that important? For this teacher, the answer was yes. And I have to admit, I know now that there is a right and a wrong way to "do school," and behavior, not just reading skills, is a big part of it. As African American parents, we have to advocate for our children if we want to move them from victims to victors. But we also have to work with our children, because from day one, their behaviors and attitudes will be judged. Isaiah is going to third grade, and we still have to remind him to keep his hands to himself and his attitude in check. But I know that his teachers also see his capabilities, his intelligence, and his curiosity, and that's the foundation of a great experience in school.

Jen's story about Isaiah is very common among parents of African American boys; unfortunately, however, many of their stories do not have a happy ending. Gwen shared a similar story about her son Joshua when he was in preschool (McMillon & Edwards, 2000). Joshua came home from preschool one day at the age of 4 and adamantly announced, "I hate school. I'm going to drop out." Like Jen, Gwen intervened on Joshua's behalf. Now, as an

11th-grade honor student in high school, Joshua has learned how to negotiate for himself. When asked if he has advice for teachers of students like himself, he stated,

> Teachers have to learn how to motivate and challenge students like me. If I'm bored, I'm not going to do my best, but if a teacher is passionate about their subject and they use interesting teaching techniques, the students usually show more interest. Right now in my Human Biology class, you can tell that my teacher loves what she's doing. She thinks of interesting ways to help us learn the material. As long as I'm focused on learning, I don't have time to talk. By the time a student is my age, either they want to learn or they don't. There's really not much for parents to do. Parents need to make sure that they work with their kids when they're little. I learned the rules early. I knew that I would be in trouble if I misbehaved in school. Some kids don't have that kind of discipline because their parents weren't hard on them when they were young. My dad never allowed us to get away with acting up in school. I learned my lesson early and I learned it well.

Classroom-Based Solutions

We believe that equal access to reading is the civil right of every child, including every African American child. Therefore, it is essential that we teach all African American children in K–12 schools to read. Classroom-based solutions are extremely important because research has shown us that teachers can make the difference in the literacy lives of African American students (Edwards, 2004; Turner, 2005; Turner & Edwards, 2009). Teachers need to approach literacy teaching for African American students in a way that we call the "cultural transparency" approach. In this perspective, teachers see themselves as school professionals and, as such, have access to the literacy conventions, norms, and behaviors associated with the culture of power (Delpit, 1995). Teachers have to become more "culturally transparent," meaning that they explicitly teach these powerful literacy discourses, skills, and conventions to African American students, and help them to acquire these literacy practices for their own uses and purposes. Importantly, the culturally transparent approach to teaching literacy means that teachers provide instruction in ways that are responsive and relevant to the cultural literacies that African American children learn in their families and communities. In this way, African American students are acquiring school-based literacy practices while affirming and embracing their community-based literacies and culture.

Classroom Instruction. Teachers who use a culturally transparent approach to teaching African American literacy learners: (a) teach them the importance of reading in and out of school; (b) motivate them to read by completing interest surveys and providing them opportunities to read books that are in their areas of interest; (c) demonstrate flexibility with reading assignments, and allow students to complete assignments using books in their areas of interest; (d) conduct read-alouds to capture students' attention/interest, build students' listening comprehension, and model fluent reading; (e) organize classroom environments and classroom libraries in ways that attract student interest and focus attention on reading by including informational and narrative texts based on students' areas of interest; (f) use various grouping formats (e.g., small groups, paired/buddy reading, guided reading, independent reading) to meet students' literacy needs; and (g) provide access to critical literacy resources (e.g., computers, the library, resource books like encyclopedias, dictionaries, and thesauri).

Parent–Teacher Relationships. Teachers need to work with African American parents in ways that honor their cultural knowledge and experiences, and also help them to understand the school-based literacy conventions, skills, and practices associated with the culture of power (Delpit, 1995). We argue that teachers must understand that African American parents value education and literacy, and they want their children to be successful, but may not know school-based literacy practices (e.g., how to read a book aloud to a child, how to help with homework, how to volunteer in the classroom and at school). We encourage teachers to help African American parents understand what school literacy is and how to enact these practices in their homes, by (a) providing flexible opportunities for parental involvement (e.g. evening/weekend conferences, meetings, workshops, etc.); (b) connecting with parents through the parent story approach developed by Patricia Edwards (1990a, 1990b); (c) providing activities that promote effective parent–child interactions; and (d) inviting parents to classroom sessions or workshops during which the teacher models "how to" read a book and "how to" talk to children in a way that promotes vocabulary development and oral language skills. The parent story approach encourages teachers to make home–school connections by collecting information from parents about home literacy practices.

Policymakers seeking to improve the education of African American students also need to encourage parent involvement. Offering various curriculum meetings during the school day, from morning, to afternoon, to evening, will ensure that parents will have an opportunity to be involved in their child's education. We also must set aside funds in Title I/Chapter 1 programs for parental involvement incentives. Some ideas for incentives could be grocery gift cards, gas cards, and so on. This has a strong impact by encouraging parents to be involved and sending a message that "we care." Presently there is a Work First program. It would be especially exciting if there was a "Child First" program that offered parents a chance to get credit for participating in various school activities that encouraged literacy learning for the family. Family literacy is vitally important and should be encouraged by teachers. Incentives could be offered for parents to obtain their GED and enroll in higher education courses. Other programs might allow families to come to school during the evening for dinner, after which children could go to one location to participate in an activity, and parents to another location to learn some necessary skills to acquire a better job or a higher education degree.

A CALL TO ACTION : AM I MY BROTHER'S KEEPER?

Paper right

As we embark on the road to redemption, we want to challenge all of us to think about our roles in (1) transforming African American students from victims to victors; (2) transforming our teachers into effective cultural mediators; and (3) transforming our own research into powerful tools that bring about change in classrooms. We will accept *no more excuses, and no more delays. Come on, people!*

We agree with Cosby and Poussaint (2007): We think it is important to face reality by making education a priority to improve the quality of life for Blacks. Freire (1970) also contended that it is the responsibility of the oppressed to liberate themselves. We could end this discussion by listing the numerous things that Black students and families need to do to improve their own quality of life, but the fact of the matter is that racism often is institutionally perpetuated, and it is incumbent upon us as African American scholars to challenge educators to help in this struggle to close the achievement gap. After all, many of you are gatekeepers at your institutions; others are policymakers at various levels, as well as teacher educators. We implore you to accept the challenge to move from talk to action.

No more excuses, no more delays. Come on, people!

It is both necessary and crucial for African Americans to understand the culture of power; and because we are speaking about people, precious human cargo, we do not have time to wait until researchers find all the plausible answers about how to accommodate, incorporate, and validate their diverse literacy practices into the curriculum of schools.

No more excuses, no more delays. Come on, people!

There are many K–12 students who dream of becoming teachers, but we have a shortage of Black teachers because, as students, African Americans struggle through school and are not admitted into teacher education programs. By failing to provide a good education for urban students, we are perpetuating this shortage. How can we expect African American students to be able to compete, get into the top institutions, and become successful if we are not giving them access to the knowledge base they need?

No more excuses, no more delays. Come on, people.

How can we expect our teacher education students to help African American students become successful border crossers if we aren't comfortable talking about racial issues, often choosing to ignore that our teacher education students are not being adequately prepared to teach Black and other minority students, especially in urban schools?

No more excuses, no more delays. Come on, people.

How can we expect our research to make a difference for Black students and parents, if we understand the problems and know the solutions but feel uncomfortable being honest and forthright with our own research subjects? We know there are problems. We have identified many of them. We need to ask ourselves: What am I doing to help close the achievement gap? What are my research findings doing to improve the subjects' quality of life?

No more excuses, no more delays. Come on, people!

African Americans and other minorities need researchers and studies that seek to improve their quality of life, not to illuminate deficiencies and deficits, but to help them develop the knowledge base and skills needed to succeed.

No more excuses, no more delays. Come on, people.

Yes, it is time to take race out of its neat little package—in our research, in our programs, in our courses, in our conversations, and in our personal lives. The achievement gap has taken on a life of its own. It has taken root and has become the source of other societal problems, such as low graduation rates, high unemployment rates, high incarceration rates, high teenage pregnancy, and so on. Remnants of its influence can be seen in areas ranging from a lack of accessibility to privileged day care services to Black students' unsuccessful experiences in the ivory tower of academia. If the achievement gap is ever going to be eliminated, every member of "the village" must mobilize for battle. We *declare war!!! Come on, people*: Join us in this fight for access, successful border crossing, and opportunities for improvement. Whatever your interests, whatever your areas of focus, you can: (1) mentor minority graduate students; (2) mentor minority junior faculty; (3) explicitly instruct teacher education students in how race and culture impact their decisions, their classroom environment, their interactions with students and parents, and their attitudes about education; (4) develop relationships with minority colleagues and invite them to critique and challenge you concerning how your work can contribute to the war on the achievement gap; and (5) make a special effort to cite minority colleagues in your work.

And, finally, challenge yourself to learn about minority issues and volunteer to make a difference. We *are* our brother's keeper.

> Everyone must join the fight. Our destiny hangs in the balance.
> The eyes of the future are looking back at us
> and they are praying for us to see beyond our own time.
> —Terry Tempest Williams,
> as quoted on the inside cover of *The Covenant* (2006)

NO MORE EXCUSES, NO MORE DELAYS. COME ON, PEOPLE!

> Rosa Parks sat so Martin Luther could walk,
> Martin Luther walked so Barack Obama could run,
> Barack Obama ran so all the children could fly;
> I'm gonna grab my wings, I'll meet you in the sky.
>
> —Jay Z (2008)

Together we can be victorious.

Change is gonna come.

References

African Americans by the numbers. (n.d.). Retrieved August 1, 2009, from http://www.infoplease.com/spot/bhmcensus1.html

Allen, J. B., & Hermann-Wilmarth, J. (2004). Cultural construction zones. *Journal of Teacher Education, 55,* 214–226.

Allington, R. (1980). Teacher interruption behaviors during primary-grade oral reading. *Journal of Educational Psychology, 72*(3), 371–377.

Allington, R. (1983). The reading instruction provided readers of different reading abilities. *The Elementary Journal, 83,* 454–459.

Allington, R., & Cunningham, P. (2007). *Schools that work: Where all children read and write* (3rd ed.). New York: Pearson.

American Council on Education & Education Commission of the States. (1988). *One-third of a nation: A report of the Commission on Minority Participation in Education and American Life.* Washington, DC: Authors.

American Federation of Teachers. (2002). Principles for professional development: AFT's guidelines for creating professional development programs that make a difference. Retrieved September 15, 2009, from http://www.aft.org/Edissues/downloads.ppd.pdf

Anderson, A. B., & Stokes, S. J. (1984). Social and institutional influences on the development and practice of literacy. In H. Goelman, A. Oberg, & F. Smith (Eds.), *Awakening to literacy* (pp. 24–37). Exeter, NH: Heinemann.

Anderson, J. D. (1988). *The education of Blacks in the south, 1860–1935.* Chapel Hill, NC: University of North Carolina Press.

Angelou, M. (1983). *I know why the caged bird sings.* New York: Random House/Mass Market Paperback.

Anyon, J. (1981). Social class and school knowledge. *Curriculum Inquiry, 11*(1), 3–42.

Apol, L. (2002). "What do we do if we don't do haiku?" Seven suggestions for teachers and writers. *English Journal, 91*(3), 89–97.

Apol, L., & Harris, J. (1999). Joyful noises: Creating poems for voices and ears. *Language Arts, 76*(4), 314–322.

Apple, M. W. (1993). *Official knowledge: Democratic education in a conservative age.* New York: Routledge.

Artiles, A., Harry, B., Reschly, D. J., & Chinn, P. (2002). Over-identification of students of color in special education: A critical overview. *Multicultural Perspectives, 4*(1), 3–10.

Asante, M. K. (1980). *Afrocentricity: A theory of social change.* Buffalo, NY: Amulefi.

Asante, M. K. (1987). *The Afrocentric idea.* Philadelphia: Temple University Press.

Asimov, N. (2008, July 17). California high school dropout rate far higher than expected. *San Francisco Chronicle.* Retrieved August 1, 2009, from http://www.sfgate.com/cgi-bin/article.cgi?f=/c/a/2008/07/16/BAS311QATI.DTL&tsp=1

Au, K. H. (2006). *Multicultural issues and literacy achievement.* Mahwah, NJ: Erlbaum.

Au, K. H. (in press). Real schools, real success: A roadmap for change. *Reading Forum New Zealand.*

Baker, L., Mackler, K., Sonnenschein, S., & Serpell, R. (2001). Parents' interactions with their first-grade children during storybook reading and relations with subsequent home reading activity and reading achievement. *Journal of School Psychology, 39*(5), 415–438.

Ball, A. F. (2009). Toward a theory of generative change in culturally and linguistically complex classrooms. *American Educational Research Journal, 46*(1), 45–72.

Ball, A. F., & Lardner, T. (2005). *African American literacies unleashed: Vernacular English and the composition classroom.* Carbondale: Southern Illinois University Press.

Banks, J. A. (1994). *An introduction to multicultural education.* Needham Heights, MA: Allyn and Bacon.

Banks, J. A. (2001). *Cultural diversity and education: Foundations, curriculum, and teaching* (4th ed.). Boston: Allyn & Bacon.

Banks, J., Cochran-Smith, M., Moll, L., Richert, A., Zeichner, K., LePage, P., Darling-Hammond, L., Duffy, H., & McDonald, M. (2005). Teaching diverse learners. In L. Darling-Hammond & J. Bransford (Eds.), *Preparing teachers for a changing world* (pp. 232–276). San Francisco: Jossey-Bass.

Beilke, P. (1986). *Selecting materials for and about Hispanic and East Asian children and young people.* Hamden, CT: Library Professional Publications.

Bell, D. (1983). Learning from our losses: Is school desegregation still feasible in the 1980s? *Phi Delta Kappan, 64*(8), 572–575.

Bell, D. (1993). *Faces at the bottom of the well: The permanence of racism.* New York: Basic Books.

Belt-Beyan, P. M. (2004). The emergence of African American literacy traditions: Family and community efforts in the nineteenth century. Santa Barbara, CA: Greenwood Press.

Bennett, C. I. (1999). *Comprehensive multicultural education: Theory and practice* (4th ed.). Boston: Allyn & Bacon.

Berger, E. H. (1995). *Parents as partners in education: Families and schools working together* (4th ed.). Englewood Cliffs, NJ: Merrill.

Berliner, D. (1986). Does culture affect reading comprehension? *Instructor, 96*(3), 28–29.

Berry, M. F., & Blassingame, J. W. (1982). *Long memory: The Black experience in America.* New York: Oxford University Press.

Billingsley, A. (1968). *Black families in White America.* Englewood Cliffs, NJ: Prentice Hall.

Bishop, R. S. (2007). *Free within ourselves: The development of African-American children's literature.* Westport, CT: Greenwood Press.

Black student college graduation rates inch higher but a large racial gap persists. (2007). *Journal of Blacks in Higher Education.* Retrieved September 21, 2009, from http://www.jbhe.com/preview/winter07preview.html

Blake, I. K. (2009). Ebonics and the struggle for cultural voice in the U.S. schools. In L. Spears-Bunton & R. Powell (Eds.), *Toward a literacy of promise: Joining the African American struggle* (pp. 127–146). New York: Routledge.

Blanchett, W. (2006). Disproportionate representation of African American students in special education: Acknowledging the role of white privilege and racism. *Educational Research, 35*(6), 24–28.

Bliss, J. R. (1991). Strategies and holistic images of effective schools. In J. R. Bliss, W. A. Firestone, & C. E. Richards (Eds.), *Rethinking effective schools: Research and practice* (pp. 43–57). Englewood Cliffs, NJ: Prentice Hall.

Boling, E. (2004). Preparing novices for teaching literacy in diverse classrooms: Using written, video, and hypermedia cases to prepare literacy teachers. In C. M. Fairbanks, J. Worthy, B. Maloch, J. V. Hoffman, & D. L. Schallert (Eds.), *53rd yearbook of the National Reading Conference* (pp. 130–158). Oak Creek, WI: National Reading Conference.

Bonner, F. A. II, & Jennings, M. (2007). Never too young to lead: Gifted African American males in elementary school. *Gifted Child Today, 30*(2), 30–36.

Braddock, J. M. (1995). Tracking and school achievement. In V. L. Gadsden & D. A. Wagner (Eds.), *Literacy among African American youth: Issues in learning, teaching, and schooling* (pp. 153–176). Cresskill, NJ: Hampton Press.

Brandon, L. T. (2004). W/righting history: A pedagogical approach with urban African American learners. *Urban Education, 39*(6), 638–657.

Bridgeland, J. M., Dilulio, J. J., Streeter, R. T., & Mason, J. R. (2008). *One dream, two realities: Perspectives of parents on America's high schools.* Washington, DC: Civic Enterprises.

Brock, C., McMillon, G. T., Pennington, J., Townsend, D., & Lapp, D. (2009). Academic English and African American Vernacular English: Exploring possibilities for promoting the literacy learning of all children. In L. Morrow, R. Rueda, & D. Lapp (Eds.), *Handbook of research on literacy instruction* (pp. 137–157). New York: Guilford.

Brophy, J. E. (1983). Research on the self-fulfilling prophecy and teacher expectations. *Journal of Educational Psychology, 75*(5), 631–661.

Bruner, J. S. (1996). *The culture of education.* Cambridge, MA: Harvard University Press.

Carter, D. J. (2005). *In a sea of White people: An analysis of the experiences and behaviors of high achieving Black students in a predominately White high school.* Unpublished doctoral dissertation, Graduate School of Education of Harvard University, Cambridge, MA.

Cartledge, G., Tillman, L. C., & Johnson, C. T. (2001). Professional ethics within the context of student discipline and diversity. *Teacher Education and Special Education, 24,* 25–37.

Casella, R. (2001). *"Being down": Challenging violence in urban schools.* New York: Teachers College Press.

Certo, J. (2004). Cold plums and the old men in the water: Let children read and write great poetry. *The Reading Teacher, 58*(3), 266–271.

Chappell, K. (2009). "Crisis of inequality" in education unites political opponents. *Jet Magazine,* p. 10.

Cherner, R., & Weir, T. (2009, January 13). *Tuesday eye-opener: Myron Rolle puts NFL on hold.* Retrieved August 1, 2009, from http://blogs.usatoday.com/gameon/2009/01/good-morning-if.html

Children's Defense Fund. (2007). *America's cradle to prison pipeline: A Children's Defense Fund report.* Washington, DC: Author.

Chorzempa, B. F., & Graham, S. (2006). Primary-grade teachers' use of within-class ability grouping in reading. *Journal of Educational Psychology, 98,* 528–541.

Christensen, L. (1999). *Critical literacy: Reading, writing, and outrage: Making justice our project.* Urbana, IL: National Council of Teachers of English.

Christensen, L. (2000). *Reading, writing, and rising up: Teaching about social justice and the power of the written word.* Milwaukee, WI: Rethinking Schools.

Clark, C., & Medina, C. (2000). How reading and writing literacy narratives affect preservice teachers' understandings of literacy, pedagogy, and multiculturalism. *Journal of Teacher Education, 51,* 63–76.

Clark, K. B. (1965). *Dark ghetto: Dilemmas of social power.* New York: Harper.

Clark, R. (1983). *Family life and school achievement: Why poor black children succeed and fail.* Chicago: University of Chicago Press.

Cochran-Smith, M. (2003a). The multiple meanings of multicultural teacher education: A conceptual framework. *Teacher Education Quarterly* (Spring), 7–26.

Cochran-Smith, M. (2003b). Teaching quality matters. *Journal of Teacher Education, 54*(2), 95–98.

Cochran-Smith, M. (2004). *Walking the road: Race, diversity, and social justice in teacher education.* New York: Teachers College Press.

Cochran-Smith, M., & Lytle, S. (1999). The teacher research movement: A decade later. *Educational Researcher, 28*(7), 15–25.

Cokley, K., & Moore, P. (2007). Moderating and mediating effects of gender and psychological disengagement on the academic achievement of African American college students. *Journal of Black Psychology, 33,* 169–187.

College Board releases 2008/2009 college cost figures. (2008, November 14). Retrieved September 20, 2009, from http://www.forefield.com/Welcome/company_

alert.aspx?ix=AL111408

Collins, M. (1992). *"Ordinary" children, extraordinary teachers.* Charlottesville, VA: Hampton Roads.

Comer, J. P. (1993). *School power: Implications of an intervention project.* New York: Free Press.

Corno, L. (1989). What it means to be literate about classrooms. In D. Bloome (Ed.), *Classroom and literacy* (pp. 29–52). Norwood, NJ: Ablex.

Cosby, B., & Poussaint, A. F. (2007). *Come on people: On the path from victims to victors.* Nashville, TN: Thomas Nelson.

Council for Exceptional Children. (2002). *Addressing over-representation of African American students in special education: The prereferral intervention process.* Arlington, VA: Council for Exceptional Children and the National Alliance of Black School Educators.

Danridge, J. C., Edwards, P. A., & Pleasants, H. M. (2003). Making kids winners: New perspectives about literacy from urban elementary school principals. In P. Mason & J. Schumm (Eds.), *Promising practices for urban reading instruction* (pp. 319–333). Newark, DE: International Reading Association.

Darling-Hammond, L. (1997). *The right to learn: A blueprint for creating schools that work.* San Francisco: Jossey-Bass.

Darling-Hammond, L., Hammerness, K., Grossman, P., Rust, F., & Shulman, L. (2005). The design of teacher education programs. In L. Darling-Hammond & J. Bransford (Eds.), *Preparing teachers for a changing world* (pp. 390–441). San Francisco: Jossey-Bass.

Darling-Hammond, L., & McLaughlin, M. W. (1995). Policies that support professional development in an era of reform. *Phi Delta Kappan, 76,* 597–604.

Dearing, E., McCartney, K., Weiss, H. B., Kreider, H., & Simpkins, S. (2004). The promotive effects of family educational involvement for low-income children's literacy. *Journal of School Psychology, 42,* 445–460.

DeBlase, G. (2003). Missing stories, missing lives: Urban girls (re)constructing race and gender in the literacy classroom. *Urban Education, 38,* 279–329.

Dekker, L. M., Krou, C. A., Wright, T. D., & Smith, D. M. (2002, April). *Effective strategies for reducing the overrepresentation of minorities in special education.* Paper presented at the annual meeting of the Classroom Action Research Conference, South Bend, IN.

Delpit, L. (1988). The silenced dialogue: Power and pedagogy in educating other people's children. *Harvard Education Review, 58,* 280–298.

Delpit, L. (1992). Acquisition of literate discourse: Bowing before the master? *Theory into Practice, 31*(4), 296–302.

Delpit, L. (1995). *Other people's children: Cultural conflict in the classroom.* New York: New Press.

DeNavas-Walt, C., Proctor, B. D., & Smith, J. C. (2009). *Income, poverty, and health insurance coverage in the United States: 2008* (No. P60-236). Washington, DC: U.S. Census Bureau. Retrieved October 7, 2009, from http://www.census.gov/hhes/www/poverty/poverty08html

Department of Education, National Center for Education Statistics. (2004). *The condition of education 2004* (NCES 2004077). Washington, DC: U.S. Government Printing Office.

Derman-Sparks, L. (1989). *Anti-bias curriculum: Tools for empowering young children.* Washington, DC: National Association for the Education of Young Children.

Diamond, B., & Moore, M. (1995). *Mirroring the new reality of the classroom: A multicultural literacy approach.* White Plains, NY: Longman.

Diamond, J. B., Lewis, A. E., & Gordon, L. (2007). Race and school achievement in a desegregated suburb: Reconsidering the oppositional culture explanation. *International Journal of Qualitative Studies in Education, 20*(6), 655–679.

Dillard, J. L. (1972). *Black English.* New York: Random House.

Diller, D. (1999). Opening the dialogue: Using culture as a tool for teaching young African American children. *The Reading Teacher, 52,* 820–828.

Douglass, F. (1969). *My bondage and my freedom.* New York: Dover Publications.

Du Bois, W. E. B. (1995). *The souls of black folk.* New York: Penguin Group. (Original work published 1903)

Duffy, G. (2002). Visioning and the development of outstanding teachers. *Reading Research and Instruction, 41,* 331–344.

Duffy, G. G., & Hoffman, J. V. (1999). In pursuit of an illusion: The flawed search for a perfect method. *The Reading Teacher, 53*(1), 10–16.

Duke, N. (2000a). For the rich it's richer: Print experiences and environments offered to children in very low- and very high-socioeconomic status first-grade classrooms. *American Education Research Journal, 37*(2), 441–478.

Duke, N. (2000b). 3.6 minutes per day: The scarcity of informational texts in first grade. *Reading Research Quarterly, 35*(2), 202–224.

Dummett, L. (1984). The enigma—The persistent failure of black children in learning to read. *Reading World, 24,* 31–37.

Duncan-Andrade, J., & Morrell, E. (2008). *The art of critical pedagogy: The promises of moving from theory to practice in urban schools.* New York: Peter Lang.

Edelman, M. W. (2008). *The sea is so wide and my boat is so small: Charting a course for the next generation.* New York: Hyperion.

Edelman, M. W. (2009). Empowering the next generation though the CDF freedom schools program. *Child Watch Column.* Retrieved August 30, 2009, from www.childrensdefense.org

Editorial Projects in Education. (2008). Diplomas count 2008: School to college: Can state P–16 councils ease the transition? *Education Week, 27*(40). Retrieved September 20, 2009, from http://www.edweek.org/ew/toc/2008/06/05/index.html

Edwards, P. A. (1989). Supporting lower SES mothers' attempts to provide scaffolding for book reading. In J. Allen & J. Mason (Eds.), *Risk makers, risk takers, risk breakers: Reducing the risk for young literacy learners* (pp. 225–250). Portsmouth, NH: Heinemann.

Edwards, P. A. (1990a). *Parents as partners in reading: A family literacy training program.* Chicago: Children's Press.

Edwards, P. A. (1990b). *Talking your way to literacy: A program to help nonreading parents prepare their children for reading.* Chicago: Children's Press.

Edwards, P. A. (1993). Before and after school desegregation: African American parents' involvement in schools. *Educational Policy, 7*(3), 340–369.

Edwards, P. A. (1995). Empowering low-income mothers and fathers to share books with young children. *The Reading Teacher, 48*(7), 558–564.

Edwards, P. A. (2004). *Children's literacy developing: Making it happen through school, family, and community involvement.* Boston: Allyn & Bacon.

Edwards, P. A. (2008). *The education of African American students: Voicing the debates, controversies, and solutions* [NRC Presidential Address]. In D. W. Rowe, R. Jimenez, D. Compton, D. Dickinson, Y. Kim, K. Leander, & V. Risko (Eds.), *57th yearbook of the National Reading Conference* (pp. 1–30). Oak Creek, WI: National Reading Conference.

Edwards, P. A. (2009). *Tapping the potential of parents: A strategic guide to boosting student achievement through family involvement.* New York: Scholastic.

Edwards, P. A., & Danridge, J. C. (2001). Developing collaborations with parents: Some examples. In V. J. Risko & K. Bromley (Eds.), *Collaboration for diverse learners: Viewpoints and practices* (pp. 251–272). Newark, DE: International Reading Association.

Edwards, P. A., McMillon, G. T., Turner, J. D., & Laier, B. (2001). Who are you teaching? Coordinating instructional networks around the students and parents you serve. *The Reading Teacher, 55,* 145–150.

Edwards, P. A., Paratore, J., & Roser, N. (2009). Family literacy: Recognizing cultural significance. In L. M. Morrow, R. Rueda, & D Lapp (Eds.), *Handbook on research on literacy instruction: Issues of diversity, policy, and equity* (pp. 77–96). New York: Guilford.

Edwards, P. A., Pleasants, H. M., & Franklin, S. H. (1999). *A path to follow: Learning to listen to parents.* Portsmouth, NH: Heinemann.

Edwards, P. A., & Turner, J. D. (in press). Do you hear what I hear? Using parent stories to listen to and learn from African American parents. In M. L. Dantas & P. Manyak (Eds.), *Connecting and learning with/from families: Disrupting deficit views.* New York: Guilford.

Edwards, P. A., & Young, L. S. (1992). Beyond parents: Family, community and school involvement. *Phi Delta Kappan, 74*(1), 72–80.

Elmore, R. F., Peterson, P. L., & McCarthy, S. J. (1996). *Restructuring in the classroom: Teaching, learning, and school organization.* San Francisco: Jossey-Bass.

Enciso, P. (1994). Integrating "cultural imagination." *The Reading Teacher, 47*(4), 336–337.

Epstein, J. L. (1985). Home and school connections in schools of the future: Implications of research on parent involvement. *Peabody Journal of Education, 62*(2), 18–41.

Epstein, J. L. (1986). Parents' reactions to teacher practices of parent involvement. *Elementary School Journal, 86*(3), 277–293.

Epstein, J. L. (2001). *School, family, and community partnerships: Preparing educators and improving schools.* Boulder, CO: Westview Press.

Evans, D., & Nelson, D. (1992). The curriculum of aspiring teachers: Not a question of either/or. In L. Kaplan (Ed.), *Education and the family* (pp. 230–242). Boston: Allyn & Bacon.

Fairclough, A. (2007). *A class of their own: Black teachers in the segregated south.* Cambridge, MA: Belknap Press of Harvard University Press.

Fanon, F. (1963). *The wretched of the earth.* New York: Grove Press.

Farran, D. C. (1982). Mother–child interaction, language development, and the school performance of poverty children. In L. Feagans & D. C. Farran (Eds.), *The language of children reared in poverty* (pp. 19–52). New York: Academic Press.

Fashola, O. (2002). *Building effective after-school programs.* Thousand Oaks, CA: Corwin Press.

Fashola, O., & Cooper, R. (1999). Developing the academic talents of African American students during the non-school hours: Four exemplary programs. *Journal of Negro Education, 68,* 130–137.

Ferguson, R. F. (2002). *What doesn't meet the eye: Understanding and addressing racial disparities in high-achieving suburban schools.* Cambridge, MA: Harvard University, John F. Kennedy School of Government. (ERIC Document Reproduction Service No. ED474390)

Fine, M. (1995). Silencing and literacy. In V. L. Gadsden & D. A. Wagner (Eds.), *Literacy among African American youth: Issues in learning, teaching, and schooling* (pp. 201–222). Cresskill, NJ: Hampton Press.

Fisher, M. (2008). *Black literate lives: Historical and contemporary perspectives.* New York: Routledge.

Florio-Ruane, S. (2001). *Teacher education and the cultural imagination.* Mahwah, NJ: Erlbaum.

Flowers, L. (2007). Recommendations for research to improve reading achievement for African American students. *Reading Research Quarterly, 42,* 424–428.

Footlick, J. K. (1990, Winter/Spring). What happened to the family? [Special issue]. *Newsweek,* pp. 15–20.

Ford, D. (1998). The underrepresentation of minority students in gifted education: Problems and promises in recruitment and retention. *Journal of Special Education, 32*(1), 4–14.

Ford, D., & Harris, J. J. III. (1994). Promoting achievement among gifted black students: The efficacy of new definitions and identification practices. *Urban Education, 29*(2), 202–222.

Fordham, S. (1996). *Blacked out: Dilemmas of race, identity, and success at Capital High.* Chicago: University of Chicago Press.

Fordham, S., & Ogbu, J. (1986). Black students' school success: Coping with the burden of "acting white." *Urban Review, 18*(3), 176–206.

Forrell, K. L. (2006). Ideas in practice: Bringin' hip-hop to the basics. *Journal of Developmental Education, 30,* 28–33.

Foster, M. (1997). *Black teachers on teaching.* New York: New Press.

Freire, P. (1970). *Pedagogy of the oppressed.* New York: Continuum International.

Fries-Britt, S. (1998). Moving beyond black achiever isolation: Experiences of gifted black collegians. *Journal of Higher Education, 69*(5), 556–576.

Fries-Britt, S. (2002, July–August). High-achieving black collegians. *About College,* pp. 2–8.

Fryer, R. G. (2006). Acting white: The social prices paid by the best and the brightest minority students. *Education Next,* 6(1), 53–59.

Fryer, R. G., & Torelli, P. (2005, May). An empirical analysis of "acting white" (NBER Working Paper No. W11334). Retrieved October 10, 2007, from http://ssrn.com/abstract=734303

Fullan, M., & Hargreaves, A. (1996). *What's worth fighting for in your school?* New York: Teachers College Press.

Fuller, M. L., & Tutwiler, S. W. (1998). Poverty: The enemy of children and families. In M. L. Fuller & G. Olsen (Eds.), *Home–school relations: Working successfully with parents and families* (pp. 257–272). Boston: Allyn & Bacon.

Gadsden, V. (1993). Literacy, education, and identity among African-Americans: The communal nature of learning. *Urban Education, 27*(4), 352–369.

Gay, G. (1983). Multiethnic education: Historical developments and future prospects. *Phi Delta Kappan, 64,* 560–563.

Gay, G. (2000). *Culturally responsive teaching: Theory, research, and practice.* New York: Teachers College Press.

Gee, J. (1991). What is literacy? In C. Mitchell & K. Weiler (Eds.), *Rewriting literacy: Culture and the discourse of the other* (pp. 3–12). New York: Greenwood.

Genevese, E. D. (1976). *Roll, Jordan, roll: The world the slaves made.* New York: Random House.

Gibson, S. C. (2009). *Critical readings: Adolescent African American girls and urban fiction.* Unpublished doctoral dissertation, University of Maryland, College Park.

Gilliam, W. S. (2005). *Prekindergarteners left behind: Expulsion rates in state prekindergarten programs.* New Haven, CT: Yale Child Study Center. Retrieved August 1, 2009, from www.fcd-us.org/usr_doc/ExpulsionCompleteReport.pdf

Giovanni, N. (Ed.). (2008). *Hip hop speaks to children: A celebration of poetry with a beat.* Naperville, IL: Sourcebooks/Jabberwocky.

Giroux, H. (1988). *Teachers as intellectuals: Toward a critical pedagogy of learning.* Granby, MA: Bergin & Garvey.

Giroux, H. A. (1994). Toward a pedagogy of critical thinking. In K. S. Walters (Ed.), *Re-thinking reason: New perspectives in critical thinking.* Albany: State University of New York Press.

Gonzáles, N., Moll, L. C., & Amanti, C. (2005). *Funds of knowledge: Theorizing practices in households, communities, and classrooms.* Mahwah, NJ: Lawrence Erlbaum Associates.

Goodlad, J. I. (1990). *Places where teachers are taught.* San Francisco: Jossey-Bass.

Goodman, K. (1989). Roots of the whole-language movement. *Elementary School Journal, 90,* 113–127.

Goodman, K. (1998). *In defense of good teaching: What teachers need to know about the "reading wars."* York, ME: Stenhouse.

Gordon, A. H. (1971). *Sketches of Negro life and history in South Carolina* (2nd ed.). Columbia: University of South Carolina.

Grant, C. (1992). *Research and multicultural education.* London: Falmer Press.

Grant, C. (2008). *Negro with a hat: The rise and fall of Marcus Garvey and his dream of mother Africa.* London: Jonathan Cape.

Grant, C. A., & Secada, W. G. (1990). Preparing teachers for diversity. In W. R. Houston (Ed.), *Handbook of research on teacher education* (pp. 403–422). New York: Macmillan.

Greene, J. P., & Winters, M. (2005). *Public high school graduation and college readiness: 1991–2002.* New York: Manhattan Institute for Policy Research.

Greene, S., & Abt-Perkins, D. (Eds.). (2003). *Making race visible: Literacy research for cultural understanding.* New York: Teachers College Press.

Gutman, L. M., & McLoyd, V. C. (2000). Parents' management of their children's education within the home, at school, and in the community: An examination of African-American families living in poverty. *The Urban Review, 32*(1), 1–24.

Haberman, M. (1993). Diverse contexts for teaching. In M. J. O'Hair & S. J. Odell (Eds.), *Diversity in teaching: Teacher education yearbook I* (pp. 1–8). Fort Worth, TX: Harcourt Brace Jovanovich.

Haberman, M. (1995). *Star teachers of children in poverty.* West Lafayette, IN: Kappa Delta Pi International Educational Honor Society.

Hacker, A. (1992). *Two nations: Black and white, separate, hostile, unequal.* New York: Scribner's.

Hale-Benson, J. (1982). *Black children: Their roots, culture, and learning styles* (rev. ed.). Baltimore: Johns Hopkins University Press.

Hale-Benson, J. (2001). *Learning while Black: Creating educational excellence for African-American children.* Baltimore: Johns Hopkins University Press.

Haley, A. (1987). *The autobiography of Malcolm X.* New York: Random House/Mass Market Paperback.

Hall, S. (1993). What is this "black" in black popular culture? *Social Justice, 20* (1-2), 104–114.

Hammond, B., Hoover, M. E., & McPhail, I. (Eds.). (2005). *Teaching African American learners to read: Perspectives and practices.* Newark, DE: International Reading Association.

Harada, V. H. (1995). Issues of ethnicity, authenticity, and quality in Asian-American picture books, 1983–93. *Journal of Youth Services in Libraries, 8*(2), 135–149.

Harley, S. (1995). *The timetable of African-American history: A chronology of the most important people and events in African-American history.* New York: Touchstone.

Harris, V. J. (1990). African-American children's literature: The first one hundred years. *Journal of Negro Education, 59*(4), 540–555.

Harry, B., & Klingner, J. (2006). *Why are so many minority students in special education? Understanding race and disability in schools.* New York: Teachers College Press.

Hart, A. C. (2009, November 13). *"Race to the top" grant rules laid out.* Retrieved November 14, 2009, from http://www.chicagotribune.com/news/chi-tc-nw-education-1112-1113nov13,0,7234226.

Hart, B., & Risley, T. R. (1995). *Meaningful differences in the everyday experience of young American children.* Baltimore: Paul H. Brookes.

Harvey, S., & Goudvis, A. (2007). *Strategies that work: Teaching comprehension for understanding and engagement* (2nd ed.). Portland, ME: Stenhouse.

Hays, S. (2004). *Flat broke with children: Women in the age of welfare reform.* Cambridge: Oxford University Press.

Heath, S. B. (1982a). Questioning at home and at school: A comparative study. In G. Spindler (Ed.), *Doing ethnography of schooling: Education anthropology in action* (pp. 102–129). New York: Holt, Rinehart and Winston.

Heath, S. B. (1982b). What no bedtime story means: Narrative skills at home and school. *Language in Society, 11,* 49–76.

Heath, S. B. (1983). *Ways with words: Life, language and work in communities and classrooms.* Cambridge: Cambridge University Press.

Heath, S. B. (1986). Separating "things of the imagination" from life: Learning to read and write. In W. H. Teale & E. Sulzby (Eds.), *Emergent literacy: Writing and reading* (pp. 156–172). Norwood, NJ: Ablex.

Heath, S. B., Branscombe, A., & Thomas, C. (1985). The book as narrative prop in language acquisition. In B. Scheiffelin & P. Gilmore (Eds.), *The acquisition of literacy: Ethnographic perspectives* (pp. 16–34). Norwood, NJ: Ablex.

Heath, S. B., & Thomas, C. (1984). The achievement of preschool literacy for mother and child. In H. Goelman, A. Oberg, & F. Smith (Eds.), *Awakening to literacy* (pp. 51–72). Portsmouth, NH: Heinemann.

Henderson, A. T. (1987). *The evidence continues to grow.* Columbia, MD: National Committee for Citizens in Education.

Henderson, A. T., & Berla, N. (1994). *A new generation of evidence: The family is critical to student achievement.* Columbia, MD: National Committee for Citizens in Education.

Henry, T. (2001, June 20). Lawmakers move to improve literacy, the "new civil right." *USA Today.* Retrieved September 20, 2009, from http://www.nrrf.org/new_USAT_6-20-01.htm

Hiebert, E. F. (1983). An examination of ability grouping for reading instruction. *Reading Research Quarterly, 18*(2), 231–255.

Hilliard, A. G. (1983). Psychological factors associated with language in the education of the African American child. *Journal of Negro Education, 52*(1, 24–34.

Hollins, E. R. (1996). *Culture in school learning: Revealing the deep meaning.* Mahwah, NJ: Erlbaum.

Hollins, E., & Guzman, M. (2005). Research on preparing teachers for diverse populations. In M. Cochran-Smith & K. Zeichner (Eds.), *Studying teacher education: The report of the AERA panel on research and teacher education* (pp. 477–548). Mahwah, NJ: Erlbaum.

Hollins, E., & Spencer, K. (1990). Restructuring schools for cultural inclusion: Changing the schooling process for African American youngsters. *Journal of Education, 172*(2), 89–100.

hooks, b. (1994). *Teaching to transgress: Education as the practice of freedom.* London: Routledge.

Hoover-Dempsey, K. V., Walker, J. M. T., Sandler, H. M., Whetsel, D., Green, C. L., & Wilkins, A. S. (2005). Why do parents become involved? Research findings and implications. *Elementary School Journal, 106*(2), 105–130.

Houston, W. R., & Houston, E. (1992). Needed: A new knowledge in teacher education. In L. Kaplan (Ed.), *Education and the family* (pp. 272–277). Boston: Allyn & Bacon.

Howard, T. C. (2002). Hearing footsteps in the dark: African American students' descriptions of effective teachers. *Journal of Education for Students Placed At Risk, 7*(4), 425–444.

Howe, N., & Strauss, W. (2000). *Millennials rising: The next great generation.* New York: Random House.

Iceland, J. (2006). *Poverty in America: A handbook* (2nd ed.). Berkeley: University of California Press.

International Reading Association. (2003). *Prepared to make a difference: An executive summary of the National Commission on Excellence in Elementary Teacher Preparation for Reading Instruction.* Newark, DE: International Reading Association.

Irons, M. (2009, March 22). *The new cool kids.* Retrieved August 1, 2009, from http://www.boston.com/news/local/articles/2009/03/22/the_new_cool_kids/

Irvine, J. J. (1990). *Black students and school failure: Policies, practices, and prescriptions.* New York: Greenwood Press.

Irvine, J. J. (2003). *Educating teachers for diversity: Seeing with a cultural eye.* New York: Teachers College Press.

Irvine, J. J., & Armento, B. (2001). (Eds.). *Culturally responsive teaching: Lesson planning for elementary and middle grades.* Boston: McGraw-Hill.

Jay Z. (2008). *My president is black.* New York: Rocafella Records. Lyrics retrieved September 20, 2009, from http://www.sing365.com/music/lyric.nsf/My-President-is-Black-Remix-lyrics-Jay-Z/400FD11C28A00A9F48257545002B4F67

Johnson, S. M. (1990). *Teachers at work: Achieving success in our schools.* New York: Basic Books.

Johnston, P. (2005). Literacy assessment and the future. *The Reading Teacher, 58,* 684–688.

Juzwik, M. M. (2004). What rhetoric can contribute to an ethnopoetics of narrative performance in teaching: The significance of parallelism in one teacher's narrative. *Linguistics and Education, 15*(4), 359–386.

Juzwik, M. M. (2006a). Performing curriculum: Building ethos through narrative in pedagogical discourse. *Teachers College Record, 108*(4), 489–528.

Juzwik, M. M. (2006b). Situating narrative-minded research: A response to Anna Sfard's and Anna Prusak's "Telling identities." *Educational Researcher, 25*(9), 13–21.

Juzwik, M. M. (2008). *The rhetoric of teaching: Understanding the dynamics of Holocaust narratives in an English classroom.* Cresskill, NJ: Hampton Press.

Kaplan, E. (1997). *Not our kind of girl: Unraveling the myths of black teenage motherhood.* Berkeley: University of California Press.

Keehn, S., Martinez, M., Harmon, J., Hedrick, W., Steinmetz, L., & Perez, B. (2003). Teacher preparation in reading: A case study of change in one university-based undergraduate program. In C. M. Fairbanks, J. Worthy, B. Maloch, J. V. Hoffman, & D. L. Schallert (Eds.), *52nd yearbook of the National Reading Conference* (pp. 230–244). Oak Creek, WI: National Reading Conference.

Kennedy, M. M. (2005). *Inside teaching: How classroom life undermines reform.* Cambridge, MA: Harvard University Press.

Kidd, J. K., Sanchez, S. Y., & Thorp, E. K. (2004). Listening to the stories families tell: Promoting culturally responsive language and literacy experiences. In C. M. Fairbanks, J. Worthy, B. Maloch, J. V. Hoffman, & D. L. Schallert (Eds.), *53rd yearbook of the National Reading Conference* (pp. 246–265). Oak Creek, WI: National Reading Conference.

Kim, D. W. (2006). Stepping-stone to intergenerational mobility? The springboard, safety net, or mobility trap functions of Korean immigrant entrepreneurship for the second generation. *International Migration Review, 40,* 927–962.

King, J. E., Hollins, E. R. & Hayman, W. C. (1997). *Preparing teachers for cultural diversity.* New York Teachers College Press.

Kirkland, D., & Jackson, A. (2009). "We real cool": Toward a theory of Black masculine literacies. *Reading Research Quarterly, 44*(3), 278–300.

Kitano, M. K., Lewis, R. B., Lynch, E. W., & Graves, A. W. (1996). Teacher in a multicultural classroom: Teacher educators. *Equity & Excellence, 29*(3), 70–77.

Kozol, J. (1991). *Savage inequalities: Children in America's schools.* New York: Crown.

Kozol, J. (1994). The new untouchables. In J. Krevotics & E. J. Nussel (Eds.), *Transforming urban education* (pp. 75–78). Boston: Allyn & Bacon.

Ladner, M., & Hammons, C. (2001). Separate but unequal: Racial bias in special education placements. In C. E. Finn, Jr., A. J. Rotherham, & C. R. Hokanson, Jr. (Eds.), *Rethinking special education for a new century* (pp. 85–110). Washington, DC: Thomas B. Fordham Foundation.

Ladson-Billings, G. (1994). *The dreamkeepers: Successful teaching of African American students.* San Francisco: Jossey-Bass.

Ladson-Billings, G. (2000). Fighting for our lives: Preparing teachers to teach African American students. *Journal of Teacher Education, 51,* 206–214.

Ladson-Billings, G. (2001). *Crossing over to Canaan: The journey of new teachers in diverse classrooms.* San Francisco: Jossey-Bass.

Ladson-Billings, G. (2005). *Beyond the big house: African American educators on teacher education.* New York: Teachers College Press.

Ladson-Billings, G., & Tate, B. (1995). Toward a critical race theory of education. *Teachers College Record, 97*(1), 47–67.

Langer, J. (2002). *Effective literacy instruction: Building successful reading and writing programs.* Urbana, IL: National Council of Teachers of English.

Lazar, A. (2004). *Learning to be literacy teachers in urban schools: Stories of growth and change.* Newark, DE: International Reading Association.

Lazar, A. (2007). Investigating African American language in literacy education courses. In D. W. Rowe, R. T. Jiminez, D. L. Compton, D. K. Dickinson, Y. Kim, K. M. Leander, & V. J. Risko (Eds.), *56th yearbook of the National Reading Conference* (pp. 319–331). Oak Creek, WI: National Reading Conference.

Lee, C. (1991). Big picture talkers/words walking without masters: The instructional implications of ethnic voices for an expanded literacy. *Journal of Negro Education, 60*(3), 291–304.

Lee, C. D. (2007). *Culture, literacy, and learning: Blooming in the midst of the whirlwind.* New York: Teachers College Press.

Leitch, M. L., & Tangri, S. S. (1988). Barriers to home–school collaboration. *Educational Horizons, 66*(2), 70–74.

LeTendre, G. K., Hofer, B. K., & Shimizu, H. (2003). What is tracking? Cultural expectations in the United States, Germany, and Japan. *American Educational Research Journal, 40,* 43–89.

Levin, R., Smith, M., & Strickland, D. (2003). Pitfalls and problems: Multicultural literature and teacher study groups. In A. Willis, G. Garcia, R. Barrera, & V. Harris (Eds.), *Multicultural issues in literacy research and practice* (pp. 263–288). Mahwah, NJ: Erlbaum.

Lightfoot, S. L. (1978). *World apart: Relationships between families and schools.* New York: Basic Books.

Lightfoot, S. L. (2004). *The essential conversation: What parents and teachers can learn from each other.* New York: Random House.

Liston, D. P., & Zeichner, K. M. (1991). *Teacher education and the social condition of schooling.* New York: Routledge & Kegan Paul.

Lleras, C., & Rangel, C. (2009). Ability grouping practices in elementary school and African American/Hispanic achievement. *American Journal of Education, 115*(2), 279–305.

Louis, K. S., & Miles, M. B. (1991). Toward effective urban high schools: The importance of planning and coping. In J. R. Bliss, W. A. Firestone, & C. E. Richards (Eds.), *Rethinking effective schools: Research and practice* (pp. 91–111). Englewood Cliffs, NJ: Prentice Hall.

MacLeod, J. (1995). *Ain't no makin' it: Aspirations & attainment in a low-income neighborhood.* Boulder, CO: Westview Press.

Mahiri, J. (1998). *Shooting for excellence: African American and youth culture in New Century schools.* New York: Teachers College Press.

Mahiri, J. (Ed.). (2003). *What they don't learn in school: Literacy in the lives of urban youth.* New York: Peter Lang.

Majors, R., & Billson, J. M. (1993). *Cool pose: The dilemmas of Black manhood in America.* New York: Simon & Schuster.

May, S. (1999). *Critical multiculturalism: Rethinking multicultural and antiracist education.* Philadelphia: Falmer Press.

May, S., & Sleeter, C. (2010). *Critical multiculturalism: Theory and praxis.* New York: Routledge.

Maynard, T. (2002). *Boys and literacy: Exploring the issues.* New York: Routledge.

McCormick, C., & Mason, J. (1986). Intervention procedures for increasing preschool children's interest in and knowledge about reading. In W. H. Teale & E. Sulzby (Eds.), *Emergent literacy: Writing and reading* (pp. 90–115). Norwood, NJ: Ablex.

McDiarmid, G. W., & Price, J. (1990). *Prospective teachers' views of diverse learners: A study of the participants in the ABCD Project* (Research Report 90-6). East Lansing: Michigan State University, National Center for Research on Teacher Education.

McDonald, J. (1999). *Project girl.* New York: Farrar, Strauss, & Giroux.

McFadden, G. J. (1993). Septima P. Clark and the struggle for human rights. In V. L. Crawford, J. A. Rouse, & B. Woods (Eds.), *Women in the civil rights movement: Trailblazers and torchbearers 1941–1965* (pp. 85–97). Bloomington: Indiana University Press.

McLaughlin, M. W., & Shields, P. M. (1987). Involving low-income parents in the schools: A role for policy? *Phi Delta Kappan, 69,* 156–160.

McMillon, G. M. T. (2001). *A tale of two settings: African American students' literacy experiences at church and at school.* Unpublished doctoral dissertation, Michigan State University, East Lansing.

McMillon, G. M. T. (2009). Pen pals without borders: A cultural exchange of teaching and learning. *Education and Urban Society, 42*(1),119–135.

McMillon, G. T., & Edwards, P. A. (2000, November). Why does Joshua "hate" school, but "love" Sunday school? *Language Arts, 78*(2), 111–120.

McMillon, G. M. T., & Edwards, P. A. (2008). Examining shared domains of literacy in the home, church and school of African American children. In J. Flood, S. B. Heath, & D. Lapp (Eds.), *Handbook of research on teaching literacy through the communicative and visual arts* (Vol. II, pp. 319–328). Mahwah, NJ: Erlbaum.

McMillon, G., & McMillon, V. (2004). Empowering literacy practices of the African American church. In F. B. Boyd, C. H. Brock, & M. S. Rozendal (Eds.), *Multicultural and multilingual literacy and language: Contexts and practices* (pp. 280–304). New York: Guilford Press.

McNeal, R. B. Jr. (1999). Parent involvement as social capital: Differential effectiveness on science achievement, truancy, and dropping out. *Social Forces, 78,* 117–144

McVee, M. (2004). On listening to what others say: Narrative as a catalyst to uncover issues of racial and cultural diversity. In F. B. Boyd, C. H. Brock, & M. Rozendal (Eds.), *Multicultural and multilingual literacy and language: Contexts and practices* (pp. 106–129). New York: Guilford Press.

Mercado, R. F. (2007). *Intersections of vision, practice, and context in the development of student teachers as reading teachers for students of diverse backgrounds.* Unpublished doctoral dissertation, University of Maryland, College Park.

Mickelson, R. A. (1990). The attitude-achievement paradox among Black adolescents. *Sociology of Education, 63,* 44–61.

Milner, H. R. (2008). Preparing teachers of African American students in urban schools. In L. C. Tillman (Ed.), *The SAGE handbook of African American education* (pp. 123–140). Thousand Oaks, CA: Sage.

Miners, Z. (2009, August 17). *Arne Duncan, Al Sharpton, and Newt Gingrich join forces.* Retrieved December 9, 2009, from http://www.usnews.com/blogs/on-education/2009/08/17/arne-duncan-al-sharpton-and-newt-gingrich-join-forces.html.

Moles, O. C. (1993). Collaboration between schools and disadvantaged parents: Obstacles and openings. In N. F. Chavkin (Ed.), *Families and schools in a pluralistic society* (pp. 21–49). Albany: State University of New York Press.

Moore, R. (1996). *Between a rock and a hard place: African Americans and standard English.* Retrieved June 17, 2009, from http://gallery.carnegiefoundation.org/collections/quest/collections/sites/moore_renee/media/files-pdf/rock_paper.pdf

Morgan, H. (1995). *Historical perspectives on the education of black children.* Westport, CT: Praeger.

Morrell, E. (2002). Toward a critical pedagogy of popular culture: Literacy development among urban youth. *Journal of Adolescent and Adult Literacy, 46,* 72–77.

Morrell, E. (2004). *Linking literacy and popular culture: Finding connections for lifelong learning.* Norwood, MA: Christopher-Gordon.

Morrell, E., & Duncan-Andrade, J. (2002). Promoting academic literacy with urban youth through hip-hop culture. *English Journal, 91*(6), 88–92.

Morrison, G. S. (1978). *Parent involvement in the home, school, and community.* Columbus, OH: Merrill.

Murrell, P. (2002). *African-centered pedagogy: Developing schools of achievement for African American children.* Albany: State University of New York Press.

Myers, W. D. (1997). *Slam.* New York: Scholastic.

National Center for Education Statistics. (2003). Retrieved September 20, 2009, from http://nces.ed.gov/pubs2007/minoritytrends

National Commission on Teaching and America's Future. (1997). *Doing what matters most: Investing in quality teaching.* New York: Author.

National Education Association. (2007). *Truth in labeling: Disproportionality in special education.* Washington, DC: National Education Association and the National Association of School Psychologists.

National Education Goals Panel. (1998). *Ready schools.* Washington, DC: Author.

National Parent Teacher Association. (2000). *Building successful partnerships: A guide to family and parent involvement programs.* Bloomington, IN: National Educational Service.

Neckerman, K. M., & Wilson, W. J. (1988). Schools and poor communities. In D. Hornbeck (Ed.), *School success for students at risk: Analysis and recommendations of the Council of Chief School Officers* (pp. 25–44). Orlando, FL: Harcourt Brace Jovanovich.

Neisser, U. (1986). New answers to an old question. In U. Neisser (Ed.), *The school achievement of minority children: New perspectives* (pp. 1–17). Hillsdale, NJ: Erlbaum.

Neuman, S. B. (1996). Children engaging in storybook reading: The influence of access to print resources, opportunity, and parental interaction. *Early Childhood Research Quarterly, 11*, 495–513.

Nieto, S. (1992). *Affirming diversity: The sociopolitical context of multicultural education.* New York: Longman.

Ninio, A. (1980). Ostensive definition in vocabulary teaching. *Journal of Child Language, 7*, 565–573.

Noffke, S. (1997). Professional, personal, and political dimensions of action research. *Review of Research in Education, 22*, 305–343.

Noguera, P. (2003). *City schools and the American dream.* New York: Teachers College Press.

Norwood, Q. T. (2002). Plantation rhymes: Hip hop as writing against the empire of neo-slavery. *Proud Flesh: New Afrikan Journal of Culture, Polities & Consciousness, 1*(1), 1–15.

Oakes, J. (1985). *Keeping track: How schools structure inequality.* New Haven, CT: Yale University Press.

Oakes, J. (1992). Can tracking research inform practice? Technical, normative, and political considerations. *Educational Researcher, 21*(4), 12–21.

Oakes, J. (2005). *Keeping track: How schools structure inequality* (2nd ed.). New Haven, CT: Yale University Press.

Obah, C. B. A. (2004). Abolition of Pell Grants for higher education of prisoners: Examining antecedents and consequences. *Journal of Offender Rehabilitation, 39*(2), 73–85.

O'Brien, S. (2009a, July). *CNN's Black in America 2.* Retrieved August 17, 2009, from http://www.cnn.com/SPECIALS/2009/black.in.america/

O'Brien, S. (2009b, July). *Interview with D. L. Hughley.* Retrieved August 17, 2009, from http://newsroom.blogs.cnn.com/2009/07/25/why-is-d-l-hughley-crying/

O'Brien, S. (2009c, August). *Interview with Michael Baisden.* Retrieved August 16, 2009, from http://www.cnn.com/2008/LIVING/06/12/bia.celebrity.interviews/index.html

Ogbu, J. (1995). Literacy and black Americans: Comparative perspectives. In V. L. Gadsden & D. A. Wagner (Eds.), *Literacy among African American youth: Issues in learning, teaching, and schooling* (pp. 83–100). Cresskill, NJ: Hampton Press.

Ogbu, J. (2003). *Black American students in an affluent suburb: A study of academic disengagement.* Mahwah, NJ: Erlbaum.

Office of the Press Secretary. (2009, March). *Fact sheet–Expanding the promise of education in America.* Retrieved September 12, 2009, from http://www.whitehouse.gov/the_press_office/Fact-Sheet-Expanding-the-Promise-of-Education-in-America

O'Gilvie, H., & Turner, J. D. (2008, May). *Teaching through language: Using multilingual tools to promote literacy achievement among African American elementary students.* Presentation at the annual meeting of the International Reading Association, Atlanta.

Orfield, G., & Lee, C. (2005). *Why segregation matters: Poverty and educational inequality.* Cambridge, MA: Harvard University, Civil Rights Project.

Pang, V. O., Colvin, C., Tran, M., & Barba, R. H. (1992). Beyond chopsticks and dragons: Selecting Asian American literature for children. *The Reading Teacher, 46*(3), 216–224.

Parker, K. (2008). *Unequal crime decline: Theorizing race, urban inequality, and criminal violence.* New York: New York University Press.

Paul, D. G. (2000). Rap and orality: Critical media literacy, pedagogy, and cultural synchronization. *Journal of Adolescent and Adult Literacy, 44,* 246–251.

Pearson, P. D. (1996). Reclaiming the center. In M. Graves, P. van den Brock, & B. M. Taylor (Eds.), *The first R: Every child's right to read* (pp. 259–274). New York: Teachers College Press.

Pearson, P. D. (2004). The reading wars: The politics of reading research and policy–1988 through 2003. *Educational Policy, 18*(1), 216–252.

Perry, T. (2003). Up from the parched earth: Toward a theory of African-American achievement. In T. Perry, C. Steele, & A. Hilliard (Eds.), *Young, gifted, and black: Promoting high achievement among African American students* (pp. 1–11). Boston: Beacon Press.

Perry, T., Steele, C., & Hilliard, A. (2003). *Young, gifted, and black: Promoting high achievement among African American students.* Boston: Beacon Press.

Pflaum, S. W. (1986). *The development of language and literacy in young children* (3rd ed.). Columbus, OH: Merrill.

Planty, M., & Devoe, J. (2005). *An examination of the conditions of school facilities attended by 10th-grade students in 2002* (NCES 2006-302). Washington, DC: U.S. Government Printing Office.

Polite, V., & McClure, R. (1997). Introduction. *Urban Education, 31,* 461–465.

Powell, L. (2009). Introduction. In L. A. Spears-Bunton & L. Powell (Eds.), *Toward a literacy of promise: Joining the African American struggle* (pp. 1–16). New York: Routledge.

Purcell-Gates, V. (1996). Stories, coupons, and the *TV Guide:* Relationships between home literacy experiences and emergent literacy knowledge. *Reading Research Quarterly, 31*(4), 406–428.

Quinn, E. (2005). *Nuthin' but a "G" thang: The culture and commerce of gangsta rap.* New York: Columbia University Press.

Randall, D. (1969/2009). Booker T. & W.E.B. In M. J. Boyd (Ed.), *Roses and revolutions: The selected writings of Dudley Randall* (p. 103). Detroit, MI: Wayne State University Press.

Raphael, T. (2009, December). *Defying gravity: Whole school literacy reform in urban schools.* Address given for the Oscar S. Causey award at the 59th annual meeting of the National Reading Conference, Albuquerque, NM.

Report of the National Reading Panel. (1998). *Teaching children to read: An evidence-based assessment of the scientific research literature on reading and its implication for reading instruction–Reports of the subgroups.* Washington, DC: National Institute of Child Health and Human Development, National Institutes of Health.

Richardson, E. (2003). *African American literacies.* New York: Routledge.

Rickford, J. R., & Rickford, R. J. (2000). *Spoken soul: The story of black English.* New York: Wiley.

Riesman, F. (1962). *The culturally deprived child.* New York: Harper.

Rist, R. C. (1970). Student social class and teacher expectations: The self-fulfilling prophecy in ghetto education. *Harvard Educational Review, 40*(3), 411–451.

Roberts, S. M., & Pruitt, E. Z. (2003). *Schools as professional learning communities: Collaborative activities and strategies for professional development.* Thousand Oaks, CA: Corwin.

Robinson, J. P. (2008). Evidence of a differential effect of ability grouping in kindergarten and first grade on the reading achievement growth of language-minority Hispanics. *Educational Evaluation and Policy Analysis, 30*(2), 141–180.

Rodriguez, R. F. (1981). The involvement of minority group parents in school. *Teacher Education and Special Education, 4,* 40–44.

Rogers, J. R. (1978, May). *Parent's responsibilities for children's reading.* Speech presented at the annual meeting of the International Reading Association, Houston.

Rohr, J., Qualls, R., & Turner, J. D. (2007, December). *Are pre-service teachers' visions of literacy instruction sustained into practice?* Paper presented at the annual meeting of the National Reading Conference, Austin.

Rosaen, C. L. (2003). Preparing teachers for diverse classrooms: Creating public and private spaces to explore culture through poetry writing. *Teachers College Record, 105*(8), 1437–1485.

Rose, T. (1994). *Black noise: Rap music and Black culture in contemporary America.* Hanover, NH: Wesleyan University Press.

Rosenthal, R., & Jackson, L. (1968). *Pygmalion in the classroom: Teacher expectations and pupils' intellectual development.* New York: Holt, Rinehart and Winston.

Ruben, G. (2009). *Disproportionate representation of minorities in special education: How bad?* Paper presented at the 3rd annual Jane H. LeBlanc Conference in Communication Disorders, State University, AK.

Rubin, B. C., & Noguera, P. A. (2004). Tracking detracking: Sorting through the dilemmas and possibilities of detracking in practice. *Equity and Excellence in Education, 37,* 92–101.

Ruddell, R. B. (1995). Those influential literacy teachers: Meaning negotiators and motivation builders. *The Reading Teacher, 48,* 454–463.

Sabol, W. J., & Couture, H. (2008, June). *Bureau of Justice statistics: Prison inmates at midyear 2007.* Washington, DC: U.S. Department of Justice.

Saddler, C. A. (2005). The impact of *Brown* on African-American students: A critical race theoretical perspective. *Educational Studies, 37*(1), 41–55.

Saint-Laurent, L., & Gaisson, J. (2005). Effects of a family literacy program adapting parental intervention on first graders' evolution of reading and writing abilities. *Journal of Early Childhood Literacy, 5*(3), 253–278.

Sampson, W. A. (2002). *Black student achievement: How much do family and school really matter?* Lanham, MD: Scarecrow Press.

Sampson, W. A. (2004). *Black and brown: Race, ethnicity, and school preparation.* Lanham, MD: Scarecrow Press.

Schiefflin, B. B., & Cochran-Smith, M. (1984). Learning to read culturally: Literacy before schooling. In H. Goelman, A. Oberg, & F. Smith (Eds.), *Awakening to literacy* (pp. 3–23). Exeter, NH: Heinemann.

Schmidt, P. R. (1998). The ABC's of cultural understanding and communication. *Equity & Excellence in Education, 31*(2), 28–38.

Schmidt, P. R., & Finkbeiner, C. (Eds.). (2006). *ABC's of cultural understanding and communication: National and international adaptations.* Greenwich, CT: Information Age.

Schott Foundation for Public Education. (2008). *Given half a chance: The Schott 50 state report on public education and black males. Executive summary.* Retrieved September 15, 2009, from http://www.blackboysreport.org

Schreiner, O. (1980). *Dreams.* Retrieved October 15, 2009, from http://www.scribd.com/doc/13979326/Dreams-by-Olive-Schreiner

Schwartz, W. (2001). *School practices for equitable discipline of African American students.* ERIC Clearinghouse on Urban Education, EDO-UD-01-5.

Sergiovanni, T. J. (1994). Organizations or communities? Changing the metaphor changes the theory. *Education Administration Quarterly, 30*, 214–226.

Shannon, P. (1989). *Broken promises: Reading instruction in twentieth-century America.* New York: Bergin & Garvey.

Shannon, P. (1990). *The struggle to continue: Progressive reading instruction in the United States.* Portsmouth, NH: Heinemann.

Shipler, D. K. (2005). *The working poor: Invisible in America.* New York: Vintage.

Shujaa, M. J. (1994). *Too much schooling, too little education: A paradox of Black life in White societies.* Trenton, NJ: Africa World Press.

Siddle Walker, V. (2001). African-American teaching in the south: 1940–1960. *American Educational Research Journal, 38*(4), 751–779.

Sims, R. (1982). Dialect and reading: Toward redefining the issues. In J. Langer & M. T. Smith-Burke (Eds.), *Reader meets author/bridging the gap* (pp. 222–232). Newark, DE: International Reading Association.

Skiba, R. J., & Leone, P. (2001). *Zero tolerance and school security measures: A failed experiment.* Retrieved July 30, 2009, from http://www.arc.org/content/view/84/36/

Skiba, R. J., Simmons, A. B., Ritter, S., Gibb, A. C., Rausch, M. K., Cuadrado, J., & Chung, C. (2008). Achieving equity in special education: History, status, and current challenges. *Exceptional Children, 74*(3), 264–288.

Skinner, E. (2007). "Teenage addiction": Adolescent girls drawing upon popular culture texts as mentors for writing in an after-school writing club. In D. W.

Rowe, R. T. Jimenez, D. L. Compton, D. K. Dickinson, Y. Kim, K. M. Leander, & V. J. Risko (Eds.), *56th yearbook of the National Reading Conference* (pp. 345–361). Oak Creek, WI: National Reading Conference.

Sleeter, C. E. (1985). A need for research on preservice teacher education for mainstreaming and multicultural teacher education. *Journal of Educational Equity and Leadership, 5*(3), 205–215.

Sleeter, C. E. (2007). *Facing accountability in education: Democracy and equity at risk.* New York: Teachers College Press.

Sleeter, C. E., & Grant, C. A. (1994). *Making choices for multicultural education: Five approaches to race, and gender.* New York: Macmillan.

Smitherman, G. (1986). *Talkin and testifyin: The language of black America.* Detroit: Wayne State University Press.

Snow, C. E., Burns, M. S., & Griffin, P. (Eds.). (1998). *Preventing reading difficulties in young children.* Washington, DC: National Academy Press.

Snow, C. E., & Ninio, A. (1986). The contribution of reading books with children to their linguistic and cognitive development. In W. H. Teale & E. Sulzby (Eds.), *Emergent literacy: Reading and writing* (pp. 116–138). Norwood, NJ: Ablex.

Sobel, M. (1988). *Trabelin' on: The slave journey to an Afro-Baptist faith.* Princeton, NJ: Princeton University Press.

Soto, G. (1993). *Too many tamales.* New York: Putnam's.

Spears-Bunton, L. A., & Powell, L. (Eds.). (2009). *Toward a literacy of promise: Joining the African American struggle.* New York: Routledge.

Spiro, R. (1991). Knowledge representation, content specification, and the development of skill in situation-specific knowledge assembly: Some constructivist issues as they relate to cognitive flexibility theory and hypertext. *Educational Technology, 31*(9), 22–25.

Steele, C. (2003). Stereotype threat and African-American student achievement. In T. Perry, C. Steele, & A. Hilliard (Eds.), *Young, gifted, and black: Promoting high achievement among African American students* (pp. 109–130). Boston: Beacon Press.

Stevenson, D. L., & Baker, D. P. (1987). The family-school relation and the child's school performance. *Child Development, 58*(5), 1348–1357.

Stovall, D. O. (2006). We can relate: Hip-hop culture, critical pedagogy, and the secondary classroom. *Urban Education, 41*(6), 585–602.

Sutherland, L. M. (2005). Black adolescent girls' use of literacy practices to negotiate boundaries of ascribed identity. *Journal of Literacy Research, 37*(3), 365–406.

Swann-Wright, D. (2002). *A way out of no way: Claiming family and freedom in the new south.* Charlottesville: University of Virginia Press.

Takaki, R. T. (1979). *Iron cages: Race and culture in 19th-century America.* Seattle: University of Washington Press.

Tan, A. (2006). *The kitchen god's wife.* New York: Penguin Books.

Tatum, A. (2000). Breaking down barriers that disenfranchise African American adolescent readers in low-level tracks. *Journal of Adolescent and Adult Literacy, 44*(1), 52–64.

Tatum, A. (2005). *Teaching reading to black adolescent males: Closing the achievement gap.* Portland, ME: Stenhouse.

Tatum, A. W. (2009). *Reading for their life: (Re) Building the textual lineages of African American adolescent males.* Portsmouth, NH: Heinemann.

Tatum, B. (2003). *"Why are all the black kids sitting together in the cafeteria?": A psychologist explains the development of racial identity* (rev. ed.). New York: Basic Books.

Taylor, B. M., Pearson, P. D., Clark, K., & Walpole, S. (2000). Effective schools and accomplished teachers: Lessons about primary-grade reading instruction in low-income schools. *Elementary School Journal, 101,* 121–165.

Taylor, D. (1983). *Family literacy: Young children learning to read and write.* Portsmouth, NH: Heinemann Educational Books.

Taylor, D., & Dorsey-Gaines, C. (1988). *Growing up literate: Learning from inner-city families.* Portsmouth, NH: Heinemann.

Taylor, M. D. (1991). *Roll of thunder, hear my cry.* New York: Penguin Books USA.

Teale, W. H. (1986). Home background and young children's literacy development. In W. H. Teale & E. Sulzby (Eds.), *Emergent literacy: Writing and reading* (pp. 173–206). Norwood, NJ: Ablex.

Thompson, M. T., & Nuckolls, M. R. (2005). *Making choices and facing consequences: Manchild in the promised land: A crime prevention program.* Bloomington, IN: AuthorHouse.

Thompson, M. T., Thompson, B. R., Thompson, M. R., Thompson, R. L., McDole, B. C., Sharper, P. K., & McMillon, G. M. T. (2009). *The preacher's kids.* Unpublished biography.

Tough, P. (2008). *Whatever it takes: Geoffrey Canada's quest to change Harlem and America.* Orlando, FL: Houghton Mifflin Harcourt

Townsend, B. L. (2000). The disproportionate discipline of African American learners: Reducing school suspensions and expulsions. *Exceptional Children, 66,* 381–391.

Traugh, C. (2002). Inquiry as a mode of renewal: Imagining the possibilities of circumstance. *CUE Point of View, 1*(1), 1–7.

Trent, S. C., & Artiles, A. J. (1995). Serving culturally deprived students with behavior disorders: Broadening current perspectives. In J. M. Kauffman, J. W. Lloyd, R. A. Astuto, & D. P. Hallahan (Eds.), *Issues in the educational placement of pupils with emotional or behavioral disorders* (pp. 215–249). Hillsdale, NJ: Erlbaum.

Turner, J. D. (2003). *To tell a new story: A narrative inquiry into the theory and practice of culturally relevant teaching.* Unpublished doctoral dissertation, Michigan State University, East Lansing.

Turner, J. D. (2005). Orchestrating success for African American readers: The case of an effective third-grade teacher. *Reading Research and Instruction, 44,* 27–48.

Turner, J. D. (2006). "I want to meet my students where they are!": Preservice teachers' visions of culturally responsive reading instruction. In J. Hoffman, D. Schallert, C. Fairbanks, J. Worthy, & B. Maloch (Eds.), *55th yearbook of the*

National Reading Conference (pp. 309–323). Oak Creek, WI: National Reading Conference.

Turner, J. D. (2007). Beyond cultural awareness: Prospective teachers' "visions" of culturally responsive literacy teaching. *Action in Teacher Education, 29,* 12–24.

Turner, J. D., & Duffy, G. (2007, December). *Powerful visions, powerful teaching: The roles of vision and visioning in reading teacher education.* Paper presented at the annual meeting of the National Reading Conference, Austin.

Turner, J. D., & Edwards, P. A. (2009). Old tensions, new visions: Implications for teacher education programs, K–12 schools, and family literacy programs. In G. Li (Ed.), *Multicultural families, home literacies, and mainstream schooling* (pp. 246–268). Charlotte, NC: Information Age.

Turner, J. D., & Mercado, R. (2009). Preparing responsive reading teachers with vision. *Academic Exchange Quarterly, 13*(1), 49–54.

Tutwiler, S. W. (1998). Diversity among families. In M. L. Fuller & G. Olsen (Eds.), *Home–school relations: Working successfully with parents and families* (pp. 40–66). Boston: Allyn & Bacon.

Tyson, K., Darity, W., & Castellino, D. R. (2005). It's not "a black thing": Understanding the burden of acting white and other dilemmas of high achievement. *American Sociological Review, 70*(4), 582–605.

Walker, A. (1994). *Everyday use.* New Brunswick, NJ: Rutgers University Press.

Ward, V. (1998). The African American Sunday school: Reclaiming its role as moral teacher. *Direction* (December 1998–February 1999), 1–2.

Weems, R. (1995). *Battered love.* Philadelphia: Fortress Press.

Wertsch, J. V. (1991). *Voices of the mind: A sociocultural approach to mediated action.* Cambridge, MA: Harvard University Press.

West, C. (1993). *Race matters.* Boston: Beacon Press.

Westmoreland, H., Rosenberg, H. M., Lopez, M. E., & Weiss, H. (2009, July). Seeing is believing: Promising practices for how school districts promote family engagement. *National Parent Teacher Association, Harvard Family Research Project.* Retrieved October 24, 2009, from http://www.hfrp.org/publications-resources/browse-our-publications/seeing-is-believing-promising-practices-for-how-school-districts-promote-family-engagement

West-Olatunji, C. A., Baker, J. C., & Brooks, M. (2006). African American adolescent males: Giving voice to their educational experiences. *Multicultural Perspectives, 8*(4), 3–9.

White, B. L. (1975). *The first three years of life.* Englewood Cliffs, NJ: Prentice Hall.

Wildsmith, E., Bennett, I., & Johnson, A. (2007). *Literacy, school connectedness, and teenage childbearing.* Philadelphia: Philadelphia Education Fund.

Williams, T. T. (2006). *The covenant.* Chicago: Third World Press.

Willis, A. I. (2002). Literacy at Calhoun colored school 1892–1945. *Reading Research Quarterly, 37*(1), 8–44.

Willis, W. B. (1998). *The Adinkra dictionary: A visual primer on the language of Adinkra.* Washington, DC: Pyramid Complex.

Wood, F. G. (1968). *Black scare: The racist response to emancipation and reconstruction.* Chicago: University of Chicago Press.

Woodson, C. G. (1933). *The mis-education of the Negro.* Trenton, NJ: Africa World Press.

Xu, S. (2000). Preservice teachers integrate understandings of diversity into literacy instruction: An adaptation of the ABCs model. *Journal of Teacher Education, 51,* 135–142.

Young, L. S., Sykes, G., Featherstone, J., Elmore, R. F., & Devaney, K. (1990). *Tomorrow's schools: Principles for the design of professional development schools* (a report of the Holmes group). East Lansing: Holmes Group, Michigan State University.

Young, V. A. (2007). *Your average nigga: Performing race, literacy, and masculinity.* Detroit, MI: Wayne State University Press.

Zeichner, K. M., Grant, C., Gay, G., Gillette, M., Valli, L., & Villegas, A. M. (1998). A research informed vision of good practice in multicultural teacher education: Design principles. *Theory Into Practice, 37*(2), 163–171.

Ziegler, E. (1979). Introduction. In W. G. Hill, P. Fox, & C. D. Jones (Eds.), *Families and schools: Implementing parent education* (Report No. 121, pp. ix–xiii). Denver, CO: Education Commission of the States.

Index